P9-BYA-174

THE BARBARIAN WAY

SOUL CRAVINGS

ERWIN RAPHAEL MCMANUS

THOMAS NELSON
Since 1798

NASHVILLE   DALLAS   MEXICO CITY   RIO DE JANEIRO   BEIJING

UNLEASH
THE UNTAMED
FAITH WITHIN

THE
BARBARIAN
WAY

Published in Nashville, Tennessee, by Thomas Nelson. Thomas Nelson is a registered trademark of Thomas Nelson, Inc.

Thomas Nelson, Inc. titles may be purchased in bulk for educational, business, fund-raising, or sales promotional use. For information, please e-mail SpecialMarkets@ThomasNelson.com.

Published in association with Yates & Yates, www.yates2.com

Interior artwork by Joby Harris

Library of Congress Cataloging-in-Publication Data

McManus, Erwin Raphael.
    The barbarian way : unleash the untamed faith within / Erwin Raphael McManus.
      p. cm.
    ISBN 978-0-7852-6432-3 (hardcover)
    ISBN 978-1-4002-8019-3 (2-in-1)
    1. Christian life. I. Title.
    BV4501.3.M374 2005
    248.4—dc22

2004027611

CONTENTS

1. The Barbarian Invasion   1

2. The Barbarian Call   19

3. The Barbarian Tribe   57

4. The Barbarian Revolt   107

Acknowledgments   145

To Mariah, my Sweet,

Who loves to live and lives to love.
From first breath you have brought to life
both celebration and adventure.
Compassionate and courageous.
Delicate and determined.
Tender and tenacious.
Lover of God and lover of people.
You are both laughter and tears.
In ancient times, you would be the warrior princess.
Always follow the steps of the One who is scarred.
May we always choose the barbarian way,

Dad

But then the worst thing happened
that could happen to any fighter,
you got civilized.

—MICK TO ROCKY,
Rocky III

1

THE
BARBARIAN
INVASION

Now Jephthah the Gileadite was a mighty man of valor, but he was the son of a harlot; and Gilead begot Jephthah. Gilead's wife bore sons; and when his wife's sons grew up, they drove Jephthah out, and said to him, "You shall have no inheritance in our father's house, for you are the son of another woman." Then Jephthah fled from his brothers and dwelt in the land of Tob; and *worthless men banded together with Jephthah and went out raiding with him.*

It came to pass after a time that the people of Ammon made war against Israel. And so it was, when the people of Ammon made war against Israel, that the elders of Gilead went to get Jephthah from the land of Tob. Then they said to Jephthah, "Come and be our commander, that we may fight against the people of Ammon."

So Jephthah said to the elders of Gilead, "Did you not hate me, and expel me from my father's house? Why have you come to me now when you are in distress?"

And the elders of Gilead said to Jephthah, "That is why we have turned again to you now, that you may go with us and fight against the people of Ammon, and be our head over all the inhabitants of Gilead."

So Jephthah said to the elders of Gilead, "If you take me back home to fight against the people of Ammon, and the LORD delivers them to me, shall I be your head?"

And the elders of Gilead said to Jephthah, "The LORD will be a witness between us, if we do not do according to your words." Then Jephthah went with the elders of Gilead, and the people made him head and commander over them. (Judges 11:1–11 NKJV, italics added)

On our way to Belfast, Northern Ireland, we made a stop in Paisley, Scotland. My wife, Kim, my twelve-year-old daughter, Mariah, and I were on a Hollywood version of a spiritual pilgrimage. (If you walk into our living room, you will find hanging as a centerpiece an exact replica of the sword that William Wallace made famous to the non-Scottish masses through Mel Gibson's *Braveheart*.) I was standing in the middle of the Paisley Abbey where Wallace was educated as a boy. I took my time as I looked reverently at the stained glass that remains a memorial to Wallace's heroics (he didn't look anything like Mel Gibson), yet it was a story about Robert the Bruce that struck me most and has stayed with me ever since.

Robert the Bruce was the Scottish noble whose character is most remembered for betraying Wallace, but he later rose up to lead Scotland to freedom after Wallace's execution. While we were standing in the abbey, Scottish pastor James Pettigrew shared a tale of Robert the Bruce that is a mixture of history and legend.

He died in 1329 at the age of fifty-four. Shortly before his death, Robert the Bruce requested that his heart be removed from his body and taken on crusade by a worthy knight. James Douglas, one of his closest friends, was at his bedside and took on the responsibility. The heart of Robert the Bruce was embalmed and placed in a small container that Douglas carried around his neck. In every battle that Douglas fought, he literally carried the heart of his king pressed against his chest.

In the early spring of 1330, Douglas sailed from Scotland to Granada, Spain, and engaged in a campaign against the

Moors. In an ill-fated battle, Douglas found himself surrounded, and in this situation death was both certain and imminent. In that moment Douglas reached for the heart strapped around his neck, flung the heart into the enemy's midst, and cried out, "Fight for the heart of your king!" One historian quoted Douglas as shouting, "Forward, brave heart, as ever thou were wont to do, and Douglas will follow his king's heart or die!" The motto of the Douglas clan to which the present duke belongs is even to this day simply, "Forward."

A TRIBE CALLED FORWARD

Although anyone who understands the heart of God knows that the Crusades were a tragic lesson in missing the point, the power of this story awakens within me a primal longing that I am convinced waits to be unleashed within everyone who is a follower of Jesus Christ. To belong to God is to belong to His heart. If we have responded to the call of Jesus to leave everything and follow Him, then there is a voice within us crying out, "Fight for the heart of your King!"

Yet Christianity over the past two thousand years has moved from a tribe of renegades to a religion of conformists. Those who choose to follow Jesus become participants in an insurrection. To claim we believe is simply not enough. The call of Jesus is one that demands action. Jesus began His public ministry with a simple invitation: "Come, follow Me." His closing instructions to His disciples can be summarized in one word, "Go!" A quick survey of the modern church would lead you to believe His invitation was "Come, and listen," and His closing mandate would be summarized in the one word "No!" The tribe of Jesus, above all people, should rightly carry the banner, "Forward."

I know the imagery of this story is nothing less than barbaric, but maybe that's the point. The invitation of Jesus is a revolutionary call to fight for the heart of humanity. We are called to an unconventional war using only the weapons of faith, hope, and love. Nevertheless, this war is no less dangerous than any war ever fought. And for those of us who embrace the cause of Christ, the cost to participate in the mission of God is nothing less than everything we are and everything we have.

Strangely enough, though, some who come to Jesus Christ

seem to immediately and fully embrace this barbarian way. They live their lives with every step moving forward and with every fiber of their being fighting for the heart of their King. Jesus Christ has become the all-consuming passion of their lives. They are not about religion or position. They have little patience for institutions or bureaucracies. Their lack of respect for tradition or ritual makes them seem uncivilized to those who love religion. When asked if they are Christians, their answer might surprisingly be no, they are passionate followers of Jesus Christ. They see Christianity as a world religion, in many ways no different from any other religious system. Whether Buddhism, Hinduism, Islam, or Christianity, they're not about religion; they're about advancing the revolution Jesus started two thousand years ago.

This is the simplicity of the barbarian way. If you are a follower of Christ, then you are called to fight for the heart of your King. It is a life fueled by passion—a passion for God and a passion for people. The psalmist tells us to delight ourselves in the Lord, and He will give us the desires of our hearts (Psalm 37:4). When Christianity becomes just another religion, it focuses on requirements. Just to keep people in line, we build our own Christian civilization and then demand that everyone who believes in Jesus become a good citizen.

It's hard to imagine that Jesus would endure the agony of the Cross just to keep us in line. Jesus began a revolution to secure our freedom. The new covenant that He established puts its trust not in the law, but in the transforming power of God's Spirit living within us. The revolution of the human heart would fuel the life and vitality of this movement. We would delight in God, and He would give us the desires of our hearts. With our hearts burning for God, we would move forward with the freedom to pursue the passions burning within us.

RAW LOVE

My daughter, Mariah, and I were eating Thai food in San Diego. We were getting some important dad-and-daughter time. There's nothing like one-on-one to create an environment for some real heart-to-heart conversation. After she reminded me that I was the only one between the two of us who liked Thai, she began to open her heart and bring me into her dreams.

"Daddy, one day I want to make a billion dollars, and I want to give it all away. I want to help the poor; I want to help the needy. I want to make a billion dollars, and I don't care if I have nothing, but I want to give it all to help people."

As I was listening to her dream, I thought, *I can fix this.* Because the dream was almost right.

But she kept saying, "I want to make a billion dollars and give it away and help the poor, and I don't care if I'm homeless or have nothing. I just want to give it away to help people."

I said, "Mariah, I want you to make a billion dollars and give to the poor and the needy, but it's not a good idea that you have nothing. Then you would be needy and somebody would have to take care of you and you wouldn't be responsible."

"I don't care if I don't have anything, Daddy," Mariah responded. "I just want to make a billion dollars and give it away. I don't care if I'm homeless. I don't care if I have nothing."

"But if you're homeless, our taxes would have to pay for you."

Looking at me as if to say, *Daddy, you just don't understand,* she continued, "I don't care if I have nothing. I just want to make a billion dollars and give it all away. I don't care if I have nothing."

I thought, *Okay, I'm not really helping here.* I was trying to help her understand that she needed to keep something, restructure it, and reinvest it so that she could make another billion and help another group of people. I just wasn't able to help her with her dream. And I thought, *A metaphor—that will help.*

"Honey, let's say you're a large tree bearing fruit for people to eat because they are hungry, and you want to give all your fruit away because you want to feed everyone, care for everyone. But because of that, you didn't care about your roots, and so you said, 'I'm going to uproot myself. Who cares about the soil and the water? I just want to bear all the fruit I can.' And then you will die. Then the next year you won't be able to bear fruit. It's better to take care of your roots, too, so that you can keep bearing fruit year after year after year."

She said, "Daddy, what in the world do roots have to do with this?"

I knew I wasn't making progress. We left the place and went to the car. I unlocked it, and she got into the car quickly. By the time I slid into the driver's seat, she was sobbing, and

I didn't know what was going on. I asked, "Mariah, are you okay?"

Just drenched in tears, she looked at me and said, "Daddy, I want to change the world, but you can't appreciate my dream. I want to change the world." She continued, "I didn't say I would be homeless; I said I didn't care if I became homeless. I want to change the world. Can't you just hear my dream?"

I realized that instead of nurturing and unleashing the dream being born out of her heart for God, I was domesticating her dream and trying to civilize her raw and untamed faith, which was ironic since I was so excited that this was her heart.

"Well, honey, I am excited about your dream," I said. "Don't you think that we were a small part of trying to nurture your heart to have that dream?"

She said, "Yeah, but I don't think you're getting it."

I said, "Well, I get it now. I get it now."

It took me a little while, but suddenly I saw it clearly. I was experiencing a barbarian invasion. Mariah's heart was beating to the rhythm of the heart of God. And her dreams were way too raw for me. I didn't see it initially, but I was trying to civilize her instead of unleashing the untamed faith within her. After all, I am her dad. It's okay if I live a life of irrational faith and breathtaking adventure. I want something different for her. I want her to have security and safety—you know, a predictable, boring, mundane life where I never have to worry about her again. In that moment I realized Mariah would have none of that. For her there is only one path. Even at twelve she has already committed to it. Be still my heart, but my daughter has chosen the barbarian way out of civilization. And it's for this simple reason that this book is dedicated to her.

OF WIND AND FIRE

Twenty-five years ago I was a part of the barbarian invasion. I knew little about God, but I wanted to know nothing else but God. I was overwhelmed that Someone as extraordinary as Jesus of Nazareth would have any interest or desire to embrace someone like me. Even before I knew what was written on the pages of the sacred text that we know as the Bible, I knew that I would give my heart fully to whatever I would learn was on God's heart. I was a follower of Jesus, and for me there was no turning back.

Over the years I have met perhaps thousands who have been a part of this barbarian invasion. From my brother, Alex, who swore allegiance to Christ, even though he had no idea that heaven existed; to my wife, Kim, who as a child growing up in a foster home cried out to Jesus that she would go anywhere He wanted and do anything He wanted her to do. In their unique voices they were committing to move forward and fight for the heart of their King.

Perhaps the tragedy of our time is that such an overwhelming number of us who declare Jesus as Lord have become domesticated—or, if you will, civilized. We have lost the simplicity of our early faith. Beyond that, we have lost the passion and power of that raw, untamed, and primal faith. Maybe John was alluding to that in the Apocalypse when he told the church of Ephesus that they had lost their first love (Revelation 2:1–4). God's command to Israel was simply, "Love the LORD your God with all your heart and with all your soul and with all your strength. These commandments that I give you today are to be upon your hearts" (Deuteronomy 6:5–6). And when Jesus was asked, "What is the greatest of all the commandments?" and "How do I inherit eternal life?" His answer was the same, except to add that we are to love our neighbor as ourselves (Mark 10:17–19; 12:28–31).

The barbarian way is about love, intimacy, passion, and sacrifice. Barbarians love to live and live to love. For them God is life, and their mission is to reconnect humanity to Him. Their passion is that each of us might live in intimate communion with Him who died for us. The barbarian way is a path of both spirit and truth. The soul of the barbarian is made alive by the presence of Jesus.

As John the Baptist reminded us, the evidence that Jesus is the Christ is that He baptizes us in both Spirit and fire. Barbarians are guided by the wind of God and ignited by the fire of God. The way of the barbarian can be found only by listening to the voice of the Spirit. The barbarian way can be known only by those who have the heart of God. The steps of the barbarian are guided by the footprints of Jesus. Barbarians see the invisible and hear the inaudible because their souls are alive to God.

If I know nothing else about you, if you are a follower of Jesus Christ, I know this without question: there is within you a raw and untamed faith waiting to be unleashed. When we come to the living God, He consumes who we are and gives us life that is fueled by His presence. You have been recreated to live in a raw and primal spirituality. Jesus came to ignite a fire within you that would consume you and ignite you. Jesus the King came to fight for your heart. If He has won your heart, then to follow your heart will always lead you to follow the heart of God. He will always lead you to advance forward behind enemy lines to win the hearts of those who do not yet know Him or love Him.

A FASHIONABLE FIGHT

One of my favorite characters in *Braveheart* was the Irish guy who joined William Wallace in his crusade. Remember him, the crazy guy who talked to God? Appropriately his name was Stephen. His most memorable quote was this: "The Almighty says this must be a fashionable fight. It draws the finest people." Of course, any civilized Christian knows why he's crazy. Every devout believer—in fact, any person of faith from any religious persuasion, whether Christian, Muslim, Buddhist, Hindu, or whatever—believes in prayer, but we all know prayer is supposed to be us talking to God. We get a little nervous when someone starts hearing from God.

What has the Almighty been saying to you lately? And when was the last time He called you to participate in a fashionable fight?

He's calling you to fight for the heart of your King. For some, doing this will be just way too barbaric, but for others, their only option will be to choose the barbarian way.

PRIMAL LEADERS

A barbarian invasion is taking place even right now. They are coming from the four corners of the earth and they are numbered among the unlikely. From the moment Jesus walked among us the invasion began. And just as with those who crossed paths with Him here on earth, those who are most religious will be most offended and indignant. Barbarians are not welcome among the civilized and are feared among the domesticated. The way of Jesus is far too savage for their sensibilities. The sacrifice of God's Son, the way of the Cross, the call to die to ourselves, all lack the dignity of a refined faith. Why insist on such a barbaric way? Why a reckless call to awaken the barbarian faith within us at the risk of endangering this great civilization we have come to know as Christianity?

Because Jesus did not suffer and die so that we could build for ourselves havens, but so that we might expand the kingdom of His love. Because invisible kingdoms are at war for the hearts and lives of every human being who walks on the face of this earth. And times of war require barbarians who are willing to risk life itself for the freedom of others. The irony, of course, is that barbarians are driven away in times of peace—they only disrupt our communities, traditions, and sensibilities. It is only in the most desperate of times—times of war or conflict—that these outcasts are welcomed or even invited to return.

Jephthah, the son of a harlot, was despised by his people and expelled from his tribe. Those who would later choose to join him were considered a band of worthless men, yet his story reminds us that the very ones who are unwanted and driven from among us are the ones we most need to lead in times of war. Barbarians can be counted as worthless when all is safe and secure, but dangerous times suddenly make them invaluable. We live in such times. And we are not ready for the great challenges set before us. We have not been prepared to take on any great quest, to battle any great enemy, or even to pursue the great dream for which we have been born. Instead,

Christianity has become our Shawshank, and our redemption will only come if we find the courage to escape the prison we have created for ourselves. Risking everything to live free is our only hope—humanity's only hope.

Jesus is being lost in a religion bearing His name. People are being lost because they cannot reconcile Jesus' association with Christianity. Christianity has become docile, domesticated, civilized. We have forgotten that there is a kingdom of darkness stealing the hopes and dreams and souls of a humanity without God. It is time to hear the barbarian call, to form a barbarian tribe, and to unleash the barbarian revolt. Let the invasion begin . . .

2

THE
BARBARIAN
CALL

After Jesus had finished instructing his twelve disciples, he went on from there to teach and preach in the towns of Galilee. When John heard in prison what Christ was doing, he sent his disciples to ask him, "Are you the one who was to come, or should we expect someone else?" Jesus replied, "Go back and report to John what you hear and see: The blind receive sight, the lame walk, those who have leprosy are cured, the deaf hear, the dead are raised, and the good news is preached to the poor. Blessed is the man who does not fall away on account of me." (Matthew 11:1–6)

If I'm right about this whole barbarian thing, then the women and men closest to God will most powerfully live out the raw and untamed spirit of the barbarian. We should ask, for instance: When Jesus walked among us, who did He choose to represent Him? Or maybe we should go back even a bit farther and ask, What kind of person did God choose to prepare the way for the coming of His Son? His name was John. We know him better as John the Baptist.

John the Baptist was a true barbarian. John was introduced to us with the full force of his personality:

In those days John the Baptist came, preaching in the Desert of Judea and saying, "Repent, for the kingdom of heaven is near." This is he who was spoken of through the prophet Isaiah:

"A voice of one calling in the desert,
'Prepare the way for the Lord,
make straight paths for him.'"

John's clothes were made of camel's hair, and he had a leather belt around his waist. His food was locusts and wild honey. People went out to him from Jerusalem and all Judea and the whole region of the

Jordan. Confessing their sins, they were baptized by him in the Jordan River.

But when he saw many of the Pharisees and Sadducees coming to where he was baptizing, he said to them: "You brood of vipers! Who warned you to flee from the coming wrath? Produce fruit in keeping with repentance. And do not think you can say to yourselves, 'We have Abraham as our father.' I tell you that out of these stones God can raise up children for Abraham. The ax is already at the root of the trees, and every tree that does not produce good fruit will be cut down and thrown into the fire.

"I baptize you with water for repentance. But after me will come one who is more powerful than I, whose sandals I am not fit to carry. He will baptize you with the Holy Spirit and with fire. His winnowing fork is in his hand, and he will clear his threshing floor, gathering his wheat into the barn and burning up the chaff with unquenchable fire." (Matthew 3:1–12)

Several things about John stand out right away. He was an unusual dresser with strange eating habits. Just in case you're uncertain, wearing clothes made of camel's hair was not the height of fashion, even during the time of Jesus. We are told he ate locusts and wild honey. I suppose the wild honey was to help get the locusts down.

He was clearly not a fan of the established religious leaders. His nickname for the Pharisees and Sadducees, who were the pinnacle of the religious elite, was "brood of vipers." Nope, that was not a term of endearment. And I think it's important to note that his fire-and-brimstone message was entirely directed toward the religious, not the irreligious. He was a barbarian in the midst of civilization. And frankly the civilization made him sick. He had no patience for domesticated religionists who were drowning in their own self-righteousness.

Oh, and by the way, he had no formal education, no degrees. His occupation was prophet, and his mailing address was the wilderness. To say the very least, he was not the person whom anyone was expecting to prepare the way for the Messiah. John was the voice that proclaimed the coming of the Christ, and through his encounters with Jesus, we can rediscover the barbarian call.

BEYOND DOUBT

John sent his disciples to ask Jesus a question: "Are you the one who was to come, or should we expect someone else?" (Matthew 11:3). It was a fair question, wouldn't you think? In fact, it's a question that all of us should ask. If Jesus is not the One, we should not follow Him. But if He is the One, we should follow Him at all costs.

I myself asked this question about twenty years ago. I hope that you have asked this question. I always feel hopeful when a person who has been indifferent begins to ask this question about Jesus. Yet for John, this question seemed entirely out of place. How could John be uncertain whether Jesus was the One? Remember, Jesus and John were cousins. Mary and Elizabeth were pregnant with their sons at the very same time. In an extraordinary story recorded by Luke, we are told,

> At that time Mary got ready and hurried to a town in the hill country of Judea, where she entered Zechariah's home and greeted Elizabeth. When Elizabeth heard Mary's greeting, the baby leaped in

her womb, and Elizabeth was filled with the Holy Spirit. In a loud voice she exclaimed: "Blessed are you among women, and blessed is the child you will bear! But why am I so favored, that the mother of my Lord should come to me? As soon as the sound of your greeting reached my ears, the baby in my womb leaped for joy. Blessed is she who has believed that what the Lord has said to her will be accomplished!" (1:39–45)

Do you see it? When John was inside his mother's womb and Jesus was inside His mother's womb, John leaped. He recognized Jesus from the fetal position. I can only imagine a little voice emanating from Elizabeth's belly, asking, "Are You the One, or should we look for another?" In the womb, John knew, but then thirty years later he was uncertain?

And it seems that God was prepared to clarify in John's adulthood what he knew before he was born. In the first chapter of the gospel of John, John the Baptist was in the middle of a controversial conversation with the religious leaders (vv. 19–28). John was clear that his one mission was to prepare the way for the coming Messiah. It was his job to point others to

Him. And that was exactly what he did. It was never his intention to gather a following to himself. His ultimate desire for any of his disciples was that they would become devoted followers of the Messiah to come.

On one occasion the apostle John told us, "The next day John was there again with two of his disciples. When he saw Jesus passing by, he said, 'Look, the Lamb of God!' When the two disciples heard him say this, they followed Jesus" (John 1:35–37).

One of those two disciples was Andrew, who became one of the Twelve that we have come to know as the apostles. He was also Simon Peter's brother. Even so early in the process, John was clear about who Jesus was. He was absolutely certain about the identity of Jesus—so much so that he led his disciples to become Jesus' followers. Why at that point wasn't John running up to Jesus and saying, "Are You the One? All you Nazarenes look the same."

BEYOND QUESTION

In between these two encounters, we find why John was so certain. The gospel tells us,

The next day John saw Jesus coming toward him and said, "Look, the Lamb of God, who takes away the sin of the world! This is the one I meant when I said, 'A man who comes after me has surpassed me because he was before me.' I myself did not know him, but the reason I came baptizing with water was that he might be revealed to Israel."

Then John gave this testimony: "I saw the Spirit come down from heaven as a dove and remain on him. I would not have known him, except that the one who sent me to baptize with water told me, 'The man on whom you see the Spirit come down and remain is he who will baptize with the Holy Spirit.' I have seen and I testify that this is the Son of God." (John 1:29–34)

John confessed that he was uncertain about whether Jesus was really the One. But His baptism removed all doubt. Matthew told us that in the moment John baptized Jesus, the heavens were opened, and John saw the Spirit of God descending on Jesus like a dove and lighting on Him. And he also heard a voice from heaven declare, "This is my Son, whom I love; with him I am well pleased" (Matthew 3:16–17).

In other words, by that time John was absolutely clear about one thing: Jesus was the One. I guarantee you, no one else whom John baptized had that kind of drama surrounding the event. A voice coming out of the heavens, and what by today's standards would be amazing special effects, would be enough to convince even the most skeptical of us. John was neither unclear nor uncertain, and in his barbaric rawness the untamed prophet defied anyone who would deny the legitimacy of Jesus.

With that knowledge John declared his subservience to the purpose and person of Jesus the Christ. Without shame or ambiguity he would declare to those who questioned him, "I baptize with water . . . but among you stands one you do not know. He is the one who comes after me, the thongs of whose sandals I am not worthy to untie" (John 1:26–27).

So what in the world was John thinking then? How could he send his disciples with a question like that? How could he be gripped with so much doubt that he would risk spreading it to his disciples? All who were close to him had heard him declare the supremacy of Jesus. All of them had to be affected by the strength of his confidence in who Jesus was. Why would he ask Jesus, "Are you the one who was to come, or should we expect someone else?" (Matthew 11:3).

HEAD GAMES

We don't have to go far to find the reason for John's confusion. Just before Matthew recorded John's question, he let us know what prompted John's crisis of faith. John was in prison. Herod arrested John and put him in prison on account of Herodias. Herodias was the wife of his brother Philip, and Herod was having an affair with her. In his expectedly barbaric way, John called it for what it was, refusing to placate Herod or cower to Herod's power. Herod wanted to kill John, but he feared the reaction of the people. The people loved John because they considered him a prophet from God.

Anyway, one day it was Herod's birthday, and the daughter of Herodias danced for him. Herod was so pleased (I think this alludes to the dark and evil kind of pleased) that he made an oath to give her whatever she asked. In a plot between Herodias and her daughter, they asked for John the Baptist's head on a platter. Though the king was distressed for political reasons, he granted what they asked (Matthew 14:1–12). That was the backdrop of John's dilemma.

John was living between prison and platter when he sent the message to Jesus. Shouldn't he expect Jesus to drop everything and come to his aid? After all, he had always been there for Jesus. Where was He when John needed Him? Was He unaware that John needed help? Was He indifferent to John's dilemma? Or was He simply not the Messiah as John had always believed?

When Jesus received the inquiry from John's disciples, He gave an impressive response: "Go back and report to John what you hear and see: The blind receive sight, the lame walk, those who have leprosy are cured, the deaf hear, the dead are raised, and the good news is preached to the poor. Blessed is the man who does not fall away on account of me" (Matthew 11:4–6).

At first glance you would think Jesus was trying to inspire John. Something like, "Don't sweat it, John. I'm doing everything that you would expect of a Messiah." You have to admit it's a pretty impressive résumé—the blind seeing, the lame walking, people with leprosy being cured, the deaf hearing, even the dead being raised, and to top it all off, the good news being preached to the poor. How do you argue with that? You just expect John to be overwhelmed with joy, come back to his senses, and wonder how he could ever have questioned whether Jesus was the One.

Except for one problem: John already knew all of that. In fact, Matthew told us that was a part of the problem: "When John heard in prison what Christ was doing, he sent his disciples to ask him . . ." (11:2–3). Well, you know the question. The amazing and inspiring work of Jesus didn't eliminate John's doubts; it actually fueled them.

Talk about a dilemma. Why would Jesus' doing so much good jeopardize John's faith? How could the very things that Jesus was doing to help others cause John to lose heart? When we look at Jesus' response to John, we see one line that just doesn't fit. After He reinforced all of the evidence that He was the Messiah, retelling His miraculous work among the people, He closed with this seemingly disconnected thought: "Blessed is the man who does not fall away on account of me."

Why would Jesus add that? Why would He even consider the thought that someone might fall away with so much good happening? I can't imagine anyone coming up to me and saying, "Too many blind people are regaining their sight.

I'm having a crisis of faith." Or someone confronting me with, "If one more person who is paralyzed rises and walks, I'm out of here." Miracles are rarely followed by a flood of recanting. Why would Jesus feel He needed to exhort John that "after all this good has been confirmed to you, you will be blessed if you do not fall away on account of Me"?

What Jesus was saying to John has been far too barbaric for us to keep in the mainstream of the Christian faith. Jesus was saying to him, "John, I'm not coming through for you. I'm not getting you out of prison. I'm not sparing your life. Yes, I have done all this and more for others, but the path I choose for you is different from theirs. You'll be blessed, John, if this does not cause you to fall away."

If that were not bad enough, we find the dissonance of this reality accentuated in one verse. In his opening chapter, Mark stated, "After John was put in prison, Jesus went into Galilee, proclaiming the good news of God" (1:14).

What exactly, one might ask, was the good news for John? Jesus knew all along that John had been imprisoned. He very well knew the fate that John would face. Even then Jesus understood His purpose was to save us not from pain and suffering, but from meaninglessness. For Jesus, John was exactly where he needed to be, fulfilling God's purpose for his life. Why would He save John from that? In that same passage Jesus explained, "The time has come . . . The kingdom of God is near. Repent and believe the good news!" (Mark 1:15).

A DANGEROUS INVITATION

So what is this good news? The refined and civilized version goes something like this: Jesus died and rose from the dead so that you can live a life of endless comfort, security, and indulgence. But really this is a bit too developed. Usually it's more like this: if you'll simply confess that you're a sinner and believe in Jesus, you'll be saved from the torment of eternal hellfire, then go to heaven when you die. Either case results in our domestication. One holds out for life to begin in eternity, and the other makes a mockery out of life.

The call of Jesus is far more barbaric than either of these. It is a call to live in this world as citizens of an entirely different kingdom. In its primitive state the good news could never be separated from the invitation of Jesus to "come, follow Me." He never lied about the danger or cost associated with becoming His follower. He told them up front, "I am sending you out like sheep among wolves. Therefore be as shrewd as snakes and as innocent as doves" (Matthew 10:16).

One danger of civilized faith is that we become so domesticated, we begin to live as shrewd as the dove. We are blind to the spiritual nature of life and the unseen reality in which we reside. Another danger is that we become as innocent as snakes. For far too long, sincere followers of Christ have had to live with the consequences of those who use religion to manipulate others and camouflage hypocrisy. Jesus made clear to those who were choosing to be His disciples what kind of leader He was and what kind of followers would be required.

When Jesus asked Peter, "Who do you say I am?" Peter answered, "The Christ of God." Jesus went on to tell him,

> "The Son of Man must suffer many things and be rejected by the elders, chief priests and teachers of the law, and he must be killed and on the third day be raised to life." Then he said to them all: "If anyone would come after me, he must deny himself and take up his cross daily and follow me. For whoever wants to save his life will lose it, but whoever loses his life for me will save it. What good is it for a man to gain

the whole world, and yet lose or forfeit his very self?" (Luke 9:20–25)

THE ROAD LESS TRAVELED

There was no pristine call to a proper religion. It was a barbaric call to a barbarian way. Peter understood that and struggled to live up to it. Jesus' words about love ignited the primal fires within Peter's faith. Longing to follow Jesus even to His death, he declared to Jesus, "Lord, why can't I follow You now? I will lay down my life for You."

Jesus' simple response was, "Will you really lay down your life for Me? I tell you the truth, before the rooster crows you will disown Me three times." (See Matthew 26:31–35.)

Yes, Peter failed in his endeavor, but he understood what Jesus was asking for. Love and sacrifice were inseparable. The barbarian way is not about violence fueled by vengeance and hatred. The barbarian way is about love expressed through sacrifice and servanthood.

After Jesus' death and resurrection, Peter and Jesus had another conversation about love and sacrifice. Three times Jesus asked Peter if he loved Him. And each time Peter responded by adamantly declaring his love. In fact, the Scriptures tell us that Peter was hurt because Jesus asked him a third time, "Do you love Me?" Peter's response was, "Lord, You know all things. You know that I love You."

Ready to move the conversation to a deeper level, Peter found himself being called to the barbarian way. Jesus said to him, "'I tell you the truth, when you were younger you dressed yourself and went where you wanted; but when you are old you will stretch out your hands, and someone else will dress you and lead you where you do not want to go.' Jesus said this to indicate the kind of death by which Peter would glorify God. Then he said to him, 'Follow me!'" (John 21:17–19).

Jesus had only one invitation for Peter, only one course set for him, only one path for him to choose if he were to journey with Christ—and that was the way of the barbarian. Jesus never watered down the cost of following Him in hopes that Peter would then choose to follow. If Peter chose the path with Christ, it would mean for him that one day he would be taken against his will and dragged off to be killed. If he wanted to live a life of love and allegiance to the Christ, it would cost him his life. We, too, are called to a path filled with uncertainty, mystery, and risk.

So how did Peter respond? He turned and made John the focus of the conversation: "Peter turned and saw that the disciple whom Jesus loved was following them. (This was the one who had leaned back against Jesus at the supper and had said, 'Lord, who is going to betray you?') When Peter saw him, he asked, 'Lord, what about him?'" (John 21:20–21).

I know exactly what Peter was doing. He was thinking, *If I'm going to die, I want to make sure everyone else has to die, especially him. After all, if the barbarian call is for all of us, wouldn't it come out the same for all of us? Wouldn't all of us have to suffer hardship and die a brutal death?* But it just doesn't work that way.

Jesus answered him, "If I want him to remain alive until I return, what is that to you? You must follow me" (John 21:22).

This is the sticky part of the barbarian call. It's not fair or equitable. When you hear the call, when you follow the call, you must recognize that it is a life-and-death proposition. When you understand what Jesus means when He says that you must follow Him, you finally realize that this is not a cattle call. He is not calling you to the same life that everyone else will live. He's not even calling you to the same path that every follower of Christ will walk. Your life is unique before God, and your path is yours and yours alone. Where God will choose to lead you and how God chooses to use your life cannot be predicted by how God has worked in the lives of others before you. Jesus' response to Peter was as straight-forward as it could possibly get: "If I want John to live and you to die, what is that to you? Your part is to follow Me. My part is to lead the way."

IT'S A RISKY BUSINESS

Christianity as a civilized religion claims to have a group plan negotiated with God. Everybody gets the same package. And of course, the package is always the premium plan—get rich, get comfortable, get secure, get safe, get well when you get God. Everybody gets the John plan; nobody gets the Peter package. The result and proof of faith are that you get to live a life without risk, which is ironic when you realize that for the early church, faith was a risky business.

Hebrews 11 has become known as the "hall of faith." It begins with the declaration "Now faith is being sure of what we hope for and certain of what we do not see. This is what the ancients were commended for" (vv. 1–2).

Throughout the chapter, the writer challenges us with the power and vitality of ancient faith. He points to individuals such as Abel, Enoch, Noah, Abraham, Joseph, and Moses. He even refers to some surprising faith heroes such as Rahab and Samson. In summarizing the exploits of this extraordinary list, the writer explains their qualifications by telling us, "Who through faith conquered kingdoms, administered justice, and gained what was promised; who shut the mouths of lions, quenched the fury of the flames, and escaped the edge of the sword; whose weakness was turned to strength; and who became powerful in battle and routed foreign armies. Women received back their dead, raised to life again" (Hebrews 11:33–35).

This is the kind of stuff that all of us think of when we think of women and men of faith. When we live by faith, we don't die by the sword. When we live by faith, every battle is won and every enemy conquered. When we live by faith, lions go hungry, executioners become unemployed, and the Grim Reaper's prospects look grim.

But faith doesn't stop here. Oh, how I wish it did. It would make life so much easier. But it really only begins here. This short list of the faithful (and I want to emphasize *short*) is pointing us not to the rule, but to the exception to the rule. These men and women are listed exactly because their lives were so extraordinary and the results were so unusual. I'm not saying that God doesn't work like this anymore. What I am saying is that God is just getting started. He has far deeper and more profound work to do in and through us.

Any understanding of faith that is genuinely rooted in the Scriptures must always make room for the "others." Who are the others? We don't exactly know. We just know how faith worked out in their lives. After all, isn't that what Jesus was preparing us for? Speaking to His disciples, Jesus said, "If the world hates you, keep in mind that it hated me first . . . 'No servant is greater than his master.' If they persecuted me, they will persecute you also" (John 15:18–20). Peter continued this theme by reminding us: "Do not be surprised at the painful trial you are suffering, as though something strange were happening to you. But rejoice that you participate in the sufferings of Christ" (1 Peter 4:12–13).

Hebrews continues describing the heroes of faith in verse 35. After telling us that women received back their dead raised to life again, the writer states,

Others were tortured and refused to be released, so that they might gain a better resurrection. Some faced jeers and flogging, while still others were chained and put in prison. They were stoned; they were sawed in two; they were put to death by the sword. They went about in sheepskins and goatskins, destitute, persecuted and mistreated—the world was not worthy of them. They wandered in deserts and mountains, and in caves and holes in the ground. These were all commended for their faith, yet none of them received what had been promised. God had planned something better for us so that only together with us would they be made perfect. (Hebrews 11:35–40)

The others experienced a different result of faith. To say the very least, their lives were far less desirable than the lives of those we've come to know from biblical fame. Yet their lives were no less expressions of a life well lived and fully lived in the presence and power of God than those we aspire to emulate. All were commended for their faith. Although the first group of the faithful have names that will be known throughout history, the others remain nameless. That is not because they lived a life of lesser faith, but because there were so many more of them.

All of them chose and walked the barbarian way, and they were blessed because they did not fall away on account of Jesus. They trusted Jesus with their lives, and they lost their lives on the journey. If you could interview any one of them, however, each would insist that even in the midst of the suffering and hardship, he was most fully alive. They were not disappointed in God because they did not misunderstand who He was. They understood His call, and they chose it willingly. John the Baptist would join their number. Some barbarians survive the night in the lion's den; others experience their darkest night and wake in eternity.

CONFESSIONS OF A DANGEROUS MIND

Mariah and I were in San Diego, and after an event, I had a mildly hostile encounter. The experience somewhat unnerved her. But more than anything else, it seemed to pique her curiosity. She asked, "You make a lot of people mad, don't you, Dad?"

"Sometimes."

Pressing further, she asked, "Has anyone ever tried to hurt you?"

"Yes."

"Has anyone ever tried to kill you?"

I said, "Sort of."

"Tell me," she insisted with as much excitement as I've seen in a father-daughter conversation.

So I described an encounter I wrote about in *An Unstoppable Force*. I told her there was an ex-convict who let me know while he was in prison that as soon as he was released, he was going to bring my life to a close. Instead of waiting for him when he hit the streets, I found him in the projects. Knowing I had Mariah captivated, I did everything I could to heighten the danger and mystery of the moment. I paused right after describing the dingy room in which only the two of us stood face-to-face—William holding open the same blade with which he had slit another man's throat; me with nowhere to go.

Before I could go on, Mariah couldn't keep it in. With panic in her eyes she blurted out, "Did he kill you?"

It may seem cruel, but I refused to tell her. It's possible

that even to this day, my daughter thinks her father is dead. (I need to add that Mariah gives me permission to share this story with you on the condition that I clearly communicate to you that she was very tired that night.)

The barbarian understands the story we're in differently from the one who is civilized. Although Mariah should have known the outcome of my story, in some ways she has a better understanding of reality than some of us. We've been taught that every story Jesus writes with our lives ends with "and they lived happily ever after." Mariah knows better. She knows that good people die, that men and women who make heroic choices do not always live to tell their own tales. Sometimes another must tell the stories of their lives, recall the memory of their courage. The civilized view of Jesus is that He always comes through for us. Like Superman, He always shows up just in time to protect us and save us from disaster. His purpose is to ensure our safety, our convenience, and our comfort.

For years I have made it my mission to destroy the influence of the Christian cliché "The safest place to be is in the center of the will of God," but just this past week my wife, Kim, introduced me to one of the earlier uses of this adage.

It's found in the diary of Corrie ten Boom. Corrie's sister, Betsie, was encouraging her with this hope. I've always had a great disdain for this statement, but I have to admit this particular context shows me how far we've strayed from how it must have been understood. For Corrie and Betsie, the promise of safety in the center of God's will was fleshed out in concentration camps during the Nazi holocaust of the Jews. And although Corrie lived to tell the story, Betsie died in the midst of it.

Clearly neither of them concluded that this expression conveyed a belief that God would keep them from suffering hardship and even death. Betsie's statement was a declaration that to walk in the character of Christ is always the right choice, regardless of outcome or consequence. We have somehow perverted this more primal understanding to a far more civilized one. Instead of finding confidence to live as we should regardless of our circumstances, we have used it as justification to choose the path of least resistance, least difficulty, least sacrifice. Instead of concluding it is best to be wherever God wants us to be, we have decided that wherever it is best for us to be is where God wants us. Actually, God's will for us is less about our comfort than it is about our contribution.

God would never choose for us safety at the cost of significance. God created you so that your life would count, not so that you could count the days of your life.

HIGH-RISK VENTURES

Do you think John the Baptist felt safe being in the center of the will of God while Jesus was busy proclaiming the good news to others, yet leaving him in prison? And when John was about to lose his head over his allegiance to the Son of God, do you think he was feeling overwhelmed by God's protecting hand?

If the safest place to be is in the center of the will of God, then how do you explain the life and ministry of Stephen—one sermon and then stoned to death? Was he really that bad? If the safest place to be is in the center of the will of God, then why is it that the biblical word for *witness* is actually the word for *martyr*?

If the safest place to be is in the center of the will of God, then how do you explain the experience of Paul? Paul walked with God, and certainly whatever the center of the will of God looks like, Paul had to have visited there at least a few times in his life. His journals, however, described not a life filled with safety and certainty, but a life of adventure and danger. Paul said of his journeys:

> I have . . . been in prison more frequently, been flogged more severely, been exposed to death again and again. Five times I received from the Jews the forty lashes minus one. Three times I was beaten with rods, once I was stoned, three times I was shipwrecked, I spent a night and a day in the open sea, I have been constantly on the move. I have been in danger from rivers, in danger from bandits, in danger from my own countrymen, in danger from Gentiles; in danger in the city, in danger in the country, in danger at sea; and in danger from false brothers. I have labored and toiled and have often gone without sleep; I have known hunger and thirst and have often gone without food; I have been cold and naked. (2 Corinthians 11:23–27)

Somebody forgot to tell Paul how safe the center of God's will was. Having been given that insight, wouldn't he have known to redirect his life? Danger would have been his first clue that he was out of God's will—unless, of course, he was a barbarian. Paul had heard the barbarian call. He knew exactly who Jesus was and the life to which he had been called. Paul had been a religionist. He had learned the art of condemning others while hiding behind his pompous self-righteousness—which, by the way, is one of the great dangers of religion.

There may not be a more dangerous weapon for violence or oppression than religion. It seems counterintuitive, but when human beings create religions, we use them to control others through their guilt and shame. True religion always moves us to serve others and to give our lives to see those oppressed find freedom. Paul persecuted followers of Christ and even instigated their deaths, but then he risked his own life so that others might live. He once personified the very worst that happens when a religion becomes civilized. It moves away from God and oppresses humanity in God's name. Paul was once consumed by religion, but then he was transformed by the living presence of God Himself.

We, too, must find the barbarian way out of civilization. How have we come to this sanitized view of the faith to which

Jesus calls us? Somewhere along the way the movement of Jesus Christ became civilized as Christianity. We created a religion using the name of Jesus Christ and convinced ourselves that God's optimal desire for our lives was to insulate us in a spiritual bubble where we risk nothing, sacrifice nothing, lose nothing, worry about nothing. Yet Jesus' death wasn't to free us from dying, but to free us from the fear of death. Jesus came to liberate us so that we could die up front and then live. Jesus Christ wants to take us to places where only dead men and women can go.

I wonder how many of us have lost our barbarian way and have become embittered with God, confused in our faith because God doesn't come through the way we think He should. Is it possible that the transforming power of the church has been lost because we keep inviting people to step into the comfort, safety, and security of Jesus Christ? We've created a religious culture in which—even though we're the most blessed society in the history of the planet—our best-selling literature still focuses on how we can be more blessed. Maybe we need to step way back to the beginning of this movement.

The original call of Jesus was so simple, so clean, so clear:

"Follow Me." He wants us to surrender our lives to Him and follow Him into the unknown. And if it means a life of suffering, hardship, and disappointment, it will be worth it because following Jesus Christ is more powerful and more fulfilling than living with everything in the world minus Him. Have we forgotten this? Have we become so refined and so civilized that the benefits of our faith have become more precious and more valuable to us than the Benefactor of our faith?

I wonder how many of us are in that place of John the Baptist, at that crucible where God is asking, "Are you willing to lose everything on My behalf to gain everything I desire for you? Rather than living a long life, are you willing to live a life worth living?"

YOU FIRST

The Church Communication Network sent me an invitation to do a session on leadership at one of their national conferences. I had actually been unaware that training was available through this satellite system known as CCN. I had been asked to do a session where I would follow one of the most credible experts on church leadership. I was honored to get to do something in partnership with the caliber of leaders that were involved. I was both excited and nervous as I prepared to follow the main speaker. Somewhere in his lecture he started to say something that totally threw me. Point-blank he instructed, "Don't be an innovator; be an early adopter."

Hearing that created a crisis for me since I place an extremely high value on innovation. At Mosaic, the community where I serve as lead pastor in Los Angeles, we don't describe ourselves as a modern church or a postmodern church, a contemporary church or an emerging church. The only description I use is that we're an experimental church. We volunteered to be God's R&D Department. Anything He wants to do that other churches do not want to do or are unwilling to do, we'd like to take on. A part of our ethos (the spirit of our congregational culture) is a value for risk, sacrifice, and creativity.

The speaker went on to explain that the innovator is the guy who eats the poisonous mushroom and dies. The early adopter is the guy right next to him, who doesn't have to eat it. He can learn from the innovator's misfortune. Made perfect sense to me. That's why he's the man. Curious to me was my perception that he had pretty much been an innovator, the kind of guy who had eaten some pretty bad mushrooms and just happened to live to tell about it.

Before I knew it, it was my turn. Whatever I had planned to talk about was irrelevant to what was banging around in my head. *Should I stop being an innovator? Was the wise choice to become an early adopter?* But my mind wouldn't stop there. *What happened if everyone became an early adopter? Who would be the innovator? If no one ate the mushroom, how would we ever know which ones are safe? Without innovators, who could we depend on to die?*

With all this running through my brain, I let my talk go where the lecture and perhaps God's Spirit guided me. After thanking him for his amazing contribution to the body of Christ and for mentoring me through his books and ministry, I went on to thank him for a new metaphor for my life. I am a mushroom eater.

I understand the risks. Perhaps more than ever before, the implications are clear—any day now might be my last supper. But without risking the poisonous mushroom, we never would have discovered the joys of portobellos. In a short time I gave this a lot of thought: *Why did that guy eat that first poisonous mushroom?* Which led me to other profound questions: *What could possibly have motivated someone to eat a sea cucumber or a jellyfish? What exactly drove that first consumer to eat a raw oyster or to decide that snails were for more than stepping on?*

My conclusion was simple: they were hungry, maybe even starving. If you're trapped at sea long enough, maybe you begin to wonder if the same jellyfish that stung you could also satisfy you. I could see a father with starving children boil up a pot of snails, call them escargot, and begin dinner by saying, "Look, children, we're rich and sophisticated." Before aristocracy dubbed fish eggs "caviar," some mother stretching the catch of the day to feed her entire family simply called it "dinner."

Innovation is a life skill. When we're surrounded by civilization, innovation tends to be motivated by boredom. When we are barbarians trying to reach barbarians, innovation is motivated by love. Barbarians are a people of the earth. We know how to survive in the wild. We understand that whoever walks in front walks closest to death, but even this knowledge does not slow us down.

The barbarian call is just this simple: we are called to be mushroom eaters. A world without God cannot wait for us to choose the safe path. If we wait for someone else to take the risk, we risk that no one will ever act and that nothing will ever be accomplished. John the Baptist was a mushroom eater, and it cost him his life. Jesus, too, was a mushroom eater, and He found Himself nailed to a tree. Neither man saw his thirty-fifth birthday. Both of them point to the barbarian way.

CALLED OUT

If you don't like the idea of being an innovator, that's fine. Just do whatever Jesus calls you to do the moment it is clear to you. Do not procrastinate; do not hesitate; do not deviate from whatever course of action He calls you to. But I want to warn you, the closer you walk with Christ, the greater the faith required. The more you trust Him, the more you'll risk on His behalf. The more you love Him, the more you will love others. If you genuinely embrace His sacrifice, you will joyfully embrace a sacrificial life. Your expectations of Jesus will change as your intimacy with Him deepens. When you begin to follow passionately after Jesus, you will inadvertently find yourself innovating. After all, Jesus is transforming lives, writing history, creating the future, and unleashing the kingdom of God. If you plan to keep step with Jesus the Pioneer, you better expect some changes.

Our civilized faith demands caviar and escargot; our barbaric faith accepts that we might have to eat fish eggs and snails. We look to Jesus not to fulfill our shallow longings or to provide for us creature comforts. We look to Him to lead us where He needs us most and where we can accomplish the most good.

Barbarians hear a call different from that of civilized Christians. We understand clearly that we follow the God who chose the way of the Cross. If Jesus would not avoid the "place of the skull," then we should not be surprised where He might lead us. If even He found Himself sweating blood at Gethsemane, then we should be certain we will stand at crisis moments where all we can do after asking for relief is declare, "Not my will, but Yours." In those moments you may find very few who stand by you to provide you comfort and strength, and strangely enough, you may find far too many trying to reason with you that God would never require so much of anyone. Yet even with all the noise pounding inside your head, you will still clearly hear the voice of Christ and His barbarian call if you listen carefully enough.

3

THE
BARBARIAN
TRIBE

As John's disciples were leaving, Jesus began to speak to the crowd about John: "What did you go out into the desert to see? A reed swayed by the wind? If not, what did you go out to see? A man dressed in fine clothes? No, those who wear fine clothes are in kings' palaces. Then what did you go out to see? A prophet? Yes, I tell you, and more than a prophet. This is the one about whom it is written: 'I will send my messenger ahead of you, who will prepare your way before you.' I tell you the truth: Among those born of women there has not risen anyone greater than John the Baptist; yet he who is least in the kingdom of heaven is greater than he." (Matthew 11:7–11)

Although John was confused about Jesus, Jesus was not confused about John. Jesus knew that everyone else was confused about John. John lacked religious pedigree, yet he clearly spoke with spiritual power. At the same time he didn't look anything like a priest or a teacher of the law. To put it bluntly, John was just plain weird. Not what you would expect when you were looking for a spiritual leader. John's faith was raw and untamed. There was nothing civilized about him.

And Jesus seemed to be either mocking or rebuking them for expecting to find someone different. If you were looking for a reed swayed by the wind (someone easily molded by the expectations of the civilized) or a man dressed in fine clothes (someone who lives to impress the political or religious elite), you were looking in the wrong place. But if you went out to see a prophet, John was your man. And he was more than a prophet. He was the one whom God chose to prepare the way for the coming of His Son. Of all the men born of women— and that pretty much covers everybody but Adam—John was the greatest. Jesus, by the way, was born of God. The assumption was that for such a job, God would choose someone with polish and refinement.

Jesus wanted to make clear that the greater the kingdom responsibility, the more a barbarian is required. But then He added something that opened up a floodgate of possibilities for the rest of us. Jesus said, "Yet he who is least in the kingdom of heaven is greater than he" (Matthew 11:11).

That means great opportunities are yet available for the rest of us. Jesus expected that John would be joined by a barbarian tribe to follow. Jesus lived in a time when Judaism had been domesticated, institutionalized, and civilized; it was only a hollow shell of what God intended. John didn't fit into the organized religion of his time because God didn't fit either. Jesus Himself, the Messiah of Israel, remained an outsider even to His death.

Jesus described this barbarian controversy as He pointed out how domesticated they had become:

> To what can I compare this generation? They are like children sitting in the marketplaces and calling out to others:
>
> > "We played the flute for you, and you did not dance; we sang a dirge, and you did not mourn."

For John came neither eating nor drinking, and they say, "He has a demon." The Son of Man came eating and drinking, and they say, "Here is a glutton and a drunkard, a friend of tax collectors and 'sinners.'" (Matthew 11:16–19)

In other words, no matter what a person who is genuinely following God does, you find a reason to disdain him. Jesus concluded, "But wisdom is proved right by her actions."

Jesus was making clear that being a disciple was never intended to be the equivalent of being molded into a stereotype. Jesus and John were considered barbarians, even though they expressed themselves in different ways. But at the core they were the same. They lived and moved in the mystical. That is, they had a unique and transcendent connection to the Creator of the universe. Guided by the voice of God, they cared little how others perceived that. What was invisible to others was clear to them. Their lives could not be explained apart from God.

While He walked among us, Jesus tried to explain this to us. He told us—as if we should understand without difficulty—that He spoke only what He heard the Father saying and did only what He saw the Father doing. He called His disciples to make this their pattern for living.

Somehow Christianity has become a nonmystical religion. It's about a reasonable faith. If we believe the right things, then we are orthodox. Frankly whether we ever actually connect to God or experience His undeniable presence has become incidental, if not irrelevant. We have become believers rather than experiencers. To know God in the Scriptures always went beyond information to intimacy. We may find ourselves uncomfortable with this reality, but the faith of the Scriptures is a mystical faith. It leads us beyond the material world into an invisible reality. We become connected to the God of eternity. Who you are at the core is spirit. God is Spirit. To walk with God is to journey in the spiritual realm.

MYSTIC WARRIORS

Our spiritual heritage is filled with people like Enoch, who walked with God for three hundred years, and "then he was no more, because God took him away" (Genesis 5:21–24). And Abram, whose spiritual journey began with the voice of God calling him to a life of reckless abandon: "Leave your country, your people and your father's household and go to the land I will show you" (Genesis 12:1). "So Abram left, as the LORD had told him" (Genesis 12:4). And then there was Samuel, who heard a voice in the night. His story began, "In those days the word of the LORD was rare; there were not many visions . . . Then the LORD called Samuel" (1 Samuel 3:1, 10). Three times he heard the voice in the night. And following Eli the high priest's instruction, Samuel responded, "Speak, for your servant is listening." And, of course, who can forget Elijah, running from the evil Queen Jezebel and hiding in a cave in a mountain? The Lord commanded him to

> "go out and stand on the mountain in the presence of the LORD, for the LORD, is about to pass by." Then a great and powerful wind tore the mountains apart and shattered the rocks before the LORD, but the LORD was not in the wind. After the wind there was an earthquake, but the LORD was not in the earthquake. After the earthquake came a fire, but the LORD was not in the fire. And after the fire came a gentle whisper. When Elijah heard it, he pulled his

cloak over his face and went out and stood at the mouth of the cave. Then a voice said to him, "What are you doing here, Elijah?" (1 Kings 19:11–13)

These people, and many others like them, were the barbarian tribe. Their stories began and ended with God. They were mystical warriors called out to advance the cause of the Creator of the universe.

Every one of us who is a follower of Jesus Christ is called to join the same tribe, to live the same way. For the early disciples, Jesus was right there for them to watch and hear. For the rest of us, we have to learn how to see the invisible and hear the inaudible. We are called to join the barbarian tribe and to embrace our call as mystical warriors. Although you can learn important things about God from others, in the end to know the barbarian way you must receive your instructions from God Himself. If this isn't enough to drive you crazy, I don't know what is. Which I guess leads me to the point: there's a level of insanity that comes with the barbarian way.

Thoreau talked about individuals who march to the beat of a different drummer. Barbarians have never met the drummer. In the civilized view of discipleship, everything and everyone moves toward the center. Discipleship is translated into standardizing everyone into the same pattern. We have equated the promise that we would be conformed into the image of Christ with a belief that all of us will be the same. Discipleship has become the mechanism for uniformity rather than uniqueness.

Yet if we learn anything about God through John, it is that God has no problem with spiritual eccentrics. The point, of course, is not that God makes us mentally or emotionally imbalanced, but that He makes us passionately and spiritually unbalanced. God steers us in the direction of His kingdom, His purpose, His passions. His desire is not to conform us, but to transform us. Not to make us compliant, but to make us creative. His intent is never to domesticate us, but to liberate us.

Is it possible that God is the cause of such abnormality? How many of us would actually expect the person who came to prepare the way for Christ to present himself wearing animal skins, eating locusts, and wandering around in the desert? If he lived today, he would be medicated and diagnosed bipolar. He would be one more certified lunatic. And that's just what would happen if the church were in charge of his diagnosis. Most of us would think that John was out of his mind.

Confronted by John, we have to stop and ask ourselves: "If this is what the person looked like who prepared the way for Jesus, then what should a disciple of Jesus Christ look like who comes after Jesus? How is it possible that, for many of us, being a good Christian is really nothing more than being a good person?" The entire focus of our faith has been the elimination of sin, which is important but inadequate, rather than the unleashing of a unique, original, extraordinary, wonderfully untamed faith.

You can't escape that John acted like a madman. God drove him out of his mind. The path to which God called him put him out of step with the cultural rhythm. Paul struggled with the same dilemma. He told us that if his only concern were for God, he would be out of his mind. But for our sake, he stayed in his right mind.

UNTAMED FAITH

You cannot meet the Creator of the universe and remain the same. If the God who is all-powerful, all-knowing, and all-present comes to dwell within your soul, you would expect at least some minor disruption. I think there's a problem when people talk about meeting God or knowing God and yet remain unchanged by God. When the Creator chooses to dwell within His creation, there is transformation. If Jesus has come to dwell within you, you are no longer suited for a normal life.

To have the Spirit of God dwelling within the heart of someone who chooses a domesticated faith is like having a tiger trapped within a cage. You are not intended to be a spiritual zoo where people can look at God in you from a safe distance. You are a jungle where the Spirit roams wild and free in your life. You are the recipient of the God who cannot be tamed and of a faith that must not be tamed. You are no longer a prisoner of time and space, but a citizen of the kingdom of God—a resident of the barbarian tribe. God is not a sedative that keeps you calm and under control by dulling your senses. He does quite the opposite. He awakens your spirit to be truly alive.

This past year my daughter, Mariah, has been my travel companion on the barbarian way. She absolutely revels in the identity of being a barbarian. She gets it—you are most fully alive when you are on an adventure with God. Mariah loves to live and lives to love. While I love adventure and seem always drawn to risk, all my life I've been an accident waiting to happen. Mariah inherited my DNA. Put us together, and some kind of medical personnel or a rescue team is usually involved.

Our family was in New Zealand visiting some of our closest friends, the Crawfords. On one of our expeditions we went ATVing in the wild and beautiful terrain of *Lord of the Rings*. Even though she was only eleven at the time, we gave Mariah her own wheels. I have to admit I was pretty nervous watching her drive trails that banked against steep drops and led through moving streams and up and down steep hills. But when we hit the mud track, things got really exciting. Racing full speed ahead while getting caked with mud is as much as a barbarian could possibly hope for. It was the barbarian version of a mud bath right up until she lost control, hit the accelerator instead of the brake, and crashed head-on into her mother's parked ATV. Next stop, emergency room—a vital locale for the barbarian. Everyone was fine.

It was a bit embarrassing since the day before we had an incident while Jet Skiing off the coast of Wellington. I had taken the Jet Ski out by myself for a few wild and wide-open runs just to make sure everything would be okay. Then I came back and got Mariah. We were having a blast. Wind in our faces, water breaking in every direction, moving freely at breakneck speed. It was exhilarating. It was nothing less than a worship experience. Then we ended up with a dead engine, and we were drifting helplessly into Cook Strait.

Here is what happened. A moment before, we were moving wide open toward the strait, and then all of a sudden I felt Mariah let go. Her arms had been tightly secured around my waist, and the moment she released, I heard her yell, "Stop!"

Knowing she was in danger, I immediately shut down the Jet Ski and turned to secure her. I shouted, "What's wrong?"

Mariah's tone made it clear she thought it was obvious: "I needed to get my hair out of my eyes."

I had flooded the engine for cosmetic reasons. I guess it was about an hour later when the Wellington Rescue Squad came out and saved us. Did I mention that the water was frigid? As you can imagine, while we were drifting, we had a lot of time to talk and reflect. Just a bit irritated, I tried to understand why it was so important to get her hair out of her eyes.

It was so simple—she couldn't see. And isn't that the whole point of choosing to live an adventure—to keep your eyes wide open and to soak in the beauty of the life all around you? Mariah was not about to live through the experience with her eyes closed. Eyes wide open is exactly how God created us to live our lives. And this is exactly what Jesus has come to ensure—that we are awakened to live life wide open as we move full speed ahead.

When you join the barbarian tribe, you begin to live your life with your eyes and your heart wide open. When the Spirit of God envelops your soul, your spirit comes alive, and everything changes for you. You are no longer the same. And to those who cannot see the invisible, to those who refuse to believe it exists, the path you choose, the life you live, may lead them to conclude that you are not simply different but insane. People who are fully alive look out of their minds to those who simply exist.

A SPIRIT TRIBE

When I was twelve years old, I had my first visit to a psychiatrist. I had a lot of brokenness to deal with and a lot of junk to overcome. And after more than two decades of walking with Christ, I'm happy to say that while Jesus can wonderfully make you healthy, He has no ambition to make you normal. The healthier you become, the freer you are to simply be yourself. The more your identity is rooted in God's value for you, the less you are controlled and limited by what others think of you. If only fools fall in love and people who are in love act like fools, then those who are changed by God's love really do become fools for Christ.

Reading the Scriptures, I find a history of people who were driven out of their minds by the living God. God would continually call them to believe things they could not see, become someone they were not, accomplish feats that were clearly beyond their abilities, and then hold them accountable for it. Certainly that would be maddening. Yet for all who accepted the barbarian call, the same thing happened—they became different aliens.

Peter put it like this: "You are a chosen people, a royal priesthood, a holy nation, a people belonging to God, that you may declare the praises of him who called you out of darkness into his wonderful light. Once you were not a people, but now you are the people of God; once you had not received mercy, but now you have received mercy" (1 Peter 2:9–10).

He went on to describe us as aliens and strangers in the world; all of us different, but a part of the same tribe; all of us walking in the same direction, but on a unique path; all of us becoming what we could not be without the One who created us. When barbarians travel together, they do not march in single file. There is no forced conformity. They are not required or expected to keep in step. They walk together as free individuals joined not by standardization, but by spirit.

MYSTICAL AND MIRACULOUS

Just a few months after becoming a follower of Jesus Christ, I found myself back at college, but on an entirely new mission. I didn't know a whole lot about Christianity, so I went to everything that looked as if it was associated with the faith. I went to Catholic Mass, to a Baptist church, to a charismatic fellowship, to an interdenominational Bible study, and I worked on a project with the Church of Christ. I pretty much covered the entire spectrum of the Christian faith. It was like a buffet—all you can eat for $2.49. You know the kind of college meal I'm talking about—high consumption with low quality. I didn't care how good it was; I just wanted all I could get.

In one of those groups I had come to know a young woman who led worship. I was just learning how to play the guitar so she lent me her guitar throughout the week. One day, to my surprise, Beth came to me and began sharing openly about her life before she met Christ. She explained that she used to live with a guy, and she had just talked to him and decided to go back to him. Her motivations to turn back to her old life were surely more complex than she explained, but all she told me was that she didn't feel God anymore. Her conclusion was that God simply didn't love her. Sometimes it's easier to believe in a love you can touch than a love that is real.

When she told me that a part of her previous life involved drug abuse, it all began to make more sense. God is not a drug, and He certainly does not create experiences and emotions that make us feel better but not become better. I have to tell you I was shocked. She looked like the perfect church girl.

I was still learning that Christians can look great on the outside and be an absolute mess on the inside.

When she unloaded all of that on me, I had no idea what to do. I was pretty new at the whole thing and certainly had not been trained as a counselor. When she told me she didn't believe God loved her, I just knew that was wrong. Looking back, I realize I should have simply pointed her to the Cross. After all, His sacrifice is proof of His love. I just didn't think of it then. I'm always smarter after the crisis and pretty stupid during.

So when Beth accused God of not loving her, I turned to her and assured her that if there was anything God could do to prove His love to her, He would do it. I know better than to say that now, but I didn't know any better then. For some bizarre reason she immediately responded by saying, "Well, then I want it to snow."

Just imagine being in my place in that moment. In a million years it never would have occurred to me that this would be her response. I can't make it snow. I guess I kind of meant God would do whatever He needed to through me or someone else. You know, something "doable." And by the way, as a guy, I think this is why it's so difficult to communicate with women. A guy would have asked for a convertible or an F "miraculously" changed to an A or a date with a cheerleader—something reasonable.

What she asked for totally confused me. What I said in response confused me even more. All of a sudden I heard a voice saying, "God is going to make it snow for you." You can imagine my surprise when I realized that voice was mine. I suppose I can appeal to being in shock. As soon as I heard myself say that, I added, "Within twenty-four hours." I meant to say it would take Him more than twenty-four hours. I got it backward and ended up giving God and myself a time limit.

She left, celebrating that God was going to make it snow for her because He loved her. I left, feeling traumatized because it wasn't very likely to happen.

I went back to my dorm, pulled down the shades, and shut off the lights, and I got down on my face before God. Have you ever earnestly, desperately cried out to God? I don't know why I said what I said, but I can tell you, in that moment I was absolutely convinced God spoke to me and in some way spoke through me. I wasn't trying to be presumptuous; I certainly wasn't trying to claim I could perform a miracle. It was like a mental hiccup; the loss of oxygen created a spontaneous response. But it was too late. It was after the fact. All I could do was to beg God to be involved.

Honestly I blame God for the encounter. I was pretty sure He had put me up to it. On that basis I asked Him to please come through. But I'm also a realist. There was a real possibility that it wasn't God, that it was all just me, and that God was up in heaven yelling, "What were you thinking?"

I obviously don't remember everything I prayed that day, but part of it went something like this: "God, I don't know why I said that. I actually thought You said it, but if it wasn't You, could You sort of adopt the idea and take this project on?" I was crying out to God, praying desperately. I was out of my mind, and I fell asleep in the midst of my exhaustion. Several hours went by before my roommate, Mark, came back and awakened me. Just for the record, I think those hours I was asleep count as intercession. It's all about intent.

To my surprise, the first words out of his mouth were, "Have you looked outside?"

The first thing that crossed my mind was that somehow he knew. I was entirely unaware that Beth felt free to tell anyone she saw that God was going to make it snow for her since He loved her. I didn't tell her to do that. It never occurred to me that she wouldn't keep my insanity a secret. I realize now that I was at a deficit since I had read only the gospel of John. If only I had read the gospel of Mark. In Mark, after Jesus performed a miracle on someone's behalf, He said, "Go and tell no one." Having that knowledge would have been really helpful. I could have reduced the level of potential humiliation and sounded spiritual at the same time.

I wasn't at all sure what was motivating Mark's question. Was he mocking me or trying to warn me that I'd better get to work if this thing was going to turn out well? With little conversation I simply got up and walked over to the window. I remember taking a deep breath just before I pulled open the shades. I don't know what I was expecting to see, but I saw snow everywhere. Evidently it had started snowing almost immediately after I began my soulful conversation with God.

Of course, this is where I'm supposed to tell you I knew the whole time that it would snow, never had any doubts, never worried. But I still don't know how it happened. I'm not trying to explain it, just trying to share this story with you as

I experienced it. I'll never forget the warm feeling I had while running across that snow and finding this young woman playing in the gift that God sent just for her. At least on that day God changed her mind. It was on the same day that God drove me out of mine. Later I would go to seminary and learn that God doesn't speak like this anymore. Essentially I was told that God exchanged the mystical and miraculous for doctrine and ritual. What the Spirit once did, programs have now replaced, and even the Scriptures became proof that God had stopped speaking.

But what was I to do? I had already experienced God in both the mystical and the miraculous. God had already turned me into a barbarian. You could put a suit on me, but underneath there would always be a savage. Once the primal fires have been ignited, fluorescent lights just won't do. I could have rationalized everything I experienced. The problem was that it wasn't an isolated event. Those who brought me to the faith did not take the time to civilize me. They brought me to the barbarian way and never tried to make me like them— only like Christ. They brought me into the presence of the living God and knew that His presence would both consume me and transform me.

CLOUDED THINKING

In the closing verses of Exodus that barbarian journey is described this way:

> The cloud covered the Tent of Meeting, and the glory of the LORD filled the tabernacle. Moses could not enter the Tent of Meeting because the cloud had settled upon it, and the glory of the LORD filled the tabernacle. In all the travels of the Israelites, whenever the cloud lifted from above the tabernacle, they would set out; but if the cloud did not lift, they did not set out—until the day it lifted. So the cloud of the LORD was over the tabernacle by day, and fire was in the cloud by night, in the sight of all the house of Israel during all their travels. (Exodus 40:34–38)

The civilized build shelters and invite God to stay with them; barbarians move with God wherever He chooses to go. The civilized Christian has a routine; the barbarian disciple has a mission. The civilized believer knows the letter of the law; the barbarian disciple lives the spirit of the law. The religiously civilized love tradition; the barbarian spirit loves challenges. The civilized are satisfied with ritual; barbarians live and thrive in the mystical. For the civilized disciple, religion provides stability and certainty; for the barbarian, a life in God is one of risk and mystery.

And maybe even a little insanity. There's no way to escape that barbarians can appear out of their minds. No reasonable person would ever fully follow God everywhere He calls. God is simply unreasonable.

No matter how we try to spin the story, the Bible is filled with tribes of irrational people. When Noah built the ark, he did not live in a flood zone. When Elijah called fire down from heaven, he had never tried it before. Go ahead. Give it a shot. See if it works for you. I didn't think so. David should have left the giant alone. Hosea never should have married a prostitute. What was Moses thinking when he pointed his staff at the Red Sea—that it would move because he commanded it? And that's just to mention the more popular and highly admired followers of God.

Those people did not live normal lives. Their actions were ludicrous and irrational if you take God out of the formula. Given proper counseling, they would have known better than to do what they did. The vitality of their life in God moved them beyond the practicality of simply being reasonable. Their lives didn't make sense, their actions defied sensibility, because God drove them out of their senses. Anyone who ever risks listening to God and following His voice knows that to everyone who is deaf to His voice, your actions will seem as if you've gone crazy.

I used to serve on the Board of Intercultural Studies at Biola University, mostly because a friend of mine asked me if I would. But after a while I wondered why I said yes. I almost never went. I hate meetings. I would much rather be outdoors than in a boardroom. Usually I asked, "Do you want me in the morning, afternoon, or evening?" I couldn't get myself to commit to the whole day.

One afternoon I happened to be there when the counseling department enthusiastically presented a plan for serving missionary personnel around the world. They were going to provide access to counseling and mental health to all those working overseas. Even while I was listening, I knew I should remain silent. I kept telling myself to keep my mouth shut: *Don't say anything; don't cause any problems; don't embarrass yourself.* But I just couldn't help myself.

Before I knew it I was blurting out, "Don't do it. Please don't do it."

They all looked at me with the strangest expressions of confusion.

Well, it was too late for me to hide in obscurity, so I knew I needed to explain. I went on, "Don't go around the world and make our missionaries mentally healthy. You'll ruin everything. You'll totally mess up the cause. I mean you have, let's say, a husband and a wife from Kentucky and they have four kids and they believe God has called them to an obscure city in Central Asia. Suddenly they find themselves in the middle of two million people who don't speak a word of English, and they don't speak a word of Mandarin or Cantonese or any form of tribal dialect. And each morning they wake up excited and confident that somehow they're going to bring that entire city to faith in Jesus Christ. You go and make them normal, and they'll be on a plane back home the next day."

The board member making the presentation graciously responded, "Erwin clearly has a different view of professional counseling than we do."

These people have got to be crazy to do what they're

doing and insane to believe that it's possible, don't they? They are not insane, but they are crazy. One day they just got up and took the barbarian way out of civilization.

If you are a follower of Christ and you have allowed yourself to be domesticated, you have lost the power of who you are and who God intends for you to be. You were not created to be normal. God's desire for you is not compliance and conformity. You have been baptized by Spirit and fire. Asleep within you is a barbarian, a savage to all who love the prim and proper. You must go to the primal place and enter the presence of the Most High God, for there you will be changed by His presence. Let Him unleash the untamed faith within you.

GOD-TAUGHT

At pentecost God unleashed His Spirit upon all who would declare Jesus their hope. In that moment a new tribe was born—a Spirit tribe. To all who would believe in His Son, the Lord God declares, "I will be their God, and they will be My people." This tribe would bear the evidence of His Spirit. They would be God-taught, God-moved, and God-inspired.

Our spiritual legacy is that we belong to this barbarian tribe. From the first human to the present, the history of God is one of conversation and transformation. The Scriptures are filled with stories of women and men who heard God speak and acted as if hearing Him were normal. Hearing God is not only to be normal, but also to be an essential proof of belonging to God. To be taught by God is one of the primal evidences that you have entered the new covenant ushered in by Jesus. In Jeremiah 31:33–34, the Lord declares:

"This is the covenant I will make with
  the house of Israel
  after that time," declares the LORD.
"I will put my law in their minds
  and write it on their hearts.
I will be their God,
  and they will be my people.
No longer will a man teach his neighbor,
  or a man his brother, saying, 'Know the LORD,'
  because they will all know me,
  from the least of them to the greatest."

To study the Bible is important, but it is not a primal evidence that you belong to God. Anyone can study the Bible, but only those who know Him can hear His voice and are taught by Him. Although the barbarian may not be formally trained, she is always God-taught. Jesus expected that those who were His followers would hear His voice, know His voice, and follow only His voice, even as He calls us out by name and leads us on the barbarian way.

HEARING VOICES

My son, Aaron, was probably five or six when he began asking me about the voice of God. He would often hear me talk about having conversations with God (most of us call this prayer), and it piqued his curiosity. On top of that, week by week he heard me teach and share mystical and miraculous experiences with God. I should have been prepared for the question, but it actually caught me off guard. When he asked me, "What does God's voice sound like?" I really didn't know how to answer. I guess when I think about it, God's voice sounds a lot like my voice. After all, the Spirit speaks to us through the conscience as well as through the Scriptures. Even when I'm reading the Scriptures, the voice I'm hearing is mine reading the text. In my experience the voice of God is an intimate experience, but not an audible one. Or at least it's not a voice coming from the outside in, but a voice coming from deep within.

I can't quite remember what I told him. Keep in mind, he was only five or six. I think my response was something like, "That's a great question. Now go watch cartoons."

A few years later, after many other similar inquiries, Aaron went off to his first junior high camp in Big Bear, about two hours from Los Angeles. Somewhere in the middle of the week, one of the other pastors at Mosaic, whose daughter was also at the camp, decided to go up with me so we could see our kids.

I expected to find Aaron having a great time, growing in the Lord, and making new friends. Instead, he had gotten himself into deep trouble. Evidently on their first lunch break he was involved in a fight. But it wasn't really a fight; it was sort of a "prefight." You know, the stuff guys do before the fight because they don't really want to fight.

Anyway, some kid said something, and Aaron said something back. The tension heightened, the smack deepened, and the next thing you know, Aaron's lunging at him and his friends are holding him back. By the time I got there two days had passed, and Aaron refused to ask for forgiveness. And if acting on his hostility wasn't bad enough, he had to go off and be the classic son of a preacher. In typical male form, he had to describe what he was going to do to his antagonist before he proceeded to do it. In short, he yelled out, "I'm going to beat the crap out of you." (In case you're wondering, *crap* is not an acceptable descriptive term used in our home.) I went to celebrate my son's spiritual pilgrimage, and I found myself in the middle of an all-out war.

I knew the Lord was working already because when Aaron tried to assault the other kid, his friends held him back. The other kid was huge and probably would have killed Aaron. We already had something to be grateful for.

When I confronted Aaron and asked him if the story I was given was accurate, he said, "Absolutely." He didn't deny anything. He also wasn't sorry for anything. I told him he needed to ask for forgiveness, and he told me that wasn't going to happen. He wasn't sorry, he would do it again, and upon reflection, he was sorry for only one thing—he didn't get at least one good punch in before they brought him down.

Trying to understand what in the world could have made Aaron so angry, I asked him to tell me what motivated him to attack the kid. Aaron said, "Dad, I don't care what you say. He said something about Mom. Anyone who says something about my mom is going to have to deal with me."

You can imagine my response: "He said something about your mom? What did he say about your mom?" I have to admit, I was with him.

Anyway, I still insisted that he needed to make things right. He said he would not, and in fact, he insisted on being allowed to leave the camp. He reminded me that I had committed to him that he would never have to pretend or play the Christian game. I told him if that's what he wanted to do, he could leave. I also told him I felt it was a mistake. He insisted and asked me if I would help him pack. I said no, I wouldn't stop him from leaving, but I wouldn't help him leave either. So for the next hour he put together his stuff, dragged it up the hill, and pushed it into the car.

Just as we were about to leave, I asked him to sit with me and talk one last time before we drove away. We sat on two large rocks in the middle of the woods. I asked him a simple question: "Aaron, is there any voice inside you telling you what you should do?"

He paused and then responded, "Yes."

"What's the voice telling you?"

"That I should stay and work it out."

I asked him, "Can you identify that voice?"

He immediately said, "Yes. It's God."

It was the moment I had waited for. I didn't expect it to come under those circumstances. Nevertheless, it was there. I turned to Aaron and said, "Aaron, do you realize what just happened? You just heard the voice of the living God. He spoke to you from within your soul. Forget everything else that just happened. God has spoken to you, and you were able to recognize Him."

I'll never forget his response: "Well, I'm still not doing what He said."

I explained to him that was his choice, but this is what would happen. If he rejected the voice of God and chose to disobey His guidance, his heart would become hardened, and his ears would become dull. And if he continued on this path, there would be a day when he would never again hear the voice of God. There would come a day when he would deny that God even speaks or has ever spoken to him. But if he treasured God's voice and responded to Him with obedience, then his heart would be softened, and his ears would always be able to hear the whisper of God into his soul.

Aaron chose to stay, I'm grateful to say. If he had chosen differently, he would have begun the path toward domestication. Perhaps he never would have rejected the faith overtly. He might have even chosen to be a faithful attender at a church and been by everyone else's estimation a good man, but he would no longer be a barbarian.

ENCOUNTERED

Years later when Aaron was about fourteen, I saw this so clearly. We were driving in the car together and had one of those gut-wrenching heart-to-heart talks. "Dad, I think that if I had not been raised in a Christian home, I would not be a Christian," he said.

You can imagine the rush of emotions going through me. It took all the restraint I had to not panic and stay calm. "Why do you think that?" I asked as if his statement had no emotional effect on me.

Aaron continued, "I have way too many doubts and questions."

"Oh," I said, sounding as relieved as I could. "I have those too. So what are you going to do?"

I'll never forget Aaron's answer. It was one of the clearest confirmations that my son was not an unwilling member of a religion, that he, too, was a true barbarian. "Well, I've met God. So what are you supposed to do?"

I affirmed, "That's a dilemma, isn't it?"

So many of us have put our hope in teaching our children about God rather than guiding them into an experience with God. We essentially civilize our children rather than guide them to the barbarian way. I am concerned that there are many who have grown up in church and have been effectively Christianized but have never genuinely met Christ. In the days of Jonathan Edwards, he faced the same dilemma when the congregation of his time had a Halfway Covenant. The children of members were essentially Christians who had never met Christ. His classic message, "Sinners in the Hands of an Angry God," was directed not to the unchurched, but to the church. Our goal must not be to populate the Christian religion but to bring people into a genuine relationship with God. We must make a clear distinction between the religion of Christianity and the revolution that Jesus began two thousand years ago.

GOD-MOVED

A second primal evidence of the barbarian spirit is unleashed when you enter into covenant with God. Not only are you God-taught as a disciple of the living God, but you are also God-moved. God informed us that He has a strategy for reestablishing His reputation among the nations:

> Say to the house of Israel, "This is what the Sovereign LORD says: It is not for your sake, O house of Israel, that I am going to do these things, but for the sake of my holy name, which you have profaned among the nations where you have gone. I will show the holiness of my great name, which has been profaned among

the nations, the name you have profaned among them. Then the nations will know that I am the LORD, declares the Sovereign LORD, *when I show myself holy through you* before their eyes." (Ezekiel 36:22–23, italics added)

God made an emphatic declaration that He will prove He is God and He is holy not through His action but through the actions of His people. A civilized faith relates to right and wrong as a moral obligation. A barbarian faith loves good and hates evil. There is no obligation fueling the actions of His people. They are passionate about the very things that are on the heart of God. Their motivation is not external, but intrinsic. They are moved from the inside out. Speaking again of this new covenant, God described what this primal transformation will look like:

I will give you a new heart and put a new spirit in you; I will remove from you your heart of stone and give you a heart of flesh. And *I will put my Spirit in you and move you to follow* my decrees and be careful to keep my laws. You will live in the land I gave your forefathers; you will be my people, and I will be your God. (Ezekiel 36:26–28, italics added)

From the moment we become citizens of the kingdom of God, we become aliens and strangers in a world that chooses to live absent of God. From the first step taken to follow Jesus, we are out of step with the rest of the world. Once your life is in sync with the story of God, you become out of sync with any story that attempts to ignore or eliminate God. You are a stranger to them, an alien among them, a nomadic wanderer who, while refusing to be rooted in this life, seems to somehow enjoy this life most.

Probably motivated by movies such as *Men in Black,* Aaron once asked me if there really were aliens among us. I told him that of course there were, and that we had to register with the government to gain peaceful admission. A bit unnerved, he asked me if I was implying that I was an alien. I told him that while I had chosen to keep this confidential in the past, it was a good time to let him know the truth: I was an alien in this land. He said, "Prove it."

I pulled out my green card that had my picture and the declaration "Resident Alien." I tried to calm him down by assuring him that he was still half human. It didn't seem to help. Okay, so I'm only from El Salvador. Not quite as glamorous as being Vulcan or Romulan, but an alien nonetheless. It's ironic that now our entire family is legitimately alien. Our citizenship is in eternity; history is our temporary residence. You are no different. Every one of us who hears the barbarian call of Christ and chooses to follow will become a foreigner and perhaps even an outcast in the time and place in which we live.

John the Baptist heard the voice of God and became an outcast among those to whom God was silent. His life was short, and if his death lacked anything, it was dignity; yet he was considered great in the sight of God. First pointing to him, Jesus then pointed to us. He promised that the least in the kingdom of heaven would be greater than even John. Jesus was pronouncing the coming of a tribe. Where there was one, there would soon be millions.

All who belong to the barbarian tribe are like Moses, who stepped toward the fire and heard the voice of God. For them the whole earth is holy ground. They do not separate between sacred and secular or real life and spiritual life. All of life is sacred; every action is spiritual. God is everywhere for them and in all things at all times.

WATER GRAVE

One Sunday morning a young woman named Nicole and her friends introduced me to Dathan. Dathan is one of those guys who stands out in the crowd—built like a rock, big smile, charismatic personality. Dathan lives in Los Angeles and is pursuing a career as an actor. He's also in the process of preparing for tryouts, hoping to make it as a defensive back in the NFL. Having grown up in Philly, he had chosen the path of hard-core crime and violence, so it was strange that my first conversation with him was about fear.

He had just become a follower of Jesus Christ, and Nicole had asked him if he was ready to be baptized. Her question evoked an unexpected response. He was terrified. So they brought him to me so that I could talk him through it. After brief introductions, I asked him to tell me what the problem was. He explained that he was afraid of water. The baptism was planned for Dockweiler Beach, and he just didn't feel he could go through with it.

I asked him if he was just afraid of the ocean or if there was more to it. He went on to explain that he was terrified of sharks. Later I learned that when he was about eleven years old, he was in the water and saw one of his friends being attacked. He was an eyewitness to a horrific and tragic event. It had been many years, but the memories of that event still haunted him.

I told him that there were other options. We could baptize him in a pool or even a Jacuzzi. That seemed to alleviate his concern a bit, and he began to relax. Then I added, "But that would sort of be the easy way out. You don't look like the kind of guy who takes the easy way out of anything." I went on, "What do you think is the likelihood you would get eaten by a shark the day you're baptized? I mean, the percentages have to be really low—like one in a million or maybe one in a thousand. Anyway, it's really unlikely that you would be attacked by a shark if you chose to be baptized in the ocean."

He nodded in agreement, but my comments clearly didn't help.

"Well, think of it like this," I said. "The likelihood is so low that you would get attacked by a shark, you would know it was God's will for your life if a shark did attack you." I don't know why, but the thought wasn't all that comforting to him. Then I added, "But if you live, if perchance no shark kills you and you survive the experience, then you will know without a shadow of a doubt that God has kept you alive, that He has a purpose for you to fulfill." I closed our conversation by concluding, "I think the pool or Jacuzzi would be okay for someone else, but I think for you it's going to have to be the ocean."

I left him with a decision to make. Would he hear the barbarian call, or would he immediately choose to be domesticated?

It wasn't long before Dathan informed me that he was headed to the beach. He had an appointment with destiny. To facilitate his experience, I asked some of my friends to take him to a shark reserve so he could spend some time with his friends. On the day of his baptism, the waves were strong and the waters rough. One man walked on each side of him as he worked his way out deeper into the ocean. A wave hit him head-on and knocked the other two men into the water, but Dathan, determined not to go under until he had to, grabbed both and willed them back up.

After he was immersed in the ocean and worked his way to the beach, he threw himself into the sand and wept. I asked him later what overwhelmed him. He said it wasn't fear; it was the knowledge that God had a purpose for his life.

Now you might be thinking this is a bit of overkill or even emotionally abusive, but if I've learned anything over the years, it's that it is a grave error to try to domesticate a barbarian. We live in a world of wandering barbarians who do not know God. They have no interest in civilized religion and no time for the games of the proper and refined. Dathan had acted on the worst of his passions, and nothing but a new passion would set him free. Dathan needed to understand that it was a life-and-death decision.

It shouldn't surprise us that Paul described baptism as a water grave. He chose this imagery to describe this sacred passage: "Don't you know that all of us who were baptized into Christ Jesus were baptized into his death? We were therefore buried with him through baptism into death in order that, just as Christ was raised from the dead through the glory of the Father, we too may live a new life" (Romams 6:3–4).

Only a few months after his baptism, Dathan landed a part in a movie pulling together a potential cast of Ed Norton, Nicolas Cage, and Taye Diggs. His, of course, was a smaller part, but in the midst of it he had to make a big decision. He was offered a scene that would be standard in the industry but was now beneath his standards. It would have been easy for Dathan to justify the fact that it's just the way of the civilized, but he chose to follow his barbarian call. He turned down a scene that could have helped establish his career and chose instead to establish his character. His decision wasn't about legalism; he was moved from the inside out to do what would bring God pleasure and honor His name. And like Dathan, all of us, if we are to follow Jesus with the passion He desires and deserves, must face the sharks and never submit to them.

We're all called to pass through the water grave. Yes, the way into the tribe of God is barbaric. You are joined with the death of Christ, buried with Him, and raised to live again. The barbarian has tasted death, has faced death, has conquered death. What do you fear when you have already died and you walked away? Your greatest fears are behind you, and you now go where only those once dead, yet alive, can go. It is here where the third primal expression of the barbarian spirit is born in every follower of Christ. The barbarian way is a path where we are God-taught and God-moved, but we are also God-inspired.

GOD-INSPIRED

The prophet Joel described the catalytic effect of the barbarian spirit ignited by the new covenant:

> I will pour out my Spirit on all people.
> Your sons and daughters will prophesy,
>   your old men will dream dreams,
>   your young men will see visions.
> Even on my servants, both men and women,
>   I will pour out my Spirit in those days.
>   (Joel 2:28–29)

God's ultimate end for our transformation is to unleash the untamed faith within. When His Spirit is poured into our lives, we are inspired to an extraordinary level of living. Barbarians never exist simply to survive. Barbarians never just get through the day. Barbarians wake to live and live life fully awake. To be filled with the Spirit of God is to be filled with dreams and visions that are too compelling to ignore. Live or die, succeed or fail, barbarians must pursue and attempt such dreams and visions. The barbarian spirit dreams great dreams and finds the courage to live them.

The barbarian call confronts us with all we love and all we fear. We resist love to avoid pain and squelch our dreams out of fear of failure. For the Spirit of God to unleash dreams and visions within our souls, we must become free to risk and to fail. Every dream born of God is fueled by love. Every conversation to be had with God challenges the boundaries of our imagination. When we turn to God, His love transforms us and ignites a new passion within us. All that we have loved is consumed by the passions of a new heart. We discover the power and force of love in its purest form. At the same time, when we turn our hearts toward God, all of our fears are consumed by one fear. We are called to fear only God. There is an important reason for this. What we fear is what we're subject to; our fears define our master. Where there is no fear, there is no control.

When we fear God and God only, we are no longer bound by all of the other fears that would hold us captive. The fear of death, the fear of failure, the fear of rejection, the fear of insignificance—all of the fears that know us by name and haunt us in the dark of the night become powerless when we know the fear of the Lord. And if this is not enough, we discover that perfect love casts out all fear. Not even God will hold us or control us by fear. When we fear Him, we in essence begin to live a life where we are fearless.

The freedom to love and the freedom from fear make the barbarian an entirely different species within the whole of humanity. This may be the most extraordinary mark of the Spirit of God within the heart of humanity: the freedom to live out dreams greater than ourselves. Yet if we were honest with ourselves, the church would be the last place most people would go to have their dreams nurtured, developed, and unleashed.

FESTIVAL OF LIFE

One of the great joys I've been privileged to experience as a result of writing *Chasing Daylight* has been receiving the stories of people from all over the world who have chosen to redirect their lives to pursue the dreams that had remained latent within them. As lead pastor of Mosaic, I regard this as an essential measure of spiritual health and vitality. When the church becomes an institution, people are nothing more than volunteers to be recruited. When the church is a movement, our stewardship becomes the unleashing of our God-given gifts, talents, and passions. My goal is not to cast a vision that everyone buys into, but to create a visional community where everyone who enters in begins to have wild and God-sized dreams and visions. There is a price to pay, of course, when you choose this particular path; you end up with an unruly barbarian tribe. They keep getting called by God to do things you didn't expect or really didn't want them to do.

From our community in Los Angeles we have social workers in New Delhi; artists in Istanbul; an aspiring chef in Paris; a dancer, a film editor, a soon-to-be doctor, and a fashion designer in New York; businesspeople in China; a psychologist and educator in Lithuania; an environmental engineer in Morocco; and the list goes on and on and on. I cannot overemphasize how difficult these people are to replace. Yet as much complexity as this brings and as much instability as this creates, it pales in comparison to watching lives being wasted on careers and occupations that were taken on as a result of obligation or lack of courage to pursue the dreams that were waiting to be realized.

While modern man keeps hoping we will evolve into something that will be godlike, the barbarian way unveils that our best future is found in our primal beginnings. Evolution is not the key to humanity's freedom; transformation is. There is a metamorphosis waiting to happen within every one of us. A part of this metamorphosis is discovering your divine destiny and knowing for the first time who you were created to become. When the Spirit of God comes to live within you, you strangely become aware of your inadequacy and your extraordinary potential. When you choose the path of a civilized religion, any change that is worth noting is at best incremental. It is only when you choose the barbarian way that the result is revolutionary.

Recently I heard an old Celtic proverb that says you should never give a sword to a man who can't dance. This couldn't be more true than on the barbarian way. Every mystic warrior finds his strength from his inner joy. This is what Nehemiah declared as he called God's people to rise up and face their impending challenge: "Go and enjoy choice food and sweet drinks, and send some to those who have nothing prepared. This day is sacred to our Lord. Do not grieve, for the joy of the LORD is your strength" (Nehemiah 8:10).

You have now joined a tribe of dreamers and visionaries,

and this is no small part of why you are passionate to bring others into this community of faith, hope, and love. You have found through the liberation of your soul that each barbarian walks a path that unleashes raw and untamed faith.

4

THE
BARBARIAN
REVOLT

From the days of John the Baptist until now, the kingdom of heaven has been forcefully advancing, and forceful men lay hold of it. (Matthew 11:12)

Not long ago Aaron asked me, "Dad, would you purposefully put us in danger?"

"Yes," I answered, "of course."

Without blinking an eye his response was simply, "That's what I thought. I was just making sure." I could tell he was tying together all the pieces of his more recent travels. In retrospect, he could see more clearly the reality of the danger and volatility of which he had been in the midst.

I wonder how many of us have actually had this conversation with God: "Abba, Father, Dad, would You purposefully put me in danger?" I think a lot of us haven't asked God that question because we went ahead and answered it for Him. Of course He wouldn't do that. We're His children. We're family. He wouldn't purposefully endanger us, not even to accomplish a higher or nobler purpose. Or would He? Maybe you should stop and ask Him. His answer might surprise you. It certainly surprised John the Baptist.

There is a barbarian revolt taking place, and its command center is the kingdom of God. Everywhere the kingdom of God advances, there is a violent engagement against a dark kingdom. To be born of God is to be made a citizen in the kingdom of God, and the kingdom of God is at war. Do not confuse this kingdom with Paradise. Salvation is not reentry into a Paradise Lost; it is enlistment in the mission of God.

Jesus is telling us in no uncertain terms that there is a battle raging. This is perhaps the most important reason why we must choose the barbarian way and resist any temptation to become civilized. Domesticated Christians are far too willing to abdicate the battle for the soul of the world. Civility focuses our energy on all the wrong places. We spend our lives emphasizing our personal development and spiritual well-being. We build churches that become nothing more than hiding places for the faithful while pretending that our actions are for the good of the world. Or we choose political and secular vehicles to try to advance our cultural values, strangely attempting to make unbelieving people act like civilized believers.

In contrast Jesus calls us to a different way. He tells us this is a battle of kingdoms. He insists that if we are His followers, we must not live in a world defined only by the material. We cannot limit our sights to what is flesh and blood. We should know better than that. To see from a kingdom perspective is to know that there is a conflict of invisible kingdoms and that people's lives are forever changed by what happens in the unseen. We are called to be warriors of light in dark places. We are mystical warriors who use weapons not of this world.

A DIVINE INSURRECTION

For centuries the nations that have considered themselves civilized have chosen weapons that wield pain and destruction on the weak and innocent. The Romans, borrowing the phrase from the Greeks, described as *barbarians* all who were not of Rome. And certainly the Romans exemplify the great virtues of civilization. From violence to decadence, they could justify the most cruel and base actions against all who were not a part of them since the "others" were beneath them.

It's appropriate that the first Christians were barbarians to Rome. History tells us there came a day when the same barbarians turned Rome upside down. Tragically it wasn't long before Rome seduced and civilized the early church. The church did, in fact, become Roman. The church became civilized. And soon the same violence and decadence defined the Christian faith rather than opposed it. We put on robes, built cathedrals, accumulated wealth and power, then lost our barbarian way.

We find Judaism in the same tragic condition during the days of Jesus. Really it's an incredibly strange scenario to watch. Given that Jesus Himself is the God of Israel, it should strike us as extraordinary that He was not welcome there. But then again, Jesus didn't like it there. One of Jesus' most violent moments took place in the temple. He became disgusted by what He saw. He was so incensed by how Judaism had become a religious retail business that He began to destroy all of the sellers' merchandise.

It's important to point out that Jesus was not against business. His anger wasn't a response to people selling something of value or providing a meaningful service. His anger was evoked because the sellers of goods had made access to God a business. They had made forgiveness something you could purchase. They had made the guilt and shame of others the marketplace for their profit. They had made the house of God into a den of robbers and thieves. They had become so good at religion that they had no need for God. They were so full of themselves that they had no room for God. When it came down to it, they loved their civilized religion far more than they longed to know the God who created them. They treasured the civilization built around their religion and despised the primal faith from which it was born. They would rather have the temple than the Presence.

So Jesus let them have it, which begs the question: What good is a house of God if God no longer chooses to live there? Speaking of His own body, Jesus challenged them to destroy the temple, and God would raise it up after three days. They thought He meant the work of art built by the hands of men. They could not for a moment imagine that God would choose so barbaric a container as flesh and blood. It shouldn't surprise us that soon after they destroyed the Temple of God, God destroyed their temple.

There may be no clearer place where we see the division between the civilized and the barbarian. We discover the painful reality that even God's people, when we become civilized, are more than willing to crucify God. When we choose a civilized faith, God becomes, at the very least, an irritant and, at worst, an enemy to our faith. We find in Jesus that the hostility of God turns toward empty religion and the mercy of God turns toward the outcast and sinner. The way that Jesus called the masses to choose was far too barbaric for those who held the positions of religious leadership. The claim that He must become the sacrificial Lamb who would take away the sins of the world was an insult to their sense of piety and self-righteousness.

But maybe the most insulting thing that Jesus said or did was to become the friend of sinners. He focused His ministry on women and men who were despised by those in spiritual authority. The path God chose for Himself was far too common for their sensibility. They couldn't imagine that God would choose that kind of life for Himself. God would be above such things. God was far too civilized to choose such barbarism.

Luke described this conflict between Jesus and the religious leaders of His time as he followed the conversion of Levi:

> After this, Jesus went out and saw a tax collector by the name of Levi sitting at his tax booth. "Follow me," Jesus said to him, and Levi got up, left everything and followed him. Then Levi held a great banquet for Jesus at his house, and a large crowd of tax collectors and others were eating with them. But the Pharisees and the teachers of the law who belonged to their sect complained to his disciples, "Why do you eat and drink with tax collectors and 'sinners'?" Jesus answered them, "It is not the healthy who need a doctor, but the sick. I have not come to call the righteous, but sinners to repentance." (Luke 5:27–32)

LOVE UNTAMED

Two thousand years ago God started a revolt against the religion He started. So don't ever put it past God to cause a groundswell movement against churches and Christian institutions that bear His name. If He was willing to turn Judaism upside down, don't think for a moment our institutions are safe from a divine revolt. I am convinced that even now there are multitudes of followers of Jesus Christ who are sick and tired of the church playing games and playing down the call of God. My travels only confirm that the murmurings of revolution are everywhere. I am convinced that there is an uprising in the works and that no one less than God is behind it.

Anyone who can picture Jesus as the great Advocate of tradition is doing some serious doctoring of biblical history. Jesus was anything but the poster child for status quo. With a band of brothers and a small community of others, Jesus instigated an uprising that He expected to reach the very ends of the earth. You must never forget that it was only to a handful of individuals that Jesus entrusted an outcome that would make disciples of all the nations of the earth. The uprising was to transcend culture, ethnicity, race, religion, status—every and any divide established by men.

The driving purpose of this barbarian revolt is to liberate every person who longs to find freedom in God. Like barbarians destroying civilization, they are to remove every nonessential obstacle between God and man. Let no one remain captive to the nefarious schemes of religionists who attempt to hold God for ransom. Let nothing prevent you or hinder you from providing mercy and forgiveness to those living under the burden of guilt and shame. Who could have guessed that a message of love could incite so much hostility?

Barbarians are entrusted with the gospel—not a message of judgment and condemnation, but good news from God to humanity. Yet the opposition and persecution came with a force that could not be expected or even imagined. Ironically Jesus was crucified not in spite of His love, but because of it. Somehow love incites both love and hate with equal force. The mission of Christ would be so easy to embrace and carry out if love always resulted in love, but it does not. It seems the world insists that love be proved. So then those who claim love are required to endure hate's most brutal tests.

Wherever the love of Christ would be spread by His disciples, they encountered rejection, persecution, suffering, and even death.

Anyone who chooses the barbarian way will learn quickly that love and sacrifice cannot be separated. This is perhaps why so many of us who know love fear love. We know that love is not the absence of pain. If anything, love is the promise of pain. No one has loved more deeply than God. Has anyone ever been more betrayed? God would not know suffering if He did not know love. But because He is Love, He chose to suffer on our behalf. Without love there is no glory in suffering.

The suffering of Christ glorifies God because it elevates love. Compelled by love, God would go where He knew suffering was certain. Love always moves to sacrifice, which is exactly where He calls us to go. We shouldn't be surprised, then, that to follow Christ is to abandon the luxury of safety and security. If we are to be like Him, we must always risk for love. We are invited to follow Him with reckless abandon. The call of God is more than a leap of faith; it is a life of faith. Even when it seems beyond our abilities, we should not be surprised when God tells us to jump.

JUMP SCHOOL

For several years we rented a two-story house in Los Angeles. Both my kids had spent a good part of their childhood enjoying that home. A unique feature of the house was that a small window from the second-story bathroom opened a path to the roof. I always figured there would be a day when one of my kids would climb up on the sink and work his or her way out on the ledge. It just seemed to be one of those things that I or my brother, Alex, would have done when we were kids.

Early one evening Kim and I were in the front yard when all of a sudden, we heard a little voice calling for us from the roof. As soon as Kim saw him, her nurturing instinct kicked in, and she started commanding him to get back inside. I have to admit I was kind of proud of him right then, but what he did next totally surprised me.

Looking past his mom, he asked me if he could jump. When Aaron shouted, "Dad, can I jump?" Kim answered on my behalf, "No, you can't jump. Get back inside."

As if he hadn't heard anything at all, he asked me again, "Dad, can I jump?"

Now I know what I was supposed to do. A dad is never

supposed to override the mom (I'm working on it). I'm just telling you what really happened. After all, he did ask me. I answered, "Yeah, go ahead."

He said, "Really?"

I said, "Yeah, sure. Go ahead and jump."

Kim looked at me as if I was out of my mind and asked, "What do you think you're doing?"

In a sort of explanation I asked Aaron, "Aaron, are you going to jump sometime?"

He said, "Yeah, I think so."

I said, "Okay. I'd rather have you jump now so if you jump and break your legs, we can take you to the hospital." It made perfect sense to me.

He responded, "Dad, do you think I'll make it?"

I said, "Oh, yeah, you'll make it." If I knew one thing for certain, it was that he would reach the ground. I just wasn't sure in what condition.

He said, "Okay. I'm going to jump."

I had one suggestion before he took off. I said, "Hey, buddy, try to clear the concrete and land on the grass. It's softer."

He thought that was a good idea, stepped as far back as

he could on the roof, and began running to jump. Just before his first step he yelled, "Dad, catch me," and I said, "I'll try."

And he jumped.

I almost caught him. It was so close. He just slipped right through my hands. I think I did slow his fall a little bit. In either case, he's recovered well since then. I'm just kidding. He was fine. (Don't try this at home.)

WILDFIRE

I know it's very unlikely that you will ever invite me to speak at a parenting conference, but hang with me for a moment. From the parenting end, I've seen far too many kids raised in Christian homes who are indifferent to Christ and often carry a great disdain for the church. Sometimes it's the result of blatant hypocrisy, but other times it's the result of nothing less than sheer monotony and boredom. We raise our children in the cocoon of a domesticated faith and wonder why they run as far as they can to find adventure.

A long time ago I decided I would never let that happen to my children. I'm a first-generation Christian, but over the years I have seen the dangers that come with being the children of the second generation and beyond. First-generation believers, even when they are barbarians, often make the mistake of raising their children to be civilized.

Paul addressed that point in a letter to Timothy:

> I have been reminded of your sincere faith, which first lived in your grandmother Lois and in your mother Eunice and, I am persuaded, now lives in you also. For this reason I remind you to fan into flame the gift of God, which is in you through the laying on of my hands. For God did not give us a spirit of timidity, but a spirit of power, of love and of self-discipline. So do not be ashamed to testify about our Lord, or ashamed of me his prisoner. But join with me in suffering for the gospel, by the power of God, who has saved us and called us to a holy life—not because of anything we have done but because of his own purpose and grace. (2 Timothy 1:5–9)

Several times Paul encouraged Timothy to be identified with Christ and to not be ashamed of doing that. Connected to his encouragement, he called Timothy to not shrink back because of the suffering that he might face. If you read his letter carefully, it is the pleading of a barbarian who is losing his son in the faith to the way of the civilized. Paul called Timothy to reignite the fire that lay dormant within him. Paul was persuaded that Timothy had a genuine faith, but he was also equally convinced that the life Timothy was living did not reflect one who was alive in the Spirit. Timothy's problem wasn't blatant sin, but latent faith. Paul was calling Timothy to choose the barbarian way out of civilization.

Just yesterday a husband and wife told me that they raised their first son to be a gentleman, and now as a man he does not walk with Christ. They went on to say, "We have a second son, and we're going to raise him as a barbarian." They understood firsthand the painful difference between a civilized Christian and the barbarian way of Jesus.

How many stories do we need of children who grow up in church being forced to act like Christians rather than being won to the heart of God? Both are an effort to shape the character of our children. The first is an external force; the latter an internal force. The civilized Christian does what is right out of fear; the barbarian does what is right out of love. The

Christian civilization is held together by rules and rituals; the barbarian revolt is fueled by the passion of God and guided by the mission of God. If our children are going to walk away from Christ, we need to raise them in such a way that they understand that to walk away from Jesus is to walk away from a life of faith, risk, and adventure and to choose a life that is boring, mundane, and ordinary.

For Aaron, the jump was fraught with danger. From my vantage point, I could see, though the jump was terrifying, he would find himself triumphant. It was important that he jumped and perhaps even more important that he knew me as the kind of father who would always call him to greater endeavors rather than send him back to the safe place.

STAND ALONE

I think God is like that. For too long we've been telling followers of Jesus Christ to climb back through the window. Our message is that "God wants to keep you safe." We can't even see the importance of growing the courage to jump. But what if our house was on fire? What if Aaron's only memory was my telling him that he couldn't do it? What if I had, in that moment, nurtured fear and apprehension? Would he become the kind of person who would die out of fear of trying? What if the courage to jump or the lack of it would be the difference in saving someone else's life?

It may seem counterintuitive, but the more civilized we seem to become, the more detached from the pain of others we end up finding ourselves. The most civilized churches have really no practical concern for people outside their congregations. The brokenness of a lost and unbelieving world is not enough to inspire the painful changes necessary to make the church relevant to the world in which we live.

One of the tragedies of a civilized society is that no one wants to get involved. What becomes appropriate is to mind our own business. When we join a community that lacks a passionate heart for the world, we soon find ourselves acquiescing to apathy. It is a painful tragedy to see a brand-new follower of Christ alive with a barbarian spirit soon conformed to the status quo.

History again and again reveals to us that we are less likely to do good when we perceive ourselves a part of a larger crowd than if we make the choice standing alone. When we are in a crowd, we are more prone toward acts of evil or at least compliance to evil. For some reason the civilized can rationalize apathy and feel themselves absolved from personal responsibility. Good needs to be done, but someone else will take care of it.

The barbarian revolt tolerates no such abdication of responsibility. Every citizen of the kingdom of God is brought into the heat of the conflict between good and evil. Everyone who swears allegiance to Christ bears responsibility for humanity. The power and force of the barbarian way are that each one who chooses His path must find the courage to jump.

I wanted my son to have the courage to jump when needed. I am convinced God wants the same thing for us. Is it possible that your Father is also calling you to jump or at least encouraging you to do so? It is the Spirit of God stirring within you, pleading with you to stop settling for the status quo.

BEHIND ENEMY LINES

The way that we've applied the wrong metaphors in the wrong places is at least partially responsible for our inclination toward domesticating new believers. The Scriptures talk in terms of a new follower of Christ having undergone a new birth. The central passage for this image is John 3. Jesus was having a conversation with Nicodemus and said to him, "I tell you the truth. No one can see the kingdom of God unless he's born again."

Nicodemus immediately concluded that Jesus was calling him to reenter his mother's womb a second time. Instead of backing off, Jesus pressed harder: "I tell you the truth, no one can enter the kingdom of God unless he is born of water and the Spirit. Flesh gives birth to flesh, but the Spirit gives birth to spirit. You should not be surprised at my saying, 'You must be born again.' The wind blows wherever it pleases. You hear its sound, but you cannot tell where it comes from or where it is going. So it is with everyone born of the Spirit" (John 3:3–8).

This, of course, leads us to perceive people who are new in the faith as nothing more than brand-new babes. They're innocent and helpless and incapable of caring for themselves, much less serving others. Yet the phrase that Jesus used can also be translated not as "born again," but as "born from above." Jesus connected this birth not with a mother's womb, but with the Spirit of God descending from heaven and moving with power.

My point is this: the metaphor of new birth has led us to some wrong conclusions. When we are born of flesh and blood, we are helpless and dependent on others even for our own survival. That is not the case when we are born of Spirit. John spoke of the first birth as one of water and the second birth as one of Spirit. Strangely enough John the Baptist made a similar distinction in Luke 3:16 when he declared, "I baptize you with water. But one more powerful than I will come, the thongs of whose sandals I am not worthy to untie. He will baptize you with the Holy Spirit and with fire."

When we are born again, we are dropped not into a maternity ward, but into a war zone. Our birthplace is less mother's womb and more battlefield earth. Maybe the first word we hear should not be "welcome," but "jump." There is no trial run, no practice life.

KNIGHTS IN DARKNESS

When you enter the kingdom of God, there is no safe zone or waiting room. There really isn't even a boot camp. It's on-the-job, on-the-field training. You get to take your first steps of new life in the middle of the battlefield. The Scriptures are quite clear about this. You are in the middle of a war. Yet the war is not against flesh and blood; the war is not against people.

Paul said it this way: "Our struggle is not against flesh and blood, but against the rulers, against the authorities, against the powers of this dark world and against the spiritual forces of evil in the heavenly realms" (Ephesians 6:12).

The barbarian revolt is an insurrection that defies the treaty between civilization and the powers of the dark world. We will not stand by and watch humanity sell its soul to gain the world. We will not be seduced by the comforts offered us if only we would compromise. We cannot pretend that all there is, is what we can see. Barbarians know the world of spirit. We know there is a darkness that subversively corrupts the hearts of men, and to do nothing is to be complicit. We are born into a war. We may feel like children, but we are warriors.

Paul wanted to ensure that we know the nature of this conflict. He wrote, "For though we live in the world, we do not wage war as the world does. The weapons we fight with are not the weapons of the world. On the contrary, they have divine power to demolish strongholds. We demolish arguments and every pretension that sets itself up against the knowledge of God, and we take captive every thought to make it obedient to Christ" (2 Corinthians 10:3–5).

Paul reminded us that not only are we dropped into the middle of a war, but the war rages in the middle of us. You cannot run or hide from the war any more than you can run or hide from yourself. You can become a prisoner of war, but you are never exempt from the war.

It is true that the enemy will essentially leave you alone if you are domesticated. He will not waste his energy destroying a civilized religion. If anything, he uses his energy to promote such activity. Religion can be one of the surest places to keep us from God. When our faith becomes refined, it is no longer dangerous to the dark kingdom.

Barbarians, on the other hand, are not to be trusted. They respect no borders that are established by powers or principalities. They have but one King, one Lord, and one mission. They are insolent enough to crash the gates of hell. For the sake of others, they are willing to risk their own lives and thrust themselves into the midst of peril.

HALO EFFECT

Years ago I learned about an avant-garde military technique used by the Special Forces described as HALO. HALO stands for "high altitude low opening." While parachuting of any kind is a risky enterprise, to add the feature of enemy fire shooting at you, picking you off like a sitting duck as you glide slowly to the ground, would make it more so. The sound of the airplane would inform the enemy that you are coming, and your slow descent would leave you helpless to defend yourself.

HALO had an answer to both problems. The plane would fly minimally at 25,000 feet and sometimes up to 40,000 feet where it was undetectable even by radar. When it was time to jump, your first instruction was not to open your parachute. You would literally move into a free fall. In a matter of seconds your terminal velocity would be 120 miles an hour, though you might hit speeds of up to 200 miles per hour. You open the chute at the last possible minute, with only enough time to save your life. With canopy deployment at 1,800 to 2,200 feet, there's just enough time to break your fall so that you land safely behind enemy territory. If you live, you get to fight the enemy.

I think this somehow is a more accurate metaphor of what it means to enter the kingdom of God, not to mention a far more dramatic picture of what it could mean to be born from above. When we become citizens of God's kingdom, we are of both heaven and earth. We become like God's HALO effect—high altitude low opening.

Paul told us that "God raised us up with Christ and seated us with him in the heavenly realms in Christ Jesus" (Ephesians 2:6). Just a few verses later he reminded us that "we are God's workmanship, created in Christ Jesus to do good works, which God prepared in advance for us to do" (Ephesians 2:10).

It's as if at the moment of our conversion, we were lifted beyond time into eternity. Seated with Christ in the heavenly realms, we can't get much higher in altitude than that. But then created by God to do good, to fulfill His purpose in the world, to advance His cause, we are God's ground troops dropped from eternity back into history. In the same world where we were once at home, we are now strangers and aliens. Where once we were enemies of God, we are now behind enemy lines.

The procedure that God chooses is clearly a low opening. After a moment of euphoria, we come crashing back down to earth, opening our chutes just soon enough to break our fall and allow us to land on the ground, advancing on enemy territory.

PRIMAL ATTIRE

Last year the men of Mosaic invited me to join them at an event set in the mountains called Highlander. In groups of twenty, the guys were divided into Scottish clans. I was a member of the one Irish clan, O'Hare (which, by the way, won the Highlander championship). On Saturday night I talked about the barbarian way. I happened to mention my admiration for the Celts. I pointed out that when the Celts went to war, they painted their bodies and wore only their primal attire—in other words, they were in the buff. You can only imagine what the Roman soldiers who warred against them, dressed in the finest battle gear, must have thought when they ran across those Celts. Maybe this reason and this reason alone explains why the Romans could never conquer the Celts. They didn't really want to catch them.

The point, of course, was for the men at the retreat to

shed their doubts, to shed their fears, to shed their timidity—not to shed their clothes. But in a study of missing the point, the next morning at the closing event, which happened to be a tug-of-war in the middle of a pool of mud, one of the men we now simply call "Nature Boy" showed up naked. Since it was a Christian camp, he was instructed to put on some clothes, so he threw on a shirt. I think once again he missed the point.

By the start of the tug-of-war, he was again unveiled in his full glory. One of my friends, John, was the first man in line on the opposing team. He is an attorney and a highly educated professional. You can only imagine what he was thinking: *Hold tight, pull hard, and keep your eyes up.*

Oh, and by the way, when Nature Boy's clan saw their fellow tribesman choose the barbarian way, they stripped in his honor. You can only imagine the whelps that resulted from pulling rope against raw flesh. Fortunately what their clan had in boldness, they lacked in muscle. Soon they were covered in mud, their nakedness to be seen no more.

When David returned to Jerusalem exhilarated by the victories that God had given him at war, he disrobed and danced before the Lord. But Michal, his wife, despised him. When she rebuked him for his inappropriate display of celebration and worship of God, David's answer was unwavering: "I will celebrate before the LORD. I will become even more undignified than this, and I will be humiliated in my own eyes" (2 Samuel 6:21–22).

I'm not saying that we should all go around naked, but I am saying that we need to find the courage and freedom to be ourselves. We need to let ourselves become the unique individuals that God created us to be. We need to stop trying to be what everyone else wants us to be and stop worrying about what everyone else thinks. Civilized people measure one another by their robes and signet rings. The barbarians measure only heart and actions. Barbarians live as if they are naked before God and naked before men. They have nothing to hide; they do not waste their energy pretending to be someone they're not. It was Nathaniel, whom Jesus saw while he was alone under a fig tree, that He described as a man without guile. God sees straight through to the heart and looks for those in whom there is nothing false. The barbarian hides nothing before God, and his tribe battles naked and unashamed.

WHEN TIGERS UNITE

Although the force of one person fully committed to God is tremendous, it pales in comparison to the force of God's people moving together. One barbarian wandering through civilization can be discarded as nothing more than an oddity. But when members of the barbarian tribe line up across the battlefield, side by side, something amazing begins to happen. Dark kingdoms tremble; the dungeons and prisons that hold men, women, and children captive crumble; prison doors open; chains unlock; and multitudes come to freedom. Whenever the barbarians of Christ pass through civilization, the oppressed and forgotten are soon found dancing in the streets.

When an opponent beheads one barbarian, he better be prepared, for we will return in force. We fight violence with peace, hatred with love, and oppression with servanthood. While never violating our uniqueness, we move together, united in heart and soul. Our greatness is unleashed in the context of community. When we move together, God is most perfectly revealed in us.

George Hunter in *The Celtic Way of Evangelism* describes

one reason why the Roman civilization was able to advance its empire, but the Celtic tribes were not. He uses an analogy given to him by a zoologist: "A tiger will defeat a lion in battle; but five lions will defeat five tigers because the lions fight together and the tigers do not, so the five lions take on one tiger at a time. Each Celtic tribe was a formidable tiger in battle, greatly respected and feared. The Romans, with legendary strength in organization and coordination, were the lions in the lengthy series of battles against specific tribes to incrementally expand their empire" (p. 18).

From the first moment I read that, I recognized the dilemma. Barbarians are far more tiger than lion. I am convinced the old adage is true, at least in this case, that a tiger can never change its stripes. More than that, we do not want to domesticate the tiger. We don't even want the tiger to try to become more like the lion. But imagine what it would be like if tigers could learn how to move together, if tigers would choose to stand side by side and engage in battle as one tribe.

Again the Scriptures describe the movement of the church as an unstoppable force. The expansion of God's invisible kingdom is the result of those of us who are passionate followers of Jesus Christ moving together united in heart, mind, and spirit. Jesus' description that "the kingdom of heaven has been forcefully advancing, and forceful men lay hold of it" (Matthew 11:12) is a call for tigers to move together, not for our untamed faith to be domesticated.

CRASH THE FUTURE

A few years ago I took my kids to a wildlife animal park near San Diego. As we rode on a tram through the open terrain, a guide pointed out the unique features of the different species that we encountered. I suppose I always knew it in part, but I had not come to realize how most groups of animals have unique names or designations when they dwell together.

With insects most of us know that bees are called swarms, and ants are called colonies. Among ocean life, I was aware that whales are pods, and fish are schools. Cattle are herds, birds are flocks, and if you watch *Lion King*, you know a tribe of lions is a pride. If you grew up in the country, you might know that crows are murders. Maybe the most unnerving one is an ambush of tigers.

I was surprised to learn that a group of buzzards waiting around together to feast on leftover carnage is called a committee. Just this one insight is worth the price of the whole book. This explains so much of what's going on in churches—a lot of committees waiting around to live off human carnage.

Groups of flamingos are called flamboyants, which for some reason reminds me of TV evangelists. And groups of the less glamorous owls are known as parliaments. They do seem sort of British.

But my favorite of all is the group designation for rhinos. You see, rhinos can run at thirty miles an hour, which is pretty fast when you consider how much weight they're pulling. They're actually faster than squirrels, which can run at up to twenty-six miles an hour. And even then, who's going to live in dread of a charging squirrel? (Sorry—that was a bit off the point.) Running at thirty miles an hour is faster than a used Pinto will go. Just one problem with this phenomenon. Rhinos can see only thirty feet in front of them. Can you imagine something that large moving in concert as a group, plowing ahead at thirty miles an hour with no idea what's at thirty-one feet? You would think that they would be far too timid to pick up full steam, that their inability to see far enough ahead would paralyze them to immobility. But with that horn pointing the way, rhinos run forward full steam ahead without apprehension, which leads us to their name.

Rhinos moving together at full speed are known as a crash. Even when they're just hanging around enjoying the watershed, they're called a crash because of their potential. You've got to love that. I think that's what we're supposed to be. That's what happens when we become barbarians and shake free of domestication and civility. The church becomes a crash. We become an unstoppable force. We don't have to pretend we know the future. Who cares that we can see only thirty feet ahead? Whatever's at thirty-one feet needs to care that we're coming and better get out of the way.

We need to move together as God's people, a barbarian tribe, and become the human version of the rhino crash. The future is uncertain, but we need to move toward it with confidence. There's a future to be created, a humanity to be liberated. We need to stop wasting our time and stop being afraid of what we cannot see and do not know. We need to move forward full force because of what we do know.

Yesterday Mariah was in a store with her mom. She saw a man working with fabrics, and for some reason he caught Mariah's attention. Mariah looked at Kim and pointed to the man, and she said, "Mom, look at the man. He's the loneliest person I've ever seen." Mariah began to weep uncontrollably.

We may not be able to see what's at thirty-one feet, but we don't have to be blind to what's right in front of us. There's a world that desperately needs God, a world filled with loneliness, hopelessness, and fear. We have somehow become deaf to a cry that reaches heaven coming from the souls of men. But God hears.

WARRIORS OF LIGHT

God heard the cries of Israel when the people lived under the tyranny of Egypt. And then He spoke and called out Moses. As one man, he went to war against an empire. He followed the barbarian way—a coward became a hero; a murderer became a deliverer; a shepherd became a prophet; a wanderer became a leader; an adopted son of Pharaoh became an adopted son of God; slaves became free—but before they became a nation, they had to learn how to survive the wilderness. The land of promise was not a land free from dangers. The milk and honey they were promised awaited them amid a land of giants.

It is no different for us. As it was for them, freedom is a return not to Paradise Lost, but to a promised land that we must win. Like Israel, who longed for Egypt because the journey was more difficult than the people expected, we must be aware of the temptation to return to the captivity from which we were freed. There is but one path to freedom. There is no easy road made available. We cannot claim to know Christ and to honor Him if we refuse the path He calls us to follow. Do not insist on binding Him or associating Him with a domesticated or civilized faith. Do not dishonor Him by claiming that a life of faith is a life without risk. This war has no room for pomp or pretension.

Jesus leads us into the heart of the dark kingdom, into the soul of what is most evil. He takes us where mankind has chosen to live. He calls us to where the darkness has made those who wander there desperate for light. He leads us as warriors of light to risk our lives for the deliverance of others. Again, our own weapons are love, hope, and faith, and they are our only defense. Yet we above all know that they and only they liberate us and fulfill the deepest longings of our souls.

If you choose to live your life in this way, if you make the insane decision to live your life for the sake of others, if you choose to follow the One whose barbarian path led Him to the brutality of the Cross, and if you embrace His invitation to take up your own cross and follow Him, then it has begun. If you dare allow God to unlock your primal spirit, He will unleash the raw and untamed faith within. Then you will know you have chosen the barbarian way out of civilization.

> Jephthah the Gileadite was a mighty warrior. His father was Gilead; his mother was a prostitute. Gilead's wife also bore him sons, and when they were grown up, they drove Jephthah away. "You are not going to get any inheritance in our family," they said, "because you are the son of another woman." So Jephthah fled from his brothers and settled in the land of Tob, where *a group of adventurers gathered around him and followed him.* (Judges 11:1–3 italics added)

ACKNOWLEDGMENTS

To Kim, whom I met on the barbarian way; my children, Aaron and Mariah, who allowed me to share their lives with all who read these words; Holly, who joined my team on the condition that I would make it my prayer that God would bring her the man of her dreams; Erik, who is now Holly's husband—live up to the dream; Tammy Borrero, who makes it possible for us to accomplish our overwhelming endeavors; my community at Mosaic and my team at Awaken who help me maximize my effectiveness and multiply the contribution we make together to serve humanity.

Also thanks to the Willow Creek Association for helping

me to get this message out. I'm always grateful for Sealy Yates and the team at Yates & Yates, who are not merely agents, but advocates. I cannot possibly thank enough Jonathan Merkh, Brian Hampton, Kyle Olund, and the entire team at Thomas Nelson Publishers. And of course to Rick, Greg, Enrique, and Robert, who have made it possible for me to accomplish more than I ever could have alone. To all who choose the barbarian way, especially to those like Steve Johnson, Paul Johnson, and Dave Olson, who find barbarians walking alone and invite them to walk with their tribe, I will always be grateful to you guys and so many others like you.

Stay off the paved road,
ERWIN

SOUL CRAVINGS

AN EXPLORATION OF THE HUMAN SPIRIT

Published in Nashville, Tennessee, by Thomas Nelson. Thomas Nelson is a registered trademark of Thomas Nelson, Inc.

Thomas Nelson, Inc. titles may be purchased in bulk for educational, business, fund-raising, or sales promotional use. For information, please e-mail SpecialMarkets@ThomasNelson.com.

Published in association with Yates & Yates, www.yates2.com

Photography by Chad Lauterbach (www.witheyeswideopen.com)

Illustrations by Joby Harris

Library of Congress Cataloging-in-Publication Data

McManus, Erwin Raphael.
    Soul cravings : an exploration of the human spirit / Erwin Raphael McManus.
      p. cm.
    ISBN 978-0-7852-1494-6 (hardcover)
    ISBN 978-1-4002-8019-3 (2-in-1)
    1. Spirituality. I. Title.
  BV4501.3.M3755 2006
  248.4—dc22   2006027950

Printed in the United States of America

08 09 10 11 12 QW 5 4 3 2 1

To ALBY KIPHUTH—

or as I know her,

Mom.

You have always been a great adventurer, a passionate lover of life,
a free spirit with a questioning mind, an insatiable curiosity,
an extraordinary resilience, and an indomitable spirit.

You are proof of the beauty of the human spirit.

CONTENTS

CRAVINGS

Intimacy

Love Is Like Stepping on Broken Glass	entry 1
I'm Living in the World's Most Dangerous Place	entry 2
Love Is a Thin Red Line	entry 3
One Is the Loneliest Number	entry 4
The Danger of Loving Nothing	entry 5
When Love Cuts Like a Knife	entry 6
Making, Taking, Faking Love	entry 7
Love Lost and Abandoned	entry 8
The Elusive Nature of Love	entry 9
What Must I Do to Be Loved?	entry 10
Chased by Love (Please Don't Run Too Fast)	entry 11
It's Murder Out There	entry 12
Being Loved to Death?	entry 13
A Vacuum of Love	entry 14
Where Do I Belong?	entry 15
God and Basketball	entry 16
Do You Know Who You Are?	entry 17
Nowhere Man	entry 18
A Force Greater Than Death	entry 19
Like a Kiss on the Face	entry 20
Love Is Not a Four-Letter Word	entry 21

SOUL CRAVING

DESTINY

Heading Down the Glory Road	entry 1
I Was Born to Run	entry 2
Destiny Calling	entry 3
Do We All Dream of Flying?	entry 4
Life Is a Dream in the Making	entry 5
Neutral Doesn't Get You Anywhere	entry 6
Destiny Calls Like a Siren	entry 7
Looking Forward	entry 8
Oxygen for the Soul	entry 9
Believing in the Future Takes Faith	entry 10
Running Out of Time	entry 11
Despair's Only Hope	entry 12
Imagine	entry 13
On Becoming Human	entry 14
A Reason to Live	entry 15
A Crisis of Success	entry 16
A Search for Significance	entry 17
Driven, Destined, and Determined to Change	entry 18
Becoming the Change	entry 19
The Secret Longing of the Soul	entry 20
A Fresh Start to a Dead End	entry 21
Standardized Testing	entry 22
Creatives	entry 23
Pathos	entry 24
A Place of Hope	entry 25

MEANING

Is It All Just Dumb Luck?	entry 1
Making Sense of This Mess	entry 2

What's the Meaning of This?   entry 3

Open Our Coffins and We're All
    Just Well-Meaning Vampires   entry 4

I've Got a Frog in My Throat   entry 5

Junk Food and the Search for Truth   entry 6

The Answer Is the Question (or the Other Way Around)   entry 7

I Don't Understand Why I Must Understand   entry 8

I Don't Know How I Know What I Know   entry 9

If It's Pitch Black, Does It Matter If You're Blind?   entry 10

We Are All Decoding   entry 11

It's All in How You Look At It   entry 12

Home Alone   entry 13

The Truth Is, It's About Trust   entry 14

Bloody Sunday Leads to Cheap Monday   entry 15

Truth Eventually Gets Personal   entry 16

You've Gotta Know Who to Trust   entry 17

Why Crawl When You Can Jump?   entry 18

A Healthy Faith in Doubts   entry 19

It's Not Supposed to Make You Sick   entry 20

Driving Blind Full Speed Ahead   entry 21

Just Follow the Signs   entry 22

SEEK

CRAVINGS

I WAKE UP EACH MORNING REMINDED THAT ALL I need to face the day is to breathe deeply of fresh air and to find my way to the nearest Starbucks. Well, actually I live in LA, so I really can live without the fresh air (my lungs have finally adapted to the smog). The caffeine, on the other hand, is essential. Each morning demands its Venti 2percent "extra hot," wet cappuccino.

Before you condemn me, let me assure you it's not an addiction but an appreciation. I can quit anytime, and so I don't need to. I'm convinced coffee is an acquired taste. The aroma is better than the flavor, not to mention the compelling nature of the effect.

Science is only now discovering the medicinal value of the sacred bean. If all goes well, it will soon be its own food group. I've never been pregnant (my wife volunteered both times), but I do know the power of cravings. Is my relationship to java a problem? No, espresso is a guilty pleasure, and I am grateful for my dealer . . . um . . . barista.

There are cravings within me, though, that pull on me like an addiction.

They have always been with me and have even at times tormented me.

They go far deeper than any physical addiction ever could.

Beyond my flesh,

    beyond my mind,

        beyond my heart,

            there seems to be a place where my deepest and
                most powerful cravings lie.

                And they do not lie silently.

My soul, it seems, always desires and demands, and no matter how I try to satisfy it, **it always craves more.** No, not more, but something I can't seem to understand.

My soul craves, but for what I don't know.

And there I tell you is at least half my problem. I've tried so many things and done so many things, certain they would satisfy my soul, but they never did.

Most of the time it was worse than leaving me empty. Not only did I find myself unsatisfied, but the craterlike vacuum inside me was now deeper than it was before.

It seems as if I've spent my whole life trying to satisfy this insatiable part of my being.

If you interviewed my soul, it would probably describe me as sadistic or masochistic. My soul would tell you I find some dark pleasure in leaving it unsatisfied. Before you jump to a conclusion, though, you need to hear both sides. It's not like I wanted to starve my soul to death. I never purposely withheld from it what it needed.

If I saw a guy crawling in the desert desperate for water, I would share whatever I had with him. If I knew where the well was, I would point the way. Heck, I'd even drag him there.

How can I be held responsible when my soul doesn't even know what it really needs?

But what if we could know? What if we must know?

In the opening page of Kurt Cobain's journal, he writes, "Don't read my diary when I'm gone. OK, I'm going to work now, when you wake up this morning, please read my diary. Look through my things and figure me out."

Kurt's life tragically ended at the age of twenty-seven. Ironically, the name of his band was Nirvana, the Hindu name for paradise. The same artist who penned the song "Come As You Are" in the end never found what he was looking for, never found the help to figure himself out.

I think we're all more like Cobain than we would care to admit. We're all struggling to figure ourselves out. We're all afraid to expose our souls to those who might judge us, and at the same time, we desperately need help to guide us on this journey. If we're not careful, we might find ourselves with everything this world has to offer and later find we have lost ourselves in the clutter.

We are all searching for ourselves, trying to understand who we are, hoping that we might discover our unique place in this world. We are all sojourners on a common quest.

A film called *21 Grams,* starring Sean Penn, Benicio Del Toro, and Naomi Watts, has a narrative that revolves around the value of a human life. Its lead-in refers to a phenomenon that happens at the time of our death.

They say we all lose 21 grams at the exact moment of our death . . . everyone."

"The weight of a stack of nickels, the weight of a chocolate bar, the weight of a hummingbird.

The question posed is simple yet profound: "How much does life weigh?" The implication, of course, is that what is lost in the twenty one grams is the human spirit, that there is more to us than simply flesh and blood. So let me put my cards on the table: I believe you are more than water and dust. At your core you are a spiritual being of infinite value. To be human is a gift. You are created by God, and you have immeasurable value to him.

Jesus once said that the kingdom of God is within us. Yet most of us don't even bother to explore the possibility that this might be true. It seems that what he is implying is that we have a better chance of finding God in the universe within us than in the one that surrounds us.

And it is on this path that I invite you to walk with me. I invite you to engage in an exploration of the human spirit, to journey deep inside yourself and search out the mystery of the universe that exists within you.

This is the question I was asked to face years ago when I found myself desperately struggling to understand myself, trying to measure the weight of this one life. There I was, making my personal contribution to the extensive research being done on the meaning of ink blots.

"What do you see?"

Even at twelve I knew this was a trick question.

He wanted to know what I saw so that he could see inside me. It really is a good question, though. Your retina may be necessary for sight, but your soul definitely shapes what you see. My soul was confused and cold and growing calloused, and I was quickly becoming blind to so many things. When your soul is sick, one of the symptoms is blindness.

Bitterness, for instance, is like a cancer that makes you blind. I had allowed hurt to make my soul toxic. From my end, I was sure that I was just becoming a realist. In fact, I was desensitizing myself. Why risk being hurt more? I didn't realize I was becoming blind to love. I couldn't see the people around me who really cared. Their sincere efforts went unnoticed. If you had asked me then, I would have said they weren't there. I look back now and realize I just couldn't see them, but they were right in front of me the entire time. Bitterness turned to skepticism, which turned to cynicism, which turned to an emptiness of my soul.

Bitterness is the enemy of love because it makes you unforgiving and unwilling to give love unconditionally.

It is the enemy of hope because you keep living in the past and become incapable of seeing a better future.

It is the enemy of faith because you stop trusting in anyone but yourself. I bring this up because I think many of us become blinded by a bitterness of the soul. If we are not careful, we will lose the ability to see such things as beauty, truth, or even affection. More importantly, you may close your eyes to what your soul needs you most to see.

IT'S NOT COINCIDENTAL THAT PSYCHOLOGY IS THE study of the soul. *Psych* comes from the Greek word for *soul, breath, life*. It is specifically the study of human conditions outside the physical domain. Is it possible that much of what we call psychosis and neurosis is really about us being soul sick?

What do you see?

If you can answer this question honestly, you'll get a pretty clear look inside yourself. But more than that, you will begin a journey of self-discovery. For this to happen, I would like to invite you into a story. It is the story of all of us.

I would like to guide you on a soul journey and help you discover that which is already there within you. And you'll ask more than simply, *What do I see?* You'll also ask, *What do I hear? What do I feel? What do I find?*

This will be an exploration of the human spirit, and I am absolutely certain that what you will discover will surprise you.

Ahead you will find a trilogy. You will find three quests that we all are on: a quest for intimacy, a quest for destiny, and a quest for meaning. They can be taken in any order. Choose the one that strikes you most at this time. Although all of us go through each of these journeys at some point in our lives and all of us carry within us these soul cravings, they are heightened at different times and places on our journeys.

I should mention that this is not a book focused on empirical evidence for God. It is about coming to know ourselves. *Soul Cravings* is a journal of the human story. It is about our story; and if God exists, we should be able to find him there. I don't know how to prove God to you. I can only hope to guide you to a place where you and God might meet.

The following pages reflect my journey, and I invite you to join me on my search. I've never believed you can or should even try to force God on someone. This book is my gift to you who are on a genuine search for God. I say it is a gift because I know I can't expect you to open your soul if I do not bare my own.

My soul craves.

If yours does, too, then let's travel together for a while.

ERWIN

INTIMACY

Intimacy

Passion

Relationships

Acceptance

Belonging

Community

Tribe

Identity

Compassion

Love

ENTRY #1   Love Is Like Stepping on Broken Glass

ONE BEAUTIFUL CAROLINA NIGHT DURING MY SENIOR year at the University of North Carolina, a group of us decided to escape the dorm and walk to Franklin Street, the mainstay of Carolina life. It was a time for catching up with old friends and making new ones. After getting some food, we all headed back to Avery dorm, and then the most unexpected thing happened. In the midst of a lot of talking and laughing, suddenly there was a loud sound of pain. The person I knew least, but frankly was attracted to most, had begun walking barefooted, and she stepped on a piece of glass.

It was impossible for her to take another step.

Everyone was concerned, and every guy wanted to help, but fate seemed to lean my direction. I was the only one who could pick her up and carry her. Thank God for hanging out with a bunch of geeks. I picked her up and carried her for what must have been nearly a mile back to the dorm, all downhill, or at least that's how it seemed. It was magic. She was really light, I was really strong, or I was highly motivated.

And like the plot of a classic novel, a romance was born—the kind you only read about and read with envy. You know, true love, an epic romance, classic Shakespeare. I believe it was Christopher Marlowe who said, "Come with me and be my love, and we will all life's pleasures prove." This had to be what was spoken of when the expression "true love" was coined—the kind that lasts forever; the stuff of which poets write for a hundred years.

It lasted a couple of months.

This brings me to the problem with love. It woos you in like a lamb headed toward the slaughter. It steals your heart with promises that seem almost too good to be true, and then you discover that was exactly right.

Perhaps John Donne said it best: "I am two fools, I know. For loving and for saying so."

There's probably no subject ever discussed among human beings that is more captivating and more elusive than love. From Aphrodite to Oprah Winfrey, we look to our mavens to guide us through this tumultuous jungle of human emotions. Every generation writes about love. From *Pride and Prejudice,* the Jane Austen novel, to *Pride and Prejudice,* the British miniseries, to *Pride and Prejudice,* the Hollywood movie, to *Bridget Jones's Diary* (aka *Pride and Prejudice* for those that don't know they like *Pride and Prejudice*), we never seem able to escape the maddening effects of love.

We are driven *by* love, driven *to* love, and even driven *from* love.

Without love there wouldn't be much to sing about, and even music seems torn when it comes to love. Some sing of love as the one compelling reason to live. From the Foo Fighters' "Everlong" to James Blunt's haunting "You're Beautiful," they describe the all-consuming power of love. At the same time you have songs like Aqualung's "Breaking My Heart" and Death Cab for Cutie's "Someday You Will Be Loved" to the old school classic "What's Love Got to Do with It" (Tina Turner for the too-young-to-know), which remind us that there may be no more dangerous place to be than in love.

> How is it that the same thing that can make your life a
> rhapsody can also leave you gutted,
> like a dead fish wrapped in day-old newspaper?

Depeche Mode asks exactly the right question in the song "The Meaning of Love."

entry 1

I've read more than a hundred books
Seen love mentioned many thousand times
But despite all the places I've looked
It's still no clearer, it's just not enough
I'm still no nearer the meaning of love

Noted down all my observations
Spent an evening watching television
Still I couldn't say with precision
Know it's a feeling and it comes from above
But what's the meaning the meaning of love
(tell me)

From the notes that I've made so far
Love seems something like wanting a scar
I could be wrong but I'm just not sure you see,
I've never been in love before

Next I asked several friends of mine
If they could spare a few minutes of their time
Their look suggested that I'd lost my mind
Tell me the answer, my Lord high above
Tell me the meaning, the meaning of love

 entry 1

ENTRY #2   I'm Living in the World's Most Dangerous Place

ROBERT YOUNG PELTON'S UNDERGROUND CLASSIC TITLED *The World's Most Dangerous Places* is over one thousand pages thick. It highlights the five-star danger zones like Colombia, Chechnya, and Liberia. Pelton ironically writes not to discourage us from going but to help us get there and maybe even survive. Nowhere, though, does he warn us about the world's most dangerous place, and he certainly gives us no guidance in how to survive when we're stuck there. Makes me wonder if he's ever been in love.

The best I can tell, no matter how powerful it feels, the staying power of love isn't that high a percentage. The intensity of love seems to have no bearing on its resilience. If anything, the more you love someone, the more capacity you have to come to hate him or her. And why, by the way, does it seem that half the time you didn't even know you were in love until you lost it? Is heartbreak the only way to know it's the real deal?

After all, the only people who can hurt you deeply

            are the ones

                  you allow to

                           get deep

                                   inside your soul.

This is what makes love so dangerous. The more you love someone, the more that person can hurt you. When you give your heart away to someone, you entrust it to that person's care. Your beloved can pretty much do whatever he or she wants with it. You are left vulnerable and defenseless. Isn't love grand? No wonder we're all searching for it.

No, let's rethink that.

Given all the problems love can create, why do we keep longing for it? How many thousands of years will it take for us to learn? How many Romeos and Juliets need to lie dead on the floor before we're willing to give up this perverse addiction? Oh, I know they weren't real, but then again, is love? If evolution is our preferred understanding of the human story, why can't we evolve ourselves out of this primal Achilles' heel we know as love? And don't give me this thing about the propagation of the species. Love isn't necessary for reproduction—just sex is. All you need is attraction, not emotion . . . If intimacy is only about attraction, we could just keep lust and dispense with love.

But it just won't go away. It's been almost four hundred years since René Descartes reasoned, "I think, therefore I am." He was the first Vulcan. We've been so long convinced that we would eventually find that higher plane where emotions no longer define us. Four hundred years after the birth of the Enlightenment, we're still not doing any better.

> How can it be that in the postinformation age, in the era of
> the technological revolution, we still need something as
> primitive as love?
> No matter how many times we fail at love or
> how many times love fails us, we plow ahead.
> Even the scars of love rarely stop us from risking at love.

Strange as it seems, in the midst of our most painful memories, we find our most treasured ones. This is powerfully portrayed in the movie *Eternal Sunshine of the Spotless Mind*. Jim Carrey and Kate Winslet come together to explore the question, Is a mind free of the pain of love filled with eternal sunshine? If you had the chance to erase all the memories of your greatest love to be free of the pain of losing it, would you? I wouldn't. I don't think many of us would.

We are addicted to love, and it's out of control.

We would give anything and everything to find it.

Here is where I begin to hold to a conspiracy theory.

There's more going on here than meets the eye.

It's as if we've been purposefully designed with a factory defect that keeps us searching . . . for love.

It seems humiliating to say it, but we need to be loved. I need to be loved. I feel like I just walked into a twelve-step program. "Hi, I'm Erwin. I'm a loveaholic."

If you try to ignore it, if you think that you can live your life without love, you're in even worse shape than the person who's desperate to find it.

To give up on love is to choose a life that is less than human.
To give up on love is to give up on life.

ENTRY #3 Love Is a Thin Red Line

WHEN YOU GIVE UP ON LOVE, EVERYTHING ELSE SEEMS TO go with it—

   joy,

       hope,

             forgiveness,

                   compassion—

                        they're all interconnected.

But you might wonder to yourself: *What if I never find love?* After all, you can't be held responsible if you've searched for love, risked in love, even fought for love, and yet have always found it unrequited. When love does not come to you, it breaks your heart, but when you do not give love away, it hardens your heart. One thing stranger than our need to be loved is our need to love, which again leads me to my conspiracy theory: We are designed for love.

I remember several years ago sitting in a theater out in Westwood watching Terrence Malick's *Thin Red Line.* Two things stood out to me: Jim Caviezel standing quietly in the lobby watching our reactions as we exited, and a haunting monologue in the middle of a war movie about the nature of love.

"My dear wife,
you get something twisted out of your insides by all this
   blood, filth, and noise.
I wanna stay changeless for you.
I wanna come back to you the man I was before.

How do we get to those other shores?
To those blue hills.
Love.
Where does it come from?
Who lit this flame in us?
No war can put it out, conquer it.
I was a prisoner.
You set me free."

Ben Chaplin's Private Jack Bell asked our soul's deepest question. What is this thing love? Where does it come from? Why are we so affected by its presence and its absence?

We cannot live unaffected by love. We are most alive when we find it, most devastated when we lose it, most empty when we give up on it, most inhumane when we betray it, and most passionate when we pursue it. The human story seems more driven by the insanity of love than the survival of the fittest. When I was seventeen, rushing off without stopping for dinner, my mom would tell me, "You can't live on love." Maybe not, but you can't live without it.

Can you be honest enough to admit how love pulls you, woos you, eludes you, torments you— sometimes all in the same day? You were created for relationship. This is and always will be at the core of your being.

All of us have an intrinsic need to belong, and all of us are on a search for intimacy. No matter how many things about us are different, in this we are all the same—we all crave love. It is as if we are searching for a love we have lost. Or perhaps more strangely we are searching for a love we have never known but somehow sense it awaits us.

The most powerful evidence that our souls crave God is that within us there is a longing for love. We are all connected by a thin red line.

ENTRY #4 One Is the Loneliest Number

HAVE YOU EVER COME FACE-TO-FACE WITH THE VACUUM of love that exists within your soul? Have you ever had an unexplainable sense of loneliness even while you're standing in the middle of a crowd? At the same time you can be all by yourself and have a wonderful sense of connectedness with the world. You can enjoy being alone, but you can become lost in aloneness. Have you ever wondered whether you are the one person who simply could not be loved or was somehow born unworthy of love? Sometimes we'll go to unimaginable extremes to earn love, to feel love, to be loved. Without love, every night is a three-dog night.

Claire Danes would be one of the last people you would expect to struggle with loneliness. Beautiful, talented, and successful, she was a hit by the age of fifteen on ABC's *My So-Called Life.* She exploded on the big screen opposite Leonardo DiCaprio in the 1996 version of *Romeo and Juliet.* In an interview with Dotson Rader she confessed, "A part of me desired fame because I associated it with love . . . that was a total mistake. Fame doesn't end loneliness." "All her life," we are told, "she has felt an innate sense of loneliness." Our need for love is intrinsic—it exists in all of us. Our souls crave intimacy.

We are created to know God and and to know love. It is love that moves God toward us and love that pulls us toward him. Follow love and it will guide you to God.

Love is the beginning of all things.

From the very beginning you were made for love.

It may be hard to accept, but you are the object of God's love. You were created out of love by him, and though you may not yet realize it, your soul longs to know this love. But it goes way beyond that. You are a creature of love. You are designed to love and be loved. Our search for intimacy explains our need for community, relationship, friendship, and acceptance; it is expressed most deeply in our need for romantic love.

We all long to belong. We are created to know love and to give love. Our need to love, though rooted in God, is not limited to him. Love is not a limited commodity. Love expands as we give it away. Love dies when we do not.

Without love there is no life. To love is to be fully human.

ENTRY #5   The Danger of Loving Nothing

IRONICALLY, SOMETIMES WHEN WE FEEL THERE IS NO PLACE for us in the world, we choose to live a life of isolation and disconnectedness—sort of our way of sticking it to all of humanity before they can get to us.

You've asked yourself the question over and over again, *Is there anyone who really cares?* And your conclusion is, *No.* So you decide to join them. You're not going to care either. You're not going to feel any more hurt.

Sometimes we take this so far that we decide the only way not to feel pain is to inflict it.

It shouldn't surprise us that Ted Kaczynski, better known as the Unabomber, had chosen a life of isolation and disconnectedness, rejecting a world that he concluded had rejected him. It wasn't enough to simply run from it; he had to find some way to destroy it. Even the designation given him is revealing—*Una*bomber. Una—

one

singular

solitary

alone

Contact with the real world—it's not optional; it's essential. We are created for relationship. We are born for community. For us to be healthy, we must be a part of others. Independence is one thing; isolation is another. The more we live disconnected lives, the more we become indifferent to the well-being of others.

The farther we move from community, thecloserwemovetoviolence.

Over the years we've come to expect urban violence. If we were honest with ourselves, we would have to acknowledge that many of us have become desensitized to crime and violence in our inner cities and especially among the urban poor, which is probably why what happened in the quiet community of Jefferson County, Colorado, so affected the American psyche. Two teenage boys planned for over a year to ruthlessly massacre as many students and teachers at Columbine High School as possible.

If I know nothing else about Eric Harris and Dylan Klebold, I know that they had given up on love. They no longer considered themselves a part of the human community. They cared for no one and cared about no one, not even themselves. Where there is no love, there is no value for life. When hate consumes our hearts, all we can think of, all we desire, is to destroy.

When there is disengagement from human community, there is the potential for inhumanity.

The human heart

        was not created

                to be a container

                        for hate.

When we allow bitterness, jealousy, envy, racism, lust, greed, and arrogance to fuel our souls, we create an environment within us to be agents of violence.

We live in a time when the most terrifying bomb is not a nuclear one, but a human one.

This is where humanity has come. This is how far we've evolved. We strap bombs around our chests, lure innocents into our presence, and then consider ourselves heroes as we destroy everything around us. If this were not bad enough, for some it has become a proof of spirituality.

There are people all around us waiting to E X P L O D E !

How many of us are walking around with fuses already lit? With the danger of oversimplifying, you are a danger to the world when you love nothing, and you're even more dangerous when you love the wrong things. When there is a vacuum of love within your soul, hate, bitterness, envy, and racism rush to fill the empty space.

There is a dramatic difference between fanaticism and love.

Fanaticism justifies and defines who you hate.

Love embraces and leaves no room for violence.

On September 1 every year, children, parents, and families gather to celebrate what is known in Russia as the Day of Knowledge. It's on this day, after hearing speeches and critical information for the new year, that the first graders give flowers to what are described as the "last graders."

It was exactly on this day that Chechen terrorists chose to seize a school in Beslan, Russia. It was September 1, 2004, when Beslan Middle School Number One was stormed by a group of approximately 30 armed men and women. Over 1,300 hostages were taken, most of whom were children under the age of eighteen. At the end of three days, the hostage crisis culminated in a barrage of gunfire between the hostage takers and the Russian security forces.

When the dust had settled, 344 civilians were killed; 186 of them were children. You don't have to understand the complexities of Russian politics to know something is terribly wrong.

> What happens inside a human being for an ideology
> to become more important than a human life?

Even those of us who disdain violence at every level could understand using force to protect the innocent, but how can any of us find a rationale for acts like this? How dark must a human soul become, how hard must a human heart become, to allow us to snuff out a life to simply make a point?

We stand in the midst of a human dilemma.
We long for community; we long to belong; we long for love.
Yet what we long for most we seem incapable of sustaining.
Humanity has no natural predators except each other.
We are safer in the jungle than in the city.
We are our own worst enemies.

ENTRY #6 When Love Cuts Like a Knife

WE MAY FEEL SAFER ALONE, BUT WHEN WE CHOOSE A LIFE of isolation, when we live without any semblance of community, it is easier to justify violence, or at least indifference to the welfare of others.

Somewhere in the archives where I keep strange things given to me, there's a hunter's knife stored away. It serves as a tragic reminder to me that, more often than we think, when we dig beneath violence, we find a place where once there was love. The knife was given to me by a man I met briefly over twenty years ago while I was traveling through Southern California.

I was speaking at an event out here in LA, and an unexpected guest drove up on his motorcycle. He had come uninvited, and in some ways it seemed his arrival was almost random. He sat through my talk and appeared genuinely moved or at least troubled. Afterward he engaged me in a conversation that was more of a confessional.

He pulled out a knife and gave it as a symbol that on that day he was letting go of all the bitterness and violence that had fueled his life. What he began to describe was a life that had left a trail of death.

He was a man of violence driven by hatred and anger.

I was somewhere between shocked and scared but decided to press him to understand what would drive a person to a life of senseless violence. It didn't take a Ph.D. in psychiatry to unravel his condition. Without hesitation he was able to take me to the core.

One day he came home early from work and found his wife in bed with his brother. Something snapped inside him. He killed them both and ran for his life, and he has hated himself and the world ever since.

It was a brief encounter with a stranger whose name I never knew and whose face I can't remember. What I can't forget is how love and hate are never far apart.

How I wish I knew the rest of the story.

Though perhaps this man's life was played out at a more intense level, his story is nevertheless the human story. It is the story of us. And it comes with a warning on the label.

The great danger of giving up on love is that we begin to give in to hate. A place where there is no love is toxic to the soul.

When we love, we are moved toward forgiveness. When we allow hate to take over, we begin to live for vengeance. If you dare to love and have felt the sting of betrayal, you could eventually justify a life of bitterness and cynicism. You might conclude, *How could anyone blame me?*

If you've never found love, if you've never been loved, how can anyone expect you to live a life of love?

After all, even the sincerest of us could eventually conclude that there is no such thing as love, that love is just a word for weakness. And most of us have been very, very weak.

ENTRY #7 Making, Taking, Faking Love

WHILE ONE PERSON MAY CHOOSE A PATH OF ISOLATION TO dull the pain of a loveless existence, others may choose a dramatically different way. Not necessarily a better way, just a different one.

Some lives can be explained only by the maddening effect of love.

I have friends who have virtually sold their souls hoping to be loved. Some mask their pain through indifference, but others through false intimacy. We all long to belong. We all need to be connected to something bigger than ourselves. Whether we like it or not, much of our self-worth is rooted in how others feel or think about us. If we belong to no one, we begin to feel that we are worthless. Because of this, we will do almost anything to belong to someone or to belong to something.

Sex, unfortunately, is used as a shortcut to love.

Sex can be the most intimate and beautiful expression of love, but we are only lying to ourselves when we act as if sex is proof of love. Too many men demand sex as proof of love; too many women have given sex in hopes of love. We live in a world of users where we abuse each other to dull the pain of our aloneness. We all long for intimacy, and physical contact can appear as intimacy, at least for a moment.

Is there any moment that feels more filled with loneliness than the second after having sex with someone who cares nothing about you?

There is no such thing as free sex. It always comes at a cost. With it, either you give your heart, or you give your soul. It seems you can have sex without giving love, but you can't have sex without giving a part of yourself.

When sex is an act of love, it is a gift. When sex is a substitute for love, it is a trap.

Have you ever met a fifty-five-year-old womanizer? It's pretty sad really. Most of the ones I've known didn't remain single on paper, just in principle. In and out of marriages, in and out of relationships, they point to their detachment as proof of their self-sufficiency. They are the guys in college guzzling the beer and swearing that they would be single for life. They probably should have kept that commitment. They looked so cool when they were twenty-two.

Most guys, if they were honest, would admit that they envied them. What a life—get drunk, sleep with a stranger, throw up, sneak awkwardly out, avoiding all eye contact, get some sleep so you can go to church the next day. No wonder we wanted to be like them. They were our heroes in college, unless, of course, we were able to see past the allure of vomit to see what was really going on.

Most of us know these guys just don't get it. Love isn't about volume. Love isn't about conquest. When we live like this, there's something deeper going on inside us that we're trying to ignore, even drown out. We are alone, disconnected, and deficient in love. Deep down inside we know we cannot fill the vacuum within our souls by consuming people. We are not only robbing others; we are pillaging our own souls.

Eventually it hits you: you cannot take love; you have to give it. Love is a gift that cannot be stolen.

You may think you're having a great time, but you're actually wasting precious time. What feels cool at twenty-two leaves you cold at fifty-five. It's funny how the people who are often described as great lovers are often unfamiliar with it. Western culture's primary male icons have been Casanova, Don Juan, and Rudolph Valentino, and now it's —— [you fill in the blank]. These, among others, are placed in the category of the world's greatest lovers. We should consider this

SOUL CRAVINGS

an insult to both men and love. Love is not about how many people we have used, but about how much we have cherished one person. I've come to find over time that players are the ones who are most afraid. They are afraid to love, and so they make it a game. They're terrified of loving deeply, and so they keep everything superficial. I think deep inside they wonder whether any woman could actually love them if she really knew who he was.

If you really believed you were capable of loving deeply and profoundly, what in the world would keep you from it? Is it that your heart so longs for love and longs to love, but you've settled for so much less?

Then there are the people who believe in love but do not believe that they are worthy of it. You find them moving from one destructive relationship to another. What they call love, any reasonable person would call abuse. It's almost impossible to understand why they choose to stay in those relationships. You can't seem to talk them out of it. If you dare say anything about their partners, they are the first to defend them. They are held hostage by their need for love. They are made victims because they don't believe they deserve love, so they settle for whatever they can get. I have met way too many women who have given their bodies to men as a trade-off for a poor imitation of love.

How can you make sense of a person who moves from one relationship to another, making her body the object of another's pleasure or abuse, except to acknowledge the painful reality that human beings fear almost nothing more than being alone?

ENTRY #8   Love Lost and Abandoned

ALL OF US HAVE ABANDONMENT ISSUES—SOME MORE THAN others. McCall would fall into the "more" category. McCall's mom left her father when McCall was two, though her parents were never married. She grew up in the land of Drew Carey—Cleveland, Ohio, that is—with an alcoholic mother and absentee father. From pretty much as early as she can remember, she struggled to figure out where she fit in—a white girl growing up in a black neighborhood going to a Jewish school, then a Catholic school, then a Quaker school. You would kind of expect her to have at least a few identity issues. Just from a cultural perspective, she felt like she never related to anyone.

But life was far more complicated than just making it through school. Going home was no safe haven for McCall. The environment that's supposed to protect children became for McCall a breeding ground for brokenness and dysfunction. She was barely twelve when she was thrown headfirst into the deep end of sexuality. This was only the beginning of a life of experimentation and devastation. McCall's childhood was a résumé of sex, drugs, mutilation, tattoos, and an attempted suicide—all by the age of fifteen. Our culture's new wisdom is that sexual freedom is far healthier than any moral guidance. Why does it continue to surprise us that a girl who is sexually active by fourteen is emotionally devastated by fifteen?

Yet underneath all the pain, all the confusion, all the noise, McCall was always keenly aware that God was quietly calling her.

With the same kind of fury with which she engaged in everything else, she began a search for her soul. If she had a motto, it was "experience everything." In fact, she describes herself as an experience vampire. As she would put it, "Suck it all up and leave it dry." So her journey included Wicca, yoga, transcendental meditation, Ouija boards, tarot cards, Ashram, and even shamanistic sweat lodges. Oh, yeah, throw in a little Baptist church she would later occasionally attend.

McCall moved to LA in 1998 and first came in contact with our community through a coworker's father. She asked if there was anyplace where she could find good music, where she could sing and be comfortable, that specifically catered to the freaks of Los Angeles. That led her to Mosaic.

On a Sunday when I wasn't speaking (great things happen when I'm not speaking), a wonderful friend named Chip Anderson was sharing. One thing he said struck McCall at the core: "If your soul is disconnected from its source, it will die." Chip explained that we were created for God and that we cannot, in essence, live without him. If we would connect to him, he would make our souls fully alive. Even with her mantra "experience everything," McCall knew this was one experience her soul was desperately lacking. "I wanted to get connected to this church so that I could get connected to my source so my soul would stop dying."

It took a little time, but McCall began to understand what her soul had been craving all along.

Her soul longed for love, for a place to belong, to be connected. Her soul longed for God.

Ironically, it was a conversation with three sorority girls who asked McCall out to lunch that pushed her over the edge—all three "blond and spunky" was how she described them. She was sure she would scare them away. I think she was more afraid of them. I mean, really, what's scarier, tattooed or spunky?

McCall explained that the spunkiest of the three asked her, "Why do you think Jesus freaks you out?"

"I have abandonment issues." McCall went on to explain, "When everyone you love seems to disappear, it's kind of hard to deal with a guy dead on a cross. Jesus left them. He didn't come through. He abandoned them. Who needs one more relationship that's going nowhere?"

They asked her when she went home to just take some time and read chapter 14 of the Gospel of John.

She read it over and over and over again until finally she wasn't reading the Scriptures, but the Scriptures were reading her. The way she described it, God began speaking to her, calling and reassuring her. Everything she had ever done began flashing before her eyes, every guy she had ever slept with, every drug she had ever taken, every lie she had ever told. Ashamed but desperate, she fell on her knees. And as McCall put it, "I turned to God, thinking he was a fool for wanting me." Which, of course, is the nature of love, isn't it?

It's a wonderful thing when your heart guides you to the very One you need the most. The strange thing about God is that the One we deserve the least is the One we need the most and the One who desires us the most (so much for abandonment issues). At the core of her story, McCall tapped into something that drives us all, although most of us don't want to admit it. There was some meaning behind her madness, going from a Klan rally to a Black Panthers meeting to a gathering at a church in a nightclub.

As she put it, "I was always seeking a place that felt like home.

"I wanted to feel like I fit in, and I was desperate for it."

I am convinced that all of us are searching for a place called home, a place where we can close our eyes and sleep, a place where there is warmth and we are somehow unafraid, a place where we gather around the fire and the room is filled with laughter and love.

My wife, Kim, has fallen in love with the story of *The Notebook*. Without giving away the plot (although it goes without saying there

entry 8

are no bombs, guns, special effects, action scenes, epic battles, just the basic chick-flick love triangle), there's one line near the end that captured my attention. When James Garner's character was asked to leave the retirement community where his wife was required to live due to her Alzheimer's and go home with his grandchildren, his answer was, *"Allie is my home."*

Later during one of my travels, I had the chance to watch John LeCarre's *The Constant Gardener* and to my surprise, the entire film culminated with the same theme. This time it was Ralph Fiennes referring to Rachel Weisz, who played his wife. When he lost her, he lost his home.

Home is ultimately not about a place to live but about the people with whom you are most fully alive. Home is about love, relationship, community, and belonging, and we are all searching for home.

The theme of a desperate search for love has been powerfully and sometimes whimsically told by Steven Spielberg. With *E. T.* we find an alien in a strange land desperately wanting to phone home. I think all of us have felt like that at some time or another.

Years later I remember sitting at the AMC Theater watching a very different Spielberg film. It was a film initiated by Stanley Kubrick. When Kubrick passed away, Steven Spielberg stepped in and finished it. And while I'm a huge fan, I have to admit this one was hard to take. Maybe you saw it. It was called *A.I.*

A.I. stands for artificial intelligence, but it's also the Japanese word for love.

It's a story about the search for belonging. Its emotional context is the painful reality of rejection and abandonment. It's the story of a piece of technology that became too human and, once human, became desperate for love.

The movie's tagline was "David is 11 years old. He weighs 60 lbs. He is 4 feet 6 inches tall. He has brown hair. His love is real, but he is not."

It is human to crave love, and like a piece of technology that could live forever, that longing for love will exist as long as we exist.

That, of course, is a part of the human dilemma—as long as we breathe, we will crave love. As long as we can take one more step, we will search for a place called home. And sometimes, like McCall, we will travel to faraway and strange places to find that which may be closer than we could ever imagine.

A.I. was like watching two hours of child abuse. David did everything he could to be loved. At one point in the film when he had inadvertently damaged himself and found himself broken, he pleaded with his surrogate parent to forgive him.

Maybe it's because he was broken that he couldn't be loved. He was so terribly sorry that he broke himself. I don't see how he's any different from us.

ENTRY #9   The Elusive Nature of Love

SOME OF US BEGIN WITH GOD AT AN EARLY AGE AND RUN far away, searching for what our hearts long for. Like Paulo Coelho's *The Alchemist,* our long journey will lead us back to where we began, but we return as changed people with new eyes to see what once we were blind to. I meet many people who are running from God, angry with God, and yet at the same time desperately searching for him. If God is love, it is maddening when we are running from God and yet searching for love.

It's like when Kim and I were first dating. It was both wonderful and volatile. We argued all the time. It seemed the more committed I was, the more conflict we had. Some people have smooth dating relationships and an exciting engagement and then a turbulent first year of marriage. We did it the other way around. We had a great first year of marriage. You never could have predicted that from how things were going right up to the wedding. For a while, it seemed that she was purposefully picking fights. I wasn't sure whether it was paranoia or whether she was doing everything possible to make me run for my life.

I remember finally confronting her and asking her what in the world was going on. When she began to open up her heart, I began to really understand. Kim was an orphan—huge abandonment issues. Abandoned by her parents at the age of eight, she grew up in a foster home. She was sure that I would do the same thing. I would eventually come to my senses and get out of the relationship. She knew it wasn't possible for me to love her unconditionally, and she was determined to prove it.

Sometimes the thing we want the most, we fear the most.

When it comes to love, often we are our own worst enemies. When we've been hurt in the past, when we feel that love has betrayed us, we can easily become the enemies of love. To see if it's real, we do everything we can to destroy it. We tell ourselves we're testing it, but actually we're resisting it.

I remember once Kim asked me why I loved her, and I made the mistake of trying to declare my unconditional love for her.

"I love you for no good reason." I was just trying to be like God.

As you might imagine, it didn't go that well.

"So there's no good reason to love me? There's nothing about me worth loving?"

Call me intuitive, but I knew somehow she had misunderstood or I had miscommunicated. There were so many things I loved about Kim, and I learned over the years that we're all actually far more comfortable with conditional love than unconditional love. "I love you because you're smart, gifted, and talented; you have beautiful blue eyes; you are unbelievably creative; you have an amazing personality; you're passionate, caring . . . " (See how much I've learned, honey?).

The truth of the matter is that we're uncomfortable with God. We're disoriented by the way he loves.

We want God to love us for an endless number of good reasons.

At the same time, we find ourselves nervous before him because he sees right through us and knows everything that isn't lovable. He tells us that he is our place of rest and acceptance and unconditional love, yet we cannot reconcile this love. We know who we are. We know all that is unlovely within us. We wonder how we have become worthy of such love, and that's what worries us—we know we're not. So we run. We run from God because he sees us best; we run from God to escape our own sense of unworthiness; we run from God because we are certain that the closer we come to him, the more guilt and shame we will feel.

> It's just too hard to believe that if you come near to God, you
>   will find yourself not drowning in condemnation, but
>   swimming in compassion.
> Jesus called to all who were weary and who found their souls
>   exhausted to come to him and find rest. He is telling us
>   that God will be for us our place called home.
> We run from God because we long to be loved and we have
>   convinced ourselves that the One who is most loving could
>   not and would not embrace us.
> We run from the One our souls crave.

It is insanity to run from God and search for love.

At least on an unconscious level, a part of our struggle with God is our discomfort with love. It seems no matter how beautiful or wanted we are, there's always something inside us that remains insecure. All of us find ourselves uncertain when it comes to love. We have no real experience of unconditional love, and it goes without saying that conditional love always leaves us wanting. But at least with conditional love we have some control over the situation. The downside is, when we don't meet the conditions, we default on the love.

Undying love has a history of premature death!

ENTRY #10 What Must I Do to Be Loved?

We speak of true love not only lasting a lifetime, but lasting forever. Forever seems to have a clear beginning and end. In the end we can't manage to meet the standards of love, and so we just accept that love isn't all it's made out to be. Prepare to be disappointed. Isn't that the history of love? We can never live up to its standards. I think we recognize this when it comes to God. If God loves conditionally, we're all in trouble. And this, when you whittle it down to its bottom line, is the basis of all religion.

God loves but on condition. Meet the conditions and gain the love. Love is something that is attained. Oh, we use different words for it—*forgiveness, mercy, acceptance, grace*—all really different words for love.

In this it appears that all religions are the same. They give God a name and then establish the rules that we must follow if we are to gain his favor and affection. I think this is why a lot of us see all religions as different ways of getting to the same thing.

Some girls want flowers; others, chocolates; others, meaningful conversation (and you thought the flowers and chocolates were expensive); all different ways of trying to get to the same place—to be loved, to find love. So some people pray five times a day facing east; others pray rosaries; still others bring offerings, light candles, and memorize incantations; all for the same purpose—to gain acceptance from their Creator.

Really it's absurd to think that any religion would somehow get you to God.

It's like being in love with a person who has no interest in you. He loves your advances only because they make him feel self-important, but really he has no motivation to pursue you. It's all one-sided. He loves being pursued, and so your desire only inspires him to be more elusive. You have to admit, if the premise of religion is valid—if you do this, then God will accept you—this is a more accurate description of God: He's just some really good-looking, smug, and arrogant Divine Being who loves being the object of all our affection.

When it relates to God, we call this one-sided love, which has, over time, become contextualized as an experience we call worship. If you thought about it long enough, it would really make you sick. If you had a friend or anyone you cared about in that kind of one-sided relationship, you would do everything in your power to convince her to dump him. But we want so much to be loved that we allow ourselves to be coerced and demeaned just by the possibility of one day being loved.

I'm often accused of being irreligious, and I suppose it's for this very reason. Whether it's Christianity, Islam, Buddhism, Catholicism, Hinduism, Judaism, or any other *ism*, when a religion is created on the subtle premise that God withholds his love and you must submit to the system to earn that love, I consider it the worst of corruptions.

But again these traps work only because of two things: we long for love, and we are convinced that all love is conditional.

Ironically, this is where so many have a problem with Jesus. For centuries the church has been telling us if we want God to love us, we need to follow the rules. It's been far more important to focus on the sin problem than the love problem. This is the only way the institution can maintain control over our lives. After all, if love is unconditional, what will keep them following our rules? Don't we want people, first and foremost, to be good? If our goal is to get people to conform, you can accomplish that without love, but you can't maintain a civilization without the rule of law.

What governments have not always been able to do, religions have accomplished with amazing effectiveness. They keep people in line.

What in the world would happen if people actually began discovering the actual message of Jesus Christ—that love is unconditional? What would happen if we began to realize that God was not, in fact, waiting for us to earn his love, but that he was passionately pursuing us with his love? What would happen if the word got out that Jesus was offering his love freely and without condition?

Would anyone actually choose to be a slave to ritual and legalism when he could have relationship and love? The answer, unfortunately, is yes. The reason religion works is that we believe in conditional love and doubt the existence of unconditional love.

I have no doubt that there are many of us who have run into religious leaders, church leaders, those who would speak on behalf of God and have held God hostage. It was our responsibility to raise the ransom to release his love. There are way too many people being duped into believing that if they give enough money, they will unlock and receive all that God has been withholding from them.

Some of us have come to our senses and realized we've been taken.

Whatever kind of love you can purchase, it isn't the love your soul longs for. If you have to buy love, it's not even worth the price. I know that many of us look to Matthew, Mark, Luke, and John for our spiritual wisdom, but in this case John, Paul, George, and Ringo got it right—*can't buy me love.*

So again we're face-to-face with a dilemma—we can't earn love, we can't buy love, and we can't live without it.

We know in the pit of our stomachs that if love is conditional, it can't really be love at all. We also know that if love is unconditional, we are neither the sources nor the instigators of such love, which again is a part of our conflict. We want what we do not give. We long for what we seem incapable of producing.

Where does the concept of unconditional love come from anyway? How can we hold such a lofty ideal when we live so far from it? Doesn't believing in unconditional love pretty much fall into the same category as believing in aliens from outer space? You know, they could exist; we've just never seen one. I would kind of like to think they're out there, but again, it's not likely. Pretty much like love—I mean, real love. Not the imitation or the homogenized version. Not lust or romance or anything and everything else that we dub as love.

If love is such a profound emotion, why is it that we love everything and anything?

Holly, who works with me on my manuscripts, if put under a hot light will confess that she loves chocolate.

I love cappuccinos, extra hot—well, actually that might not be love, but maybe more of an addiction.

We are a culture of great lovers.

We love great movies.

We love ice cream.

We love our pets.

We love rainy days in Los Angeles.

We love sunny days in Seattle.

We love shopping.

We love great meals.

We love weekends.

We love rock and roll.

The French love their wine; the Germans love their cars; the Swiss love their watches (and, I'm reminded by Holly, their chocolate); the Italians love their lattes and their pasta; the Chinese love their feng shui; the Japanese love their sushi; the Brazilians love, well, pretty much everything.

Maybe the fact that we love even the most meaningless of things tells us more about our capacity to love than we think.

What we have described as love has become something so superficial, something so thin and without substance, that pretty much anything qualifies as love. If we really knew love, if we knew deep, profound, unending love, maybe we wouldn't love chocolate. While I'm sure God appreciates all these things (after all, he is the Creator of all that is good and perfect), creation is not the object of his affection. When it comes to love, you exist in a unique category. There are a lot of things that are dispensable to God. He can re-create whatever he wants. You, however, are not on that list. You are unique and irreplaceable.

You are the object of God's love.

In Solomon's sensual Song of Songs, he describes a lover pursuing the one who has won her heart. He captures the hopelessness that one feels on this desperate search for love.

> At night on my bed,
> I looked for the one I love;
> I looked for him, but I could not find him.
> I got up and went around the city,
>   in the streets and squares,
>   looking for the one I love.
> I looked for him, but I could not find him.
> The watchmen found me as they patrolled the city,
>   so I asked, "Have you seen the one I love?"

Solomon is describing the desperation that comes when we seem unable to capture the heart of the one we love. I wonder if it ever occurs to us that God feels like this. But if God's love is immeasurable and unending, as the Hebrews describe him, how deep and profound must be his sense of sorrow and rejection. If anyone knows the pain of a love unreturned, it must be God.

ENTRY #11 Chased by Love
(Please Don't Run Too Fast)

IN *CHASING DAYLIGHT*, I DESCRIBE A TIME WHEN A TEAM of us were in the Middle East. I had been invited to speak to a group of Muslims, specifically about the history of Christianity. Pressed by my translator to answer a question that I had somewhat evaded, I was left with nowhere to go but to talk more specifically and personally about Jesus. I had been describing to them my own sense of disappointment with and even disdain of the religion of Christianity. They all quickly agreed that as a religion, there were deep problems and inconsistencies between beliefs and practices.

But eventually they wanted to know what exactly was the meaning behind the coming of Jesus. Somewhat apprehensively I began my best effort to translate back into a Middle Eastern context the story of Jesus (after all, this was Jesus' home turf) and, more specifically, why it would be necessary for God to become human. This, from my vantage point, was the story of God. It's a love story, by the way.

"I once met a girl named Kim."

My translator looked at me confused. I'm sure he was wracking his brain, trying to remember some biblical character named Kim. He stopped translating and just looked at me. I encouraged him to simply translate.

"I once met a girl named Kim, and I fell in love."

I continued, *"I pursued her with my love and pursued her with my love until I felt my love had captured her heart. So I asked her to be my wife, and she said no."* I could feel their empathy, if not their pity.

 entry 11

SOUL CRAVINGS

"I was unrelenting and asked her again, pursuing her with my love, and I pursued her with my love until she said yes."

There was huge relief throughout the entire room.

I went on, *"I did not send my brother, nor did I send a friend. For in issues of love, you must go yourself.*

"This is the story of God: he pursues you with his love and pursues you with his love, and you have perhaps not said yes. And even if you reject his love, he pursues you ever still. It was not enough to send an angel or a prophet or any other, for in issues of love, you must go yourself. And so God has come.

"This is the story of Jesus, that God has walked among us and he pursues us with his love. He is very familiar with rejection but is undeterred. And he is here even now, still pursuing you with his love."

The images we often receive of Muslims are that they're angry, hostile, and violent people. I can tell you that in this moment I knew there was something transcendent that connected all of our hearts and souls together. A belief that was supposed to divide us strangely united us, and I feel most certain that I know why. Every human being longs for love. The possibility that God is love is an almost overwhelming prospect.

In that moment the story of Jesus was not about who is right and who is wrong, what God's name is and who his prophet is, but what exactly God's motivation toward humanity is. If the message that God wants to get across to us is just about getting our beliefs right, then he didn't need to come himself. If God's entire intent was to clarify right from wrong, no personal visitation was necessary. If the ultimate end was simply to overwhelm us with the miraculous so that we would finally believe, then even God taking on flesh and blood and walking among us was far from necessary.

There is only one reason for God to come himself, because in issues of love, you just can't have someone else stand in for you.

When it comes to love, it has to be face-to-face. There has to be contact. Love cannot exist where there is only distance. Love can survive distance, but only by the strength of what comes through intimacy.

Like Solomon's lover, God is going up and down the streets of the city, traveling the most obscure paths and untamed wilderness, walking on unnamed roads in the most desolate of places, searching for the one he loves—and that one is you and me and every human being who has ever walked this earth, has taken a breath, and has longed for love.

Religion exists not because God loves too little, but because we need love so much. In the end all religions misrepresent God. They either dictate requirements for love or simply become a requiem for love. I think many of us have rightly given up on God on this basis alone. We've been told that God is a reluctant lover and that his standards must be met before there can be any talk of love. This is lunacy. Love exists because God is love. Our souls will never find satisfaction until our hearts have found this love that we so desperately yearn for.

God is not passive, for love is never passive, but always passionate; and passion always leads to action.

ENTRY #12 It's Murder Out There

HAVE YOU EVER CARED SO MUCH FOR SOMEONE THAT YOU would do anything to prove your love for that one? Have you ever been so much in love that you would even give your life to protect that one from harm? That God could feel this way somehow seems to elude us. A small glimpse of this came to me in the unlikeliest of ways.

I've spent my life living in cities, from San Salvador to Miami to Queens to Raleigh to Dallas to Los Angeles to several others in between. I am right at home with city lights, skyscrapers, and rush-hour traffic. I feel totally at ease moving to the concrete beat.

After a decade in LA, things finally came together for us to buy a house. During our first spring, a pair of mallards adopted us. They evidently thought our pool was a lake or really more like a pond or a puddle. In any case, they chose to make it their spring home. Next thing we knew they had laid a nest full of eggs. To our surprise, we woke up one day to nearly a dozen baby mallards swimming in our pool. The male mallard was there every day until the chicks were hatched. Once they were born, he flew the coop. He was nothing more than a deadbeat duck. My kids were excited and quickly adopted them as their own.

We've never been good with pets. We've pretty much tried them all. They would always seem to run away. This time, the exact opposite happened; we couldn't get rid of them. So they took over our backyard, and we were the reluctant managers of a wilderness camp. We gave them full run of the pool and the backyard. We expected to enjoy the experience of watching them grow up and then one day fly away.

Little did we know that we were about to enter into our own personal nightmare.

One by one we watched those little ducklings being hunted and eliminated. From cats to skunks to crows, our backyard was open for duck season. To put it mildly, it was a jungle out there. We did everything we could to save their lives. We watched the female mallard face one sleepless night after another. Once I even had the misfortune of watching a crow swoop down, grab a duckling, and fly away as its mother pursued to no avail. It was more than I could bear. I had moved to the city to avoid violence like this. I soon found myself having nightmares. All I could think about was how to save the remaining ducklings. I would spend time in the backyard trying to keep the crows away. Every couple of days I would discover another one had disappeared.

One evening I woke up in the middle of the night breathing heavily, my heart pounding against my chest. I found myself leaping out of bed, shouting, "Did you hear the quack?" Kim, who had grown up in the country, was sleeping soundly until my panic attack woke her up. She tried to calm me down and encouraged me to go back to sleep. As I lay there in bed, haunted by what I knew were the implications of the sounds I had heard, I found myself having an entirely different conversation.

God crashed into my brain and allowed me to see something—no, more accurately, to *feel* something—from his perspective.

I know it was just inside my head, but it was as if I could hear God screaming, "*Do you know how you feel about that duckling? The anguish that you're feeling this very moment, that's how I feel for every human being who walks the face of this earth. If you could just care about people the way you're caring about that mallard this moment, it would make you a different person. You would know the heart of God.*"

The world is full of crows, mallards, and ducklings. There are crows that swoop down on helpless children in Thailand and steal them away to turn them into child prostitutes; there are crows that use a caste system to keep millions oppressed and in poverty in India; there are crows in the priesthood who hide behind their collars while they abuse children. It doesn't surprise me any longer that a cluster of crows is called a "murder." And this is how Jesus describes the evil one. His summary of the spiritual reality in which we live is pretty simple: "The thief comes to steal and to rob and to kill, but I have come to give you life and life in abundance."

ENTRY #13 Being Loved to Death?

A FRIEND OF MINE NAMED RONALD LOPEZ HAS BEEN LIVING in Istanbul for the past several years working among Muslim artists, and he has recently published his first book, *Does Religion Kill?*

The implied answer is, of course, yes.

Emphatically, yes.

Tragically, yes.

Way too many times the crows that have swooped down are wearing the robes of religion. It's not that they're tormenting the innocent, for our sense of defenselessness is that we know that we're not innocent, but they are tormenting the helpless. How could we ever guess that God would be the friend of the broken, the outcast, and the guilty? Because of religion, we have run from God when, in fact, he has been the only One ready to stand in our defense.

There was a moment in the life of Jesus when an unnamed woman was surrounded by the crows.

Jesus went to the Mount of Olives. But early in the morning he went back to the Temple, and all the people came to him, and he sat and taught them. The teachers of the law and the Pharisees brought a woman who had been caught in adultery. They forced her to stand before the people. They said to Jesus, "Teacher, this woman was caught having sexual relations with a man who is not her husband. The law of Moses commands that we stone to death every woman who does this. What do you say we should do?" They were asking this to trick Jesus so that they could have some charge against him.

 entry 13

But Jesus bent over and started writing on the ground with his finger. When they continued to ask Jesus their question, he raised up and said, "Anyone here who has never sinned can throw the first stone at her." Then Jesus bent over again and wrote on the ground.

Those who heard Jesus began to leave one by one, first the older men and then the others. Jesus was left there alone with the woman standing before Him. Jesus raised up again and asked her, "Woman, where are they? Has no one judged you guilty?"

She answered, "No one, sir."

Then Jesus said, "I also don't judge you guilty. You may go now, but don't sin anymore."

If those who are the religious elite are closest to God, why is it that they are so rarely closest to love?

If God is love, those who know God best would love people most. Jesus said he came not to condemn the world, but to bring the world life. Why is it that so many who represent him are ever so quick to condemn? All her accusers could see was a woman guilty of adultery. There's always so much more behind these stories—a woman abused by her husband searching for love; a little girl abused by a relative, who would forever confuse love with sex; a prostitute who would sell love for a price but had none to give.

If Jesus' encounter with this unnamed adulterous woman tells us anything, it reveals the unexpected truth that the safest place for a sinful person to go is to God. He and he alone is the only One who will neither condemn us nor leave us in our brokenness. On the mount of Olives she found herself most alone and discovered the unimaginable—God wanted her. God was her place to belong, and this reality became the beginning of new things. That may be the most powerful thing about love. Love gives us a fresh start. Love gives us a reason to live.

When life isn't what it should be, love gives us the strength to endure whatever may come.

Nichole was raised in a destructive environment. Her mom was sixteen and her dad seventeen when she was born. She was a child born to children. Her dad was a drug addict who was physically abusive to her mom. Her childhood memories are filled with the endless number of women her father brought home and the many nights she found her mother in bed with different men. Her childhood was marked by the sexually violent environment where on numerous occasions her mom would be gang raped by her father's friends.

When she was eight years old, Nichole moved from the insanity of Los Angeles to what one would expect to be the safe environment of Oklahoma to live with her great-grandmother. But it was there that she was molested by her great-grandfather. Every relationship in her life that was supposed to promise her safety and protection brought her only pain and confusion. A year later she was sent back to live with her mother, who had remarried. She was thrown back into the family turmoil, and now she had the added responsibility, the raising of her three brothers. She had to raise herself while she raised them.

Sometimes it's hard to understand why love hurts so much.

When Nichole was a senior in high school, she was determined to leave home but stayed in response to her mom's pleadings. Her mom had not earned her love, but love just doesn't work that way. Sometimes, to our detriment, love can be irrational. It was during this time Nichole became friends with a guy named Mark. Their friendship deepened as she became close not only to Mark, but also to his family. She was rarely allowed to escape the dark environment of her own family, but whenever possible she treasured the retreat of Mark's home. There was something different about his family. It was a family that worked. There was real community, real love. It wasn't perfect, but it was honest, it was healthy, and it was healing.

Nichole was experiencing for the first time the kind of community that Jesus longs to create for all of us.

She writes, "Their home and church for me was a safe place. It was the only place I felt okay. I loved going to church with them, and any chance I could get away, that was the first place I ran to."

Too often church is seen as a place that lacks genuine, authentic community, but this time it was different. Nichole found what her soul longed for. She left home at eighteen unready for the challenges ahead. Just as in the world she had come from, she now found herself drowning in the abyss of drugs, alcohol, and sex.

"It was a dark time for me until God placed an amazing woman, Marisol, in my life. . . . She invested in me, and through that process I became more involved and felt like I belonged and had a family, and God began to work in all the ugly parts of my life. He still is. I now see God's hand in my life. God has brought me out of so much and spared me from so much to give me even more."

You will spend your life working through relationships trying to understand your need for love, your inadequacies in love, your desperation for love, and all the time you might miss the signs that your heart is giving you, that you're searching for God.

We need each other; we need people; we need community; we need relationship; we need God.

They are all interconnected, and it flows in both directions. We try to fill our vacuum for God with people, and we find ourselves frustrated and empty.

When we turn to God, we find our hearts open to people and discover our need for them more than ever before.

ENTRY #14 A Vacuum of Love

IN OUR OWN WAY WE ARE ALL TRYING TO FIND OUR TRIBE. When Jesus was asked what the most important commandment is, His response was simple and straightforward: "You are to love God with all your heart, soul, mind, and strength." And then He added, "And you must love your neighbor as yourself."

It seems Jesus simply couldn't restrain Himself to one commandment, but gave His inquirers two of them. Maybe it's because He couldn't separate the effect that connecting to God would have on our relationship to people. Really, Jesus is saying that the most important thing to God is love. Love, it seems, has two arenas where it's played out—in our relationship with God and in our relationship with people. What's on God's heart is not a list of rules or commands, but the expansion of love. . . . All God wants for us in this is that we live in healthy, loving relationships.

At first glance this would seem pretty easy, yet life experience tells us that this may be the most difficult task we've ever been called to, which is why the order of the Great Commandment is not incidental but absolutely critical. When we live in an intimate relationship with God, we are able to love ourselves and become passionate about loving others. When we are disconnected from God, we find ourselves increasingly empty of love.

Jesus, it seems, is certain that the more you love God, the more you will love people.

Nichole's life is not the story of one person journeying in isolation. Her quest, like so many of ours, is a search for belonging. Her story began with a painful realization that those who are supposed to love us the most often hurt us the worst. The dark side of human community can lead us to give up on God or to recognize he is exactly what we need most. When people hurt us, we blame God. We wonder why God would allow such horrible things to happen.

We wrongly conclude that God is indifferent to our pain and suffering. Many of us give up on love because those who were supposed to love us never came through.

After all, we instinctively know that those who are closest to us are supposed to love us the most. I sat last night and listened to a mother describe how much she hated her daughter. The daughter never said a word, just sat there in silence. Both of them knew that this is not how God intended life to be lived. You don't have to be a genius to know that a mother is supposed to love her daughter; that a father is supposed to love his son; that children are intended to be born into a world of doting parents who love their children as if they've received the world's most extraordinary gift. If you need evidence that something is broken in the human spirit, just look carefully here. There's something wrong with us when we cannot love even those who are our flesh and blood.

There's something desperately wrong with us when we find ourselves experiencing animosity or, at best indifference, toward the ones with whom we should be sharing intimacy.

Yet many of us grow up in a vacuum of love, and it doesn't have to be abusive for this to be true. I know way too many people who have grown up with responsible parents who were entirely unresponsive. Some of the adults who have the most difficult time with love are the ones who were given everything they ever wanted as kids except love. There is no substitute for warmth, affection, and intimacy. The truth is, we were designed for relationship, and when our relationships don't work, they affect how we see God, how we relate to God, and even whether we will believe in him.

We are born to belong, we are created for connection, and whether we admit it to ourselves or not, we spend our whole lives trying to fit in, get in, and stay in. It almost doesn't even matter what "in" is; we just want to belong somewhere.

ENTRY #15 Where Do I Belong?

WE ARE A WORLD OF JOINERS. EVEN LONE WOLVES SEEM to run in packs. Part of the trauma of high school is trying to figure out which clique you belong to. There are the freaks and the geeks and the jocks and the nerds and the vandals and the rebels and then, of course, the invisibles. I really liked the freaks but just couldn't see a future in dropping acid. You had to have higher than a straight D average to get into the geeks, so I was disqualified. I participated with the jocks, but my brother was the star quarterback for the football team. Who wants to be part of the tribe where your brother is chief? No need to explain why I didn't want to join the nerds. You don't actually join the nerds anyway; you get placed there by acclamation.

I didn't see a future in the vandals either. Besides, I was trying to break the stereotype of being a Latino and having a criminal record. Have you ever noticed that if there's ever a Latin on screen, you know he did it? So that pretty much left the invisibles or the rebels—and aren't the rebels really just the ones who are desperately trying not to be invisible while knowing they don't fit in anywhere else? This is maybe why I'm so attracted to Jesus. If James Dean was the rebel without a cause, Jesus was the rebel with one.

This desperate need to belong doesn't end with our high school graduation; it haunts us the rest of our lives.

I like to think of myself as a person who is not trapped by the need to be a joiner, but then I opened up my wallet as an experiment in self-awareness. I pulled out my Starbucks card, my AMC Theater card, my Blockbuster card, my YMCA card, my 24-Hour Fitness card—yes, I have both of those, and I'm still out of shape—my VISA card. (But not just *a* VISA card, it's my United Airlines VISA card. And not just United Airlines, I'm part of the Star Alliance. Not to mention, of course, that I finally worked my way up to belong to the 1K Club.) I also have my Red Carpet Club card, my Costco card, my AAA card, and my Pacific Care insurance card, but that one my wife makes me carry.

There are an endless number of symbols of belonging all around us. We join clubs, teams, sororities, fraternities, unions, guilds, churches, synagogues, organizations, political parties, and unfortunately, even Klans. We mark our tribes through labels, tattoos, piercings, colors, symbols, music, language, and style, and this is just the surface of an array of ways we find to belong, to fit in, to be insiders . . . ironically the less genuine community we have, the more we create artificial communities.

We live in a world of planned communities and virtual communities that are growing as fast as the human community is disintegrating. I don't think it's incidental that over the past twenty years the labels on our clothes moved from the inside to the outside. We know who we are by our symbols, and we can identify those who belong to our tribe by simply reading the signs. Izod has an alligator, Polo has a rider,

SOUL CRAVINGS

Abercrombie & Fitch has a moose, Lucky Brand has a shamrock, Hollister has a seagull, Modern Amusement has a crow, American Eagle has, well, an American eagle, and Penguin has, you guessed it, a penguin—not to mention True Religion, which has a Buddha, and may give us insight to what's really going on.

Something as meaningless as moving the labels to the outside could actually have deeper spiritual implications. Is it possible that we all are created with a need to belong to something, to belong to someone, and the less we actually belong to each other, the more symbols we need to feel like somehow we're making a connection? It goes much deeper than what we wear. We will reshape, redesign, and remake ourselves to be a part of a broader community.

We will go to great lengths and great pain to become insiders.

At one end of the spectrum, we will pierce ourselves, tattoo ourselves, and mutilate ourselves to be our unique selves, who look like a lot of other people. At the other end of the spectrum, we will use Botox, collagen, and plastic surgery to become what we hope other people will love. We will go through hell weeks, allow ourselves to be demeaned during hazing, and even commit unimaginable acts of violence to make it through an initiation just so that we can belong, so that we can be part of a tribe.

In the end, we are all tribal. We are created by a relational God for relationship.

God made us for relationships, and we only begin to experience life fully when we move toward healthy relationships and healthy community. Your soul will never be satisfied with anything less.

When we are estranged from God, we drift from love. Without God we lose our source of love but not our need for love.

What was once our source of endless pleasure would become the soul's deepest longing. What was intended to be an unlimited resource would become rare. We would spend the rest of history searching for love. And we would find ourselves far too often all too alone . . . I think all of us in our own way build strategies to avoid aloneness.

Some people are related to each other, and others are connected to each other.

Some people share the same space, and others share the same heart.

Some people live in proximity to each other, and others live in intimacy with each other.

Why is it so hard to move from "me" to "us"? In our guts we know we're not supposed to live simply for ourselves. Even the central character of the LA riots, Rodney King, asked, "Can't we all just get along?" It's time to recognize the opposite of "me" isn't "you," but "we."

Our need for relationship comes from the core of our being. It would be the greatest of tragedies to sacrifice others in the effort to find ourselves. Our souls crave to belong. The experience of love, though it emanates from God, is not limited to him.

We are created for each other.

We are all far more affected than we would like to admit by the community we are a part of. It is hard to believe in God when our world is deficient in love. It's just not that hard to convince people who have been loved deeply and freely that there is a God who also loves them.

> While our brains may deny it, our hearts know it:
> love is proof of God.

The further we move from love, the more distant God becomes.

To live without God is to carry a loneliness that goes to the deepest part of our being. There's an old expression about frigid winters being cold to the bone. Without love we get cold to the bone—cold gets inside you so deep that nothing gets you warm. It's amazing how the love of just one person can make you warm again. Inside of love there is always a fire burning where we can warm our hands, our hearts, and our souls.

> All of us know how cold it is outside.
> It's almost unbearable out there.
> Especially when we're there
> alone,
> isolated,
> lonely.

> You were never meant to be . . .

alone

ENTRY #16 God and Basketball

LOVE CAN NEVER BE SIMPLY BETWEEN YOU AND GOD. IT can never be limited to that relationship. Jesus makes that clear. Love is more than the relationship between a man and a woman, no matter how extraordinary it may be. Love is ever expanding. Love always grows, not just deeper, but wider. Love always loves people more and always loves more people. Love calls us to community; love calls us to humanity; love calls us to each other.

When we belong to God, we belong to each other.

There are no outsiders. All outcasts are welcome. If it isn't enough of a gift to receive God's endless and unconditional love, it even gets better than that—he gives us each other. Our belonging to each other is not incidental, but absolutely essential. It was no one less than Jesus who said the proof of God is found in our love for one another. Where there is no love, there is no God. At the same time, if there were no God, there would be no love.

Jesus is telling us that without love, without genuine belonging, without the power of authentic community, no one should believe that we have come to know God. This might be exactly why you have been hesitant to trust your heart to Jesus Christ. You've been to church, you've been around Christians, and you've been hurt by both. You've created all these intellectual arguments to justify your unbelief, but in the end, you've just been burned. Your conclusions may be wrong, but your instincts are right.

If God is at the core of something, if he exists at the hot, flaming center, what you're going to find is love. Jesus knew this all too well.

He warned us against the trappings of hypocrisy. When those who claim to represent him are unloving, those searching for God might conclude he is as well. The problem, of course, is that we are all hypocrites in transition. I am not who I want to be, but I am on the journey there, and thankfully I am not whom I used to be.

A healthy community is not a place of perfect people.

That place just doesn't exist. We all are flawed. If there was a perfect community, it would be ruined the moment I joined it. And it's easier to be patient with people when you realize they're being patient with you. When we don't come clean up front, it creates an unhealthy environment that leads to pretension and hypocrisy.

Strangely enough, the best opportunity for building meaningful relationships is admitting up front that you're not perfect and that you've got issues. Honesty is the only context in which intimacy can develop. For either of these to have a chance, there has to be trust. Love, no matter how you come at it, is a huge risk. It makes it easier for me to remember that God will never reject me because I'm not good enough and that any community that has His heart will embrace me as I am. Jesus invites us into a community where imperfect people can find acceptance, love, forgiveness, and a new beginning.

Eventually, though, this will require you to have to take the chance and see if God can really love you through people.

We were playing basketball in the backyard, and after we were good and exhausted, I sat down with a guy named Ben, who still had some serious questions about God. Most of our conversation revolved around whether Jesus is God or not. He was more than willing to embrace Jesus as a great teacher, philosopher, or even spiritual guru. His real hang-up was the divinity thing. After a while it hit me.

I just stopped everything I had been trying to do and said, "You're afraid God's going to burn you."

He looked at me and said without hesitation, "Yes, that's exactly right." He went on to acknowledge that pain and baggage from his past definitely factored in to his present doubts.

We're all like that. Jesus knew this. When others hurt us, it becomes a reflection on God. If we risk entering a community that claims access to God and we find ourselves betrayed in the process, it becomes the fastest way to become a practical atheist. If religion can bring us to God, it can certainly take us from him. I can only hope that Ben, as he shares life with our community, will experience the presence of God through the love we have for each other and for him.

ENTRY #17 Do You Know Who You Are?

I WAS RECENTLY TALKING TO MY FRIEND MICK, WHO HAS struggled with alcoholism throughout his life. There were even times while he was working with our sound team that I knew the smell of alcohol wasn't from the club we met in. There have even been times when Mick has disappeared and we've wondered if we'd lost him for good. It was great talking to him this past weekend. I asked Mick what he thought has kept him in our community over all these years filled with great highs and tremendous lows.

He said, "Oh, that's easy. There was always a place for me here. No one ever asked me to leave. No matter what I did, no one ever asked me to leave."

There may be no greater proof of God than the power of community.

There may be no greater gift than a place to belong. While it may seem that you're selling out to admit you need people, the irony is that you'll never really know yourself until you're in a healthy community. We only truly come to know ourselves in the context of others. The more isolated and disconnected we are, the more shattered and distorted our self-identity.

We are not healthy when we are alone.

We find ourselves as we connect to others.

Without community we don't know who we are.

On one of my trips to the land of Oz, I met an Aussie named Yanni. He told me how years before he had been working on a train and found himself having problems with one of the passengers. Evidently one particular passenger felt he was not being treated in

entry 17

accordance with his importance and started yelling at Yanni, "Do you know who I am? Do you know who I am?"

So Yanni calmly called all the passengers to attention and asked, "Does anyone know who this man is? He seems to have forgotten." He went on to describe how the man quietly and sheepishly found his seat.

I think many of us out there have forgotten who we are, or maybe we've never really known. It's been only in the past few years that the concept of self-awareness has become popularized. I think this is largely due to the fact that we are increasingly less self-aware. We're more self-absorbed but less self-aware. We don't know who we are.

Have you ever watched the early stages of *American Idol*—you know, the part where unimaginably untalented people audition for the show? Have you ever wondered whether it's really possible that a person could be so unaware of a lack of talent? How could a person be twenty-four years old and not know? Didn't anyone ever bother to tell them? Wouldn't it be the loving thing to do? Yes, and that's the whole point. In a healthy context of loving relationships we come to know ourselves.

When we live outside of healthy community, we not only
    lose others,
but we lose ourselves.

Sometimes the most irrational things we do are in response to our lack of identity or to our pursuit of a sense of identity. When we don't know who we are, when we have no clue as to who we were meant to become, we try to become something that we are not. Who we understand ourselves to be is dramatically affected for better or worse by those we hold closest to us. Sometimes that can even be someone we've never really even known.

ENTRY #18 Nowhere Man

EVERY ONCE IN A WHILE I'LL GOOGLE THE WORD *ANCESTORS* and try to explore some system that will guide me into my past. So far it's been pretty much a dead end. You see, sometimes you're as affected by the people you don't know as the people you do, or maybe it's really more like the people you should know or were supposed to know. I never knew my biological father. I almost called him my real father, but that wouldn't be accurate, would it? I have about a sixty-second memory of what must have been a chance meeting in a hotel lobby when I was probably no more than eight years old. I can understand my need to know him at eight or eighteen or even twenty-eight, but it just never went away. The longing that lingers has come as a surprise to me. I have a feeling even at eighty-eight there will still be something there.

There's something inside all of us that longs to know who we belong to.

Where we come from informs us where we're going. All of us long to be rooted somewhere.

I remember when Kim and I were traveling through Ireland. I love being from El Salvador, but I have adopted Ireland as my other country. After all, my last name is McManus. And even though it's only an alias (long story), you've got to take what you can get. Besides, Kim actually is Irish. Her mom was a McMahan. It was fun traveling through county Clare, walking through cemeteries and finding all the McMahans marked with Celtic crosses. We walked into a store, and the owner of a small studio asked us questions about our travels. As we began to share our excitement to be in the place where Kim's family comes from, she made a statement I'll never forget: "I don't know how people can live without knowing where they come from."

The Irish are a people of tribes. Their identity is rooted in their community. There's both strength and danger laced within the connection between community and identity. The power of community is that it helps us understand ourselves. In a healthy community we come to know ourselves and find strength in that knowledge. In community we learn how to live a life beyond ourselves, we begin to discover our potential and our strengths, and we are best positioned to make our greatest contribution. When community happens the way God designed us to live, it is always inclusive and never exclusive . . . Healthy communities are always permeable. You are never forced in, but you're always welcome.

Some communities like communism can't afford to give you a way out; other communities like fascism give you no way in. When God is not involved in the forming of a community, it becomes exclusive even when God's name is used.

Belfast was left in ruins because Protestants and Catholics could not bring themselves to come together in genuine community.

In Africa, the Tutsi and Hutu tribes could not see themselves as one people, and so became determined to annihilate one another.

In India, Hinduism justifies a caste system where Brahmans need never be moved with compassion or concern with the plight of the untouchables since karma determined where they belonged.

From the Nazis of Germany to the Ku Klux Klan of the American South, human history is flooded with endless examples of exactly what human community was *not* intended to become. Our need for identity is so powerful that we will choose a clearly defined destructive community rather than live without community at all.

What is overlooked in all this chaos is that no matter where we choose to join, what community we choose to be a part of, how we choose to identify ourselves, all of us are longing for the same thing— we are longing to belong.

I think a lot of us are like I have been, having never known my father. So many choices I have made in my life have been affected by the one person I haven't known. I think a lot of us are like that with God. We've never known the Father who created us, and we were never created to live apart from him. My mom remarried, and thanks to Bill McManus, I was never fatherless in the classic sense, and for that I am grateful. Yet at the same time, there was always that nagging, that longing, that craving in my soul to know the man who would be my father.

It is no different for us with God. If anything, it is far deeper and more profound. Our ability to know ourselves is dramatically diminished when we do not know our God and Father. Ironically, even if you do not believe in God, your life may be more shaped by your lack of relationship to Him than any other relationship in your life. Of this I'm convinced.

ENTRY #19 A Force Greater Than Death

I'VE KNOWN JESSE AND LAURA FOR EIGHT YEARS, AND OVER the years they've become two of our family's dearest friends. We met them in the middle of their search for God and before they had become followers of Christ. When I first met them, I figured they were either insatiably curious or two of the most earnest pursuers of truth I had ever known.

From Catholicism to Buddhism to Scientology to New Age to Mosaic, they were open to every possibility. All they wanted was to find something that was real and true and beautiful. If I remember correctly, my first conversation with them was when I was teaching a series about the meaning of water.

Somehow we know there are secrets in the universe waiting to be unlocked. The earth dangles in space somehow perfectly positioned to produce the only environment that would allow us to live. Any closer to the sun and we fry; any farther and we freeze. Make sense of that. Why should the liquid that covers almost all of the earth carry the exact composition necessary to sustain life?

What if, instead of the blue planet, we were the green planet?

Everything in creation speaks of God. God has created an entire universe to point us to Himself. Creation is thick with meaning. Everything around us demands that we explore, that we discover, that we understand.

> The signs are there.
> We live in a universe that is elegant.
> On a planet perfectly created for life.
> In a world filled with beauty.

The Jewish, Muslim, and Christian view of creation is all rooted in Genesis. The same text tells us that God is love. If this is true, then love is the motive behind all creation. Love is waiting to be discovered. The whole cosmos is wooing us to its Creator.

Water was not what we came to know, but instead more like radiator fluid. It wouldn't make any difference where the planet was positioned in our solar system, the water would ruin everything. The air we breathe—how do you make sense of it? Why is it oxygen and not nitrogen? Why is it life to us and not toxic instead? We're doing the best we can to change that, but it didn't start that way.

We're polluting the water and the air, destroying the ozone, creating global warming. We're pretty much making a wreck of the planet, but whoever designed it did a really great job. We're supposed to be the highest and most advanced species in the ecosystem, but we're ruining it all.

Our best thinking isn't even solving the problem, yet we think it all happened by accident. No intelligent design needed; it was all just an accident. How is that possible when we can't even keep it in its former condition on purpose? It's so much easier to believe that God was involved. It takes far less faith than it does to believe that coincidence can result in something so complex, something so amazing.

Anyway, they came when we were talking about water.

I remember Jesse telling me he also wondered what the meaning of water was, and now it made sense to him. Even now, I'm drinking from a bottle of water on my desk. It's called *Ethos*. When I wrote about ethos years ago in *An Unstoppable Force*, I never imagined it would end up as a part of our common language as quickly as it has.

Ethos is about essence.

Ethos water gives meaning to drinking a bottle of water. The company's focus is helping children around the world get clean water. On their mission statement they explain, "We tap your thirst to help solve this problem."

It makes it easier to spend an outrageous amount of money for something that once flowed freely for all of us on earth, knowing that in some small way I'm also helping children in countries such as Ethiopia, Honduras, India, and Kenya get the water they need to live. Tapping your thirst to help solve the problem—originally this was God's idea. He made us thirsty and then provided water to quench our thirst and supply refreshment and replenishment. He then tells us he is the Living Water, and if we drink of him, we will never thirst again . . . It is as if God has left us clues within creation of our need for him.

Over the next several years, Jesse and Laura's adult children came to trust God with their lives. The last of them was their youngest son. We were at a mountain retreat with a couple hundred guys. I was doing a talk on *The Barbarian Way*, which was an earlier book where I describe the primal nature of true spirituality. It was there where Jesus (that's pronounced *hey-soos*) reconnected to God. You would think, or at least hope, that this is the point from which the story only gets better, but all of us know that life is not always like that.

Less than a year later, Jesus was riding home on his motorcycle in Hacienda Heights and tragically lost his life. He was only twenty-four years old.

It was just that year that everything seemed to be coming together. He was working with his father in their family business; he was married to a beautiful young woman named Rong; he had a son named Solomon, who was less than a year old. He was an amazing human being with a great future in front of him. He had a wonderful, loving family.

He had parents who loved him, a wife who loved him, and a son who adored him. Then he was gone.

It's hard to make sense of life when you lose the one you love. Yet in the midst of all the pain, the momentum of his life could not be stopped.

Love can't be stopped.

Grief is proof that love prevails over death.

You cannot kill love.

I'm not talking about the pervasive counterfeits we so often call love. But the kind that fables like *The Princess Bride* speak of—"true love." The kind of love that lasts beyond life, that does not end with death, that fills you when you breathe deeply of it and wounds you when you lose it. Love is the most powerful force in the universe. God is love, and he is everywhere.

Love is the essence of the cosmos. Love is the ethos of God.

With the loss of Jesus, Jesse and Laura brought Rong and Solomon into their home and have become as one family. Jesse and Laura are of Mexican descent, and Rong's family is Vietnamese. Their love created a new community. Because of love they belonged together.

Solomon is the result of two different worlds coming together in love. And what a great name he was given, a wonderful reminder that God can lead you through even the most painful tragedies if you ask him for his wisdom and allow him to help you make sense of your life. It would have been easy for the loss of the one they loved so much to have caused them to have lost their faith in God, yet through the pain and grief they have been a comfort to others and a source of inspiration and hope for many.

ENTRY #20 Like a Kiss on the Face

WHEN WE TREAT EACH OTHER WITH VALUE, WHEN WE CARE for each other, when we love, we experience the presence of God. More powerful than any data or doctrine, love is the proof of God our souls long for.

An earthquake devastated Managua, Nicaragua, when I was in my early teens. It was one of the few times I remember my mom opening up her heart and sharing her struggles with faith. She told me that night that tragedies like this make it impossible for her to believe in a personal God. As she put it, it was easier for her to be Jewish, to believe that if there was a God, he got everything started but was disconnected from the course and experience of human history. I understand now that what she was describing was really the views of a deist, yet at the same time I know many Jews who would agree with her. At that same time she was reading a book by Rabbi Harold Kushner titled *When Bad Things Happen to Good People.* The conclusion is that God is good but is powerless to do anything about the problems in the world.

As traumatic as earthquakes, hurricanes, and tsunamis may be, they are not the cause of the violence that tears our souls most deeply. What tears at us the most, what leaves us shattered and broken, is what we do to each other. A tidal wave has no moral compass, no capacity to feel deeply. Nature isn't supposed to care about anything, but we are. We want God to stop nature from wreaking havoc on us, and God is trying to get us to stop destroying each other.

Why is it that the most dangerous place in the world to be is in the hands of a human being unmoved by love?

Like far too many people, Ann was unwanted when she was born, and she was raised in an abusive environment where she was physically, emotionally, and sexually abused. One of her earliest memories is at the age of three, standing in front of her mother while being screamed at for doing something wrong that she cannot remember. What she does remember is that while facing the barrage of noise, she thought to herself, if she could just hold her breath long enough, she could go away and never come back—three years old and already trying to end her life.

Years later she jumped from one abusive environment to another. She married a man who was a drug addict and alcoholic, and liked to beat her up. She recalls how one night, only weeks after her second son's birth, her husband was out with another woman. She remembers getting up for the 2:00 a.m. feeding and feeling very much alone in the world. It was pouring down rain.

She sat at the window and told God that she had always believed that he was out there, but if this was it, if this was the way life was, there was no point in living.

In her own words she writes, "I began to suffer from the Mack truck syndrome. 'Dear God, please let a Mack truck run over him.' I thought of ways to kill my husband, kill myself, and kill my children so that my husband would not be able to lay a hand on them. Realizing the futility of these thoughts, I asked God to reveal himself to me if life mattered to him at all. He did. That night at 2 AM, I went into the basement and searched through storage boxes to find an old Bible. I was Catholic. We didn't read the Bible, but I knew God was in those pages. So I read about Christ in the Garden of Gethsemane, the suffering he endured for love."

In a dark basement on a rainy night, a now grown-up three-year-old girl found a reason to breathe again—it was love. Something she had

entry 20

never really known, something she had never really experienced, came to her from the pages of an ancient text. God's entire motivation toward her was love. God, too, had endured a dark night of the soul. He suffered for love so that she could find love in her suffering. When telling her story, she used this as her opening line: "Unwanted when I was born." God would passionately disagree with that. He would insist on rewriting the story: "Wanted before you were conceived; loved from your very first breath."

Maybe the most amazing thing about Ann's story is that she recognized love when she saw it.

On the other hand, Judas, the most infamous of Jesus' disciples, looked straight into the face of love and remained blind to it.

When he chose to turn against Jesus, he betrayed Him with nothing less than a kiss.

This is the great irony of the human story.

When God does come to embrace us, to meet us face-to-face, to bring us into relationship with him, we far too often find ourselves betraying love.

Yet his love is undeterred.

He still pursues us with his relentless compassion.

God is the passionate lover of humanity.

He created you for love.

You cannot live without love, and you do not have to.

Yes, there is an insanity to love. You will go mad in pursuing it.

You will despise life itself if you do not find it.

Your soul craves love and will find satisfaction with nothing less.

You shouldn't be surprised that as you look for love, you keep running into God.

Listen to your soul. You have not given yourself to a futile search.

You are not alone in your pursuit.

Love searches for you.

Is it possible this is why the story won't go away? Two thousand years later and somehow it is still strangely compelling.

On a cross, Jesus of Nazareth hung naked and beaten for love.

Talk about rejection.

It would be easy to conclude that God made a fool of himself.

What was he thinking to die for love?

He gambled everything on the power of love. That love was more powerful than hate. That love was more powerful than death. What was he thinking to die for us, to give himself for you and for me, knowing we might just kiss him in the face and then walk away?

Love's just crazy like that.

ENTRY #21 Love Is Not a Four-Letter Word

ALL YOU NEED IS LOVE.

God Is Love.

DESTINY

Destiny

Dreams

Desires

Ambition

Becoming

Success

Significance

Progress

Optimism

Hope

ENTRY #1 Heading Down the Glory Road

Are you a coward? This is not for you. We badly need a brave man. He must be 23 to 25 years old, in perfect health, at least six feet tall, weigh about 190 pounds, fluent in English with some French, proficient with all weapons, some knowledge of engineering and mathematics essential, willing to travel, no family or emotional ties, indomitably courageous and handsome of face and figure. Permanent employment, very high pay, glorious adventure, great danger. You must apply in person, 17, rue Dante, Nice, 2me etage, appt. D.

I PROBABLY WASN'T MORE THAN ELEVEN YEARS OLD when I first read Robert A. Heinlein's *Glory Road*. It became my bible throughout my adolescence. Everyone has a bible, it's just not always the same book. I might have forgotten everything else in this sci-fi novel, but that one paragraph would forever capture me.

It was an ad placed in the personals specifically for the story's main character. His name was Evelyn Cyril Gordon. You can't even begin to imagine how wonderful it was to read of a hero whose name is Evelyn when your name is Erwin. He would later upgrade to Oscar, and that was good for me too.

I didn't match the ad in any way, but it didn't matter—that was my personal ad. They didn't know it, but they were looking for me. I desperately wanted to find myself on that glory road, regardless of the danger and in spite of the small detail that I was a coward. Even then I had a sense of destiny. We all do. But we don't all do something about it.

If you're presently a coward desperately trying to avoid any stress, unnecessary pressure, or unforeseen danger, you might call it a design flaw, but we humans are most alive when we passionately pursue our dreams, live with purpose, and have a sense of destiny. Again, if you're currently a cynic, skeptic, or pessimist, you might not appreciate the fact that as Martin Seligman points out in *Learned Optimism*, we thrive when we are optimistic about the future. It seems failure is no match for the person who believes in the future. When we see failure as personal, pervasive, or permanent, we become paralyzed.

Bottom line: we cannot live the life of our dreams without an irrational sense of destiny.

And all of us have dreams.

More than that, all of us need dreams.

Some of us sadly are just sleeping through them.

ALL OF US LONG TO BECOME SOMETHING MORE THAN WE are. We are driven to achieve, moved to accomplish, fueled by ambition. It burns hotter in some than in others, but it is within all of us. We're all searching for our unique purpose, our divine destiny, or simply a sense of significance or some measure of success. When we are optimistic about the future, we find the energy to create it.

We may disagree violently about what success is; we may even change our own minds about what makes our lives actually significant. But all of us are united in our desperate attempt to make a future for ourselves. We all desperately want to achieve something, to accomplish something; we just don't know what. Worse than that, we don't even understand why. Yet that doesn't stop us from searching.

ENTRY #2   I Was Born to Run

FOR ME, THERE IS ALMOST NOTHING AS TERRIFYING AND as rewarding as writing a book. The feeling you get when you're done, the sense of accomplishment when your publisher finally approves the manuscript, the overwhelming feeling of gratitude when someone you don't know takes the time to tell you that even in the smallest of ways you made a difference in their life—all of this keeps you writing through the blistering responses from your editor as he reacts to your first draft and from those who sincerely and passionately are convinced you should do the world a favor and only read books and give up on writing them (they, on the other hand, are sure my thoughts are from the devil). But I can't stop. It's not a profession for me; it's a passion—really more than a passion, more like a disease. In fact, on one of my many trips to Borders, I found an obscure book entitled *The Midnight Disease: The Drive to Write, Writer's Block, and the Creative Brain* by Alice Weaver Flaherty that proposes an interconnection between the compulsion to write and mental illness. I totally understand the diagnosis. When I get going, I would rather write than sleep or eat, and I find human contact an invasion of privacy.

As far back as I can remember, I wanted to become a writer. It's one of those childhood dreams come true. Funny when you think about it—not the idea of being a writer, but the concept of becoming something.

How is it that as children we imagine a life we have never known? How is it possible to engage in such a complex thinking process years before we are capable of even surviving on our own? You're five years old and you want to be a doctor. Why? You don't need a job. All your bills are being paid. You have food, shelter, clothes, toys, chauffeurs, a personal bodyguard, and a private chef—you have it all! What's the motivation to change? You'll never have it better.

What did you want to be when you grew up?

Even when we were little, we thought big. We want it all. We wanted to play sports. We wanted to be movie stars. We wanted to be taller. We even wanted to be older.

What were we thinking?

We wanted to be eleven when we were six, then sixteen, then eighteen, then twenty-one, then at twenty-nine we came to our senses and wished we were twenty-five and counting (down).

Remember when all we could do was crawl?

Come on, think back.

We had it made! We were carried everywhere. Grown-ups jumped to meet our every need. We could cry, whine, and act like a baby, and still the world would revolve around us. Oh!

Those were the days, my friend.

But you couldn't leave well enough alone, could you?

You had to start trying to walk, and at what cost?

Falling over and over again, you certainly weren't a natural. But you insisted. You stumbled your way through it. You stood on your own two feet, and you started walking on your own. As soon as you could, you made a run for it. You may not be like that now, but when you were two, you were one stubbornly ambitious hominoid.

There is something inside us that drives us. Call it ambition, passion, rebellion, competition, independence, whatever—it manifests itself in different ways, but it's in there from the very beginning. The human spirit longs to become. "Become what?" you ask. It hardly seems to matter. We are motivated by an endless number of things, but they're always big.

 entry 2

We humans are dreamers. We don't so much grow into this as much as it's a factory defect. In fact, when we're young and less grounded in reality, we dream bigger and more ridiculous dreams. Our ambitions and aspirations can be absolutely out of control when we're eight years old. We're like young Leo in the Oscar-dominating film *Titanic,* standing on the bow of the ship, shouting for all creation to hear, "I'm the king of the world." He wasn't, you know.

Though we seem to get it in different measures and intensities, all of us long to become. We are born with an instinct for not only survival but also accomplishment. There is a fire inside every one of us that propels us forward. We are designed to learn, to adapt, to grow, to change, to develop, to progress, to become. Especially when we are children, we have endless energy that fuels play, curiosity, and imagination. From childhood we naturally move toward the future. George Bernard Shaw lamented that imagination was wasted on the young; Einstein, on the other hand, attributed the key to his genius as never losing his childhood curiosity.

As we grow, these intensify into passion, desire, drive, and ambition. Throughout our lives, we express these as we aspire and strive to achieve, to accomplish, and to attain. We are custom made for a future. All of us long for our lives to count in some way. We all have an internal need to achieve some kind of success or to somehow find significance. Pursuing the future we desire energizes and inspires us. For me, it was a longing to write that drove me to what may be considered a form of insanity. It appears in different forms, but in this we all share the same disease. Every one of us longs to create even when we don't know exactly what. All of us, at the very least, want to create a better life, a better future, a better us. When we surrender these aspirations, we find ourselves drowning in apathy and atrophy.

ENTRY #3   Destiny Calling

WHETHER IT'S STRIVING FOR SUCCESS OR LONGING FOR
significance, whether it's trying to create a better world or become a better person, there is a drive within us all. We are designed with a need to
move forward. Without it our lives become only shadows of what they
could have been. You can live without pursuing a dream, you can function without passion, but with each passing moment, your soul will
become more and more anemic.

Your soul longs to become, and you can try to ignore it, but soon
you will find yourself hating your life and despising everyone who
refuses to give up on his or her dreams.

And you can't write this off as cultural conditioning. This is not a
characteristic that forms in adulthood; this is something that reveals
itself from the earliest stages of our lives. No one has to encourage infants
to crawl. With every fiber in our being, we are struggling to move. There
comes a point where crawling isn't enough. Though we fall over and over
again, we fight our way to our feet, and we begin to walk. Walking is
great until we can run, and running is great until we can drive, and for
some of us, driving is not fast enough—we just have to fly.

Our intrinsic need for progress can be seen from our earliest dreams
and childhood longings. We humans are instinctively ambitious. When
we dream, our dreams naturally gravitate toward greatness. No one ever
dreams of becoming an Olympic swimmer who, after years of hard work
and personal sacrifice, manages to come in fourth. Can you imagine a
ten-year-old swimmer passionately describing to you how she is working
toward the Olympic Games and her ambition is to finish just one place

short of a medal? The dream that drives her is to know that she is in the same water with the very best in the world.

Walk the streets of Brooklyn. Interview those kids playing ball until the dark of night. Ask them what they want to do when they grow up.

They'll tell you they want to play in the NBA; they want to be the next Michael Jordan. Not one of them will get misty-eyed, look off in the distance, and say, "I want to be just good enough where I can ride the pine for the last place team in the NBA."

What's really strange about this phenomenon is that if we were brutally honest, most of those kids don't have what it takes to make it as an Olympic swimmer or a professional basketball player. If they could just get a contract to sit on the bench or ever manage to even qualify for the Olympic Games, it would be nothing short of a miracle. For most of us, coming in last among the best would be a far-fetched dream, yet we don't dream like this.

We were living in Miami, Florida, when I met a Filipino kid named Billy. He was a couple years older than me and ten times cooler. He was popular, edgy, got all the girls, and played the sax. I quickly concluded I needed to play the sax. I signed up for band and for the next two years played third chair in a section of three. No matter how hard I tried, it just wasn't going to happen. I wasn't born to play the sax, but I have always loved music. Years later I picked up a guitar, messed with a piano, and wrote a lot of music, but there are miles between me and Miles—Davis, that is. I may not have the skills of a world-class musician, but I have the soul of one.

My house looks like a Guitar Center has been robbed—sound equipment, microphones, keyboards, acoustic guitars, electric guitar, bass guitar, flute, drums, and yes, even a saxophone. While I think it's not an exaggeration to say I have been the unquestioned impetus for my children's love for music, their aspirations are fueled not by me, but by Neal Pert, Geddy

Lee, and Lenny Kravitz. For me it was John Lennon and Paul McCartney when I was young, and Bono and Chris Martin since then. There have been a lot of great bands since the Beatles and Rush and Radiohead and Coldplay, but if we're going to dream, if we're going to pursue a standard of greatness, once again the human spirit naturally gravitates toward the extraordinary. We dream of greatness; we dream ambitiously.

While my son, Aaron, has a poster of James Dean in his room, my thirteen-year-old daughter has a poster of Albert Einstein. Underneath his matted hair it says, "It is only to the individual that a soul is given." Mariah loves Einstein. Having read some of his life story, she knows that he had real problems. There were things in his life that she doesn't admire, but as a scientist, he is James Dean. The reason is simple—she loves science.

Ever since I can remember, she has aspired to be a scientist. I'm sure somewhere in her earlier years she had a great science teacher who inspired her toward this field. I can't remember her name. Unfortunately, that's the way it really works in this world. If my son is inspired to play basketball because I spend endless hours in the backyard with him, he's never going to say, "One day I hope I play as well as my dad." I will pretty much be forgotten on the court, and Dwyane Wade will serve as his inspiration.

As children we assume that greatness is within our grasp. Whatever inspires us, we begin to dream that one day we will be the best. It is only as we lose our childlike innocence that we begin to settle for far less. A part of growing up seems to be acquiescing to mediocrity. It's easy to say that we're just becoming realistic, that it's just a part of growing up. But, in fact, it's the death of our souls. When we stop dreaming, we start dying. For some of us, this has been a slow, painful death. Others are just walking dead. They died a long time ago, and it's nothing less than a freak of nature that they're still breathing.

ENTRY #4   Do We All Dream of Flying?

I WAS AT THE CLUB MAYAN (THE PLACE OUR COMMUNITY of faith meets each Sunday night here in LA) last night saying good-bye to one of the most extraordinary people I have met this past year. His name is Randy Bradford. I remember the first time I met him, how he struck me with an unusual confidence for a man of his stature. You see, Randy stands less than four feet tall, "depending on which convenience store tape you're looking at," as he puts it. Everyone has a unique story, but I had a feeling that Randy's was more unusual than most of ours.

A few months ago we were sitting together after one of our gatherings, and I asked him to share with me a little of his journey. His intro caught me off guard: "I'm a bumblebee." I had no idea what he meant. He is sort of short and stocky, so at first I thought he was being descriptive, but actually he was leading into one of his greatest passions—Randy loves to fly. Though he has a much broader story, for him the fact that he is a pilot is symbolic of his greater journey. I have to admit when he told me he owned an airplane, I was surprised. When he told me he was actually the pilot of the plane, I was stunned. I must confess I had jumped to the conclusion that Randy required a caretaker, you know, someone who would help him through the day— at least a driver and facilitator. Man, was I wrong. This guy hadn't let anything stop him. No challenge seemed too big—no challenge for which he was too small (pun intended).

He was five years old when he knew that someday he would fly. In the late 1960s his parents took him to the Portland airport to watch planes take off and land. As a child he enjoyed watching the cadre of Boeing 707s and 727s and McDonnell Douglas DC-8s land and take off. It was there that his dream was born. This, he felt, was his destiny. His mother, of course, struggled with how she was going to tell him that this would not be possible. It turns out, she never had to, which is where the bumblebee effect comes in.

Randy explained that by all theories of aerodynamics and physics, the bumblebee should not be able to fly, but it can. No scientific reason why it should; it just does. I guess no one bothered to tell it that flying wasn't possible. There were many people along the way who told Randy that his dream to fly would never come to fruition. He was told again and again it was impossible, but somehow in his gut he knew it wasn't true. There were glimpses of hope along the way. Another person of short stature had done it, and prosthetic devices were being developed for people with missing limbs. In 1989, finally a flight instructor named Bob Wallace took him on as a student, and Randy began preparing for takeoff. A year later, after several trials and

SOUL CRAVINGS

revisions of adaptive equipment and a demonstration of his ability to an FAA examiner, Randy went solo.

In that moment, his dreams took flight.

On April 15, 1998, Randy purchased a 1968 Cessna 150 and started flying for a nonprofit organization called Challenge Air for Kids and Friends, an organization that gives plane rides to children who are either disabled or in some way disadvantaged. The bumblebee effect had gone full circle. But really it went much deeper than this. Randy was born with a genetically inherited bone dysplasia called diastrophic dwarfism. This disorder is characterized by very short limbs and a number of other orthopedic and cartilage defects. Imagine being forty-three years old and barely standing forty-five inches. Beyond his physical challenges, Randy was not expected to survive too far beyond birth, much less into adulthood.

We live in a time when, given the information of Randy's condition, many would choose to terminate the pregnancy. The argument, of course, would be about the quality of life. What kind of life could you expect for someone who was born with such an extraordinary disadvantage? Would it be fair to bring someone into the world when he would so quickly leave it? Yet four decades later, Randy is a walking reminder that the future often holds far more than we can imagine. He holds a degree in chemical engineering from Oregon State University and for the last twenty years has been working to write software that automates chemical plants.

According to Randy, "I am living proof that Darwin was wrong—or at least had a poor definition of who was the most fit to survive."

With all that Randy had overcome, there were still many other struggles and challenges that he had to face. When he found himself reaching the age of forty, he began to wonder if he had a future worth living for. He had never been married and wondered if he would ever know love. He knew his stature came into play and questioned why God would ever do this to him. He found himself struggling with addictions. As he describes it:

"I became a lost soul."

I was struck that while his physical challenges were very different from most of ours, his internal struggles were very much the same. He longed to be loved. He was trying to make sense of his life. He needed to know whether his life had a purpose or whether his entire struggle was for nothing. Are we nothing more than biological anomalies? Are we simply the product of chance—the result of bad luck? Is our existence just an accident, or is there a reason for our being? There is a difference between being unusual and being unique. Randy knew he was different, but more than that he somehow knew he was destined to soar.

It's amazing how much we can endure when we are convinced there is a purpose to our struggle.

It was while Randy was in Washington State that he came to grips with his need for God. He found God while searching for his destiny. He wasn't on a religious search, but without realizing it, he was on a profoundly spiritual journey. Like Randy, every one of us has a longing to become. Our souls crave progress. We need to believe in the future. The bumblebee doesn't just point us to God; it points us to us—to our own unique design. There is a destiny that awaits us all. It calls us, and if we ignore it, we are soon haunted by it. We all dream of flying. Don't let the fact that no one thinks you can do it keep you off the runway.

Recently Randy moved back north. He had planned to sell his plane to pay for his relocation. It seems after he shared his story, he couldn't bring himself to sell the plane. He sent me a note saying thank you and good-bye, and then he signed off, "The Bumblebee still flies."

ENTRY #5   Life Is a Dream in the Making

WE TRAVEL THROUGH LIFE LOOKING FOR OUR OWN *17, rue Dante, Nice, 2me etage, appt. D.*

That door once passed through changes our lives forever; not because life is now better than it has ever been, but because we know we are on the path we were created to walk. It is our glory road, our glorious adventure. We have been called out of the mundane into a life beyond our wildest imagination. We have a mission, a purpose, a destiny. Randy's finding his unique path does not bring us to a happy ending of his story—only to a new beginning.

Before I met Randy, I was well acquainted with the butterfly effect, but it took Randy to bring me face-to-face with the bumblebee effect. The butterfly effect proposes that small and apparently insignificant incidents can set in motion a chain of events with far-reaching consequences. The bumblebee effect describes how great and apparently impossible dreams can set in motion a chain of events resulting in a seemingly insignificant person living an extraordinary life. We are capable of far more than we think.

Now, I have never bought into the adage "If you can dream it, you can do it." That's not because of lack of imagination, but because of an abundance of it. There are just so many things I can dream that I was not designed to do. I can dream of being a gymnast, but I guarantee you it's not in the realm of possibility. Winning the NBA slam dunk contest: I can dream it—can't do it. Becoming the lead singer of U2: I can dream it—not going to happen.

Some of our dreams are meant to be just that—dreams.

We may not be able to accomplish everything we can dream, but we will not accomplish anything without our dreams. That's not to say that things don't happen beyond our wildest dreams, but that effect seems to come into play only when we are actually pursuing wild dreams.

The bumblebee effect is a reminder that you may be underestimating what you're capable of doing. Certainly design matters. But even in nature purpose overrides design. The bumblebee has a purpose that makes it necessary for it to fly, and so it does. Bumblebees are a great reminder that we should never underestimate potential. Randy Bradford has become a great proof of God. In fact, every life that is pulled out from the mundane and ordinary and finds unexpected flight becomes proof of God.

Think about it for a minute. What is it that causes us to dream? How can this just be a function of evolution? Don't get me wrong here. My goal isn't to build an argument against evolution; I'm just saying there's more going on than Darwin was thinking about when he was studying plants.

What do dreams have to do with the survival of the fittest?

If anything, daydreaming can be a real liability. I mean, dreams are great while you're in one, but eventually you have to wake up.

What happens when your life just can't live up to your dreams? There comes this huge sense of dissatisfaction with life. If you're not careful, you might actually develop a real disdain for life itself.

Big dreams + nightmare for a life = dangerous combination.

Dreams can become a way of escape—

    a

        way

            of

                going

                    somewhere

that

gets

us

away

from

the

real

world.

What I find curious is that we even have this capacity to see, to imagine, to dream of a life other than the one we have. If God were in his nature sinister, this would be a great way to torment us. We could come to this conclusion easily enough if it were not for one thing—we can't live without dreams. In our worst moments, dreams haunt us, but when things are working the way they should, our dreams inspire us.

Without dreams we have nothing to pull us forward.

It is, in fact, our dreams that energize us to literally go to war against reality and make what only exists in our imagination our future. There may be no more uniquely human capacity than the ability to anticipate. Anticipation ignites a thrill in the present caused by nothing more than a possibility in the future. Anticipation is like tasting a great meal even before taking the first bite.

We dream of a destiny, and it fuels our desire.

When we dwell on the past, we tend to want to live there. When we dream of the future, we want to go there. *Our dreams are where God paints a picture of a life waiting to be created.* Dreams are God's way of fueling the future, and in this we are all the same.

All of us need to believe in tomorrow.

When we live without dreams, we are functionally dysfunctional.

We have given up on the creative process.

We have abdicated responsibility for our own future to chance or fate or something else . . . A life in God is never absent of dreams.

God designed us to dream because he created us to create. We are made to be actively involved in the process of creating the future. The future doesn't just happen; it is ushered in. Our need for progress is all around us. It's probably screaming at you, but maybe you just haven't noticed.

Even while I was reflecting on this section, I went through my daily ritual of getting on the scales. Yeah, I know, it's a vain activity in both senses of the word. It's vain in that I shouldn't care, and it's vain in that it's a losing battle. So there I was interacting with that lying piece of machinery. Most of the time, it simply taunts me for being trapped in the status quo, and other times, it sends me a stark warning I'm headed in the direction I don't want to go. But in a moment of reflection, I looked underneath the numbers that define my value, and I saw the name of the manufacturer of this instrument of torment.

Guess what the name is?

It's "Thinner."

If we're looking for accuracy in advertising, shouldn't anyone who makes scales be called "Thicker" or "Futile"? Oh, but the marketing gurus were way too smart for that.

You could just hear them plotting, "We've got to keep them believing that they can make progress. First they get the bad news, and then they'll unconsciously drop their heads in despair and see our name. It will be more than a name; it will be a sign to them, a voice of hope. You can be . . . you will be thinner."

(We just ordered pizza.)

ENTRY #6 Neutral Doesn't Get You Anywhere

SOMEWHERE DOWN THE ROAD, MANY OF US EITHER lose our ambition, or we come to believe that ambition is a bad thing. We were told that if we are going to be truly spiritual, we have to free ourselves from all ambition. The tragedy, of course, is that this is not true. Not only is ambition a good thing; it is also a God thing.

It is God who has placed within you the fuel of ambition.

You cannot live the life God created you to live without being ambitious. The reason your heart leaps when you see greatness is that your spirit is drawn to it. The reason we can experience the vicarious exhilaration of a great victory or an amazing accomplishment is that the human spirit resonates with greatness.

While many of us have come to believe ambition is unhealthy, the truth is when you lose ambition, you lose your future. When you lose your future, you lose hope. And no one can live well without hope. Without ambition we have no dreams worth living. When we let our dreams die, we start dying with them.

Every human being has a need for progress.

This is not accidental. God created us with an intrinsic need to become. We are connected not only to the past and the present, but also to the future. There is a reason why you have a sense of destiny. It was placed there by God, and it woos you to pursue it.

The point here is not about what we strive for but the very fact that we strive.

And we strive and strive and strive.

It was Niccolò Machiavelli who observed, "Ambition is so powerful

entry 6

a passion in the human breast that however high we reach, we are never satisfied."

You can conclude ambition is a bad thing, but like blaming the gas for fueling the car of a drunk driver or even blaming the alcohol, the problem isn't ambition; it is what we are ambitious for.

To lack ambition is to become complacent.

To lose our passion is to become apathetic.

If this is our only option, now that's **pathetic**!

Have you noticed, by the way, that those with great ambitions have a disproportionate effect on the future? The future is not simply entered into; it is created. To create we must first dream, then act.

The future doesn't happen by accident; it happens through engagement.

We were created to strive for progress and to pursue it with passion. It is God who designed us this way. He made us creative, and he makes us responsible. Somehow there are many of us who have missed this point. We have allowed human history to be shaped by those who are distant from God and hostile toward people.

Evil never looks for permission.

Tyrants never consider the appropriateness of their actions. One of the great tragedies of human history is that while those who are motivated by greed and power and violence have forged the future of their liking, too many of those who long for a better world have sat passively by, watching and wishing the world could be different.

I think I understand, at least in part, why. Sometimes it has been indifference, but I think quite often it has been a misunderstanding about God. We think it's God's job to fix everything. Sincere people have deferred their responsibility while waiting on God to do something, but it has created a spirituality that lacks initiative and engagement. This goes against the nature of the human spirit, and it goes against the way God has created us. We might actually conclude God is apathetic and indifferent just because we are. God created us to engage, solve problems, meet needs, do something with our lives. He made us to get involved and expects us to act. That's why someone like Mother Teresa helps us believe in God. Human compassion reflects God and moves us toward God.

Did I mention that the future doesn't happen by accident?

We were created to believe in progress and to pursue it with passion. It is God who designed us this way. He made us creative, and he holds us responsible. Somehow there are many of us who have missed this point. We have allowed human history to be shaped by those who do not reflect God's value for love, for beauty, and for justice.

ENTRY #7   Destiny Calls Us Like a Siren

IN 1977, STEVEN SPIELBERG CAME OUT WITH ANOTHER classic film that captured this sense of destiny that haunts us all. It was titled *Close Encounters of the Third Kind*. The story line at first glance seems pretty straightforward—aliens from outer space making contact with the planet Earth. Are they good guys or bad guys? Have they come in peace, or are we now moving from world war to war of the worlds? The subplot, however, is far more mystical than we would have expected.

There are signs that will guide your journey.

They are waiting to be discovered,

but you must search for them.

There is something happening inside you that no one else can understand. You are being called out but don't know to what or by whom. It feels trapped within you, rises to the surface, and becomes all-consuming.

For Roy Neary, played by Richard Dreyfuss, it was a mystical and maddening experience. His journey cost him everything—it caused him to lose his job, alienated him from his family, and drove him to nearly lose his mind. He was haunted by a vision that he could not bring into focus. There were clues everywhere, but he could not make sense of any of them.

There were the sounds, unintelligible noises that somehow promised to reveal their secrets if he would pay close attention. They could easily be dismissed as nothing more than noise, except their meaning haunted him. He was being called. He had been chosen. Five notes riddled with meaning in what seemed a cosmic game of *Name That*

Tune. There was somewhere he was supposed to go, something he was supposed to do. He just didn't know what it was. But to ignore it was not an option. To close his eyes and cover his ears would only ensure he would lose his mind.

We all hear voices in our heads and have visions erupting out of our brains that disrupt our daily routine and beg us to tear ourselves away from the mundane of life. Something stirs deeply within us, calling us out, inviting us to pursue and discover that which we do not know.

All of us are called to a place we have not been. Our lives were always intended to be journeys into the unknown. The invitation is both personal and mystical. No one else may fully understand what you are being called to. You may not even fully understand. The path you must walk may appear to others as strange or unreasonable, but you know there's more going on than meets the eye.

When I began to search for God, he opened my eyes, my mind, and my imagination to a future I never could have dreamed of. I began to see what life could be if I would read the signs and choose this great quest.

> God calls us out of the life we have known
> and calls us to a life we have never imagined.

The signs are all around you, but even more the signs are all within you. Your soul is being pulled forward. You are being called to a God whose voice your ears have never heard. You are having visions of a life you could not possibly create alone. You are no longer satisfied with where you are, and now you are on a quest for where you do not know. You were created not to live in the past, but to create the future. Your soul craves to become, and you will never be satisfied with less.

entry 7

ENTRY #8 Looking Forward

IT IS IMPORTANT TO FULLY LIVE EACH MOMENT, BUT EQUALLY important to make sure that we do not live only for this moment. If we don't believe in an afterlife, we try to find purpose in the here and now. Yet we can do this only if we at least believe in the "after now." We have to believe in tomorrow to function well today. It will never be enough for us simply to exist, and if all we have is now, our souls will starve from lack of nourishment. Without a future there is no hope, and hope is essential for our souls to thrive. Hope exists only in the future, and if the future does not exist, there is no hope. Our minds can work out an endless number of scenarios; our souls, however, are quite inflexible when it comes to this. Without hope there is only despair.

A sense of destiny is what you begin to experience when you are filled with hope. Every one of us is on a search for destiny. We all need to believe we have a future and a hope. These two are impossible to separate. If you don't believe you have a future worth living for, your spirit loses all hope, and your soul was not designed to live without hope. In fact, when we lose all hope, we lose all desire to live. Hope moves us from pessimism to optimism.

It is impossible to get into the heart and mind of a person who has chosen to take his or her life. As if suicide were not tragic enough, sometimes it seems the scenarios around stories make it even worse. Over the years I've had many friends struggle with thoughts of suicide. For some people, the contrast between the life they have and the life they long for is more than they can bear. What has struck me, though, is how little it sometimes takes for a person to change his or her mind. You would think something as final as deciding to commit suicide would take some life-shaking event to circumvent it. I haven't found that always to be the case.

I knew a young woman who decided to take her life that day at work. She was walking to the window in the high-rise building where the company's offices were, and just before she walked out to the ledge, someone walked through the hall and asked her if she knew where the Coke machine was. It was just enough that day. Instead of pointing the way to the machine, she showed the person the way. She said it gave her something to do, something that needed to be done by her, a reason to live.

Anna, on the other hand, was a dancer in Los Angeles who had grown up in a world of divorce, drug abuse, and homelessness. Barely out of her teens, she couldn't see herself making it through one more day. She went to an infamous spot in Pasadena called "suicide bridge." It was there that she decided to bring her story to an end. She couldn't think of one more reason to live. In that moment, she decided to call out to God one last time—one of those gauntlets. "If you have anything to say about this, God, speak now or forever hold your peace."

She didn't know her cell phone was on. There had been no good reason to take it with her. No one ever called. And suddenly it rang—an unexpected call. Someone needed her, had been looking for her, was wondering where she was, what she was doing. How could she end her life that day? There was something for her to do. Someone needed her. She had a reason to live. It doesn't take much to keep us wanting to live—just a little hope.

ENTRY #9   Oxygen for the Soul

WHEN THERE IS NO FUTURE, THERE IS NO HOPE. WHERE there is no hope, there is no reason to live. There is only despair. Our souls are not designed for despair. It's not where we are intended to live. If we live there too long, we will find ourselves soul–sick.

Martin Luther King Jr. had a dream and was killed for it.

When we have no dream, it kills us.

It's the same way with hope. Hope pulls us into the future. When you consider that the future is overwhelmingly uncertain, you can see why hope would have such immense value. Yet as essential as hope is for life, we live in a world that seems determined to take it from us. Hope is rare, but we don't need much of it to experience its power.

When we are full of hope, it's not because everything in the future is certain to us, but because the future itself is filled with promise.

At the same time, like the promise of a future, hope comes only from something we do not yet have, something we have not yet attained. In other words, how much you have in the world has no bearing on how much hope you have. In actuality, everything you have no longer qualifies as a conduit of hope. Once you have it, it's out of the arena of hope.

Anything you have already received or experienced no longer qualifies as a source of hope. Hope pulls you into the future because it comes from there. If you no longer believed in the future, you would lose all hope. And what's strange about this is that while hope is connected to the future, it is impossible to thrive in the present without it. There's a simple reason for this. It's exactly how God has designed you. We tend to take for granted the things that are most obvious to us.

It's sort of like we worry about paying the bills but never worry about having air to breathe. But really which one is more critical to life?

ENTRY #10 Believing in The Future Takes Faith

WE NEVER THINK ABOUT THE FACT THAT WE'RE EVEN AWARE of the future. Do you really think that animals are aware of time? Imagine being a mayfly with a life span of twenty-four hours. From the moment you came into this world you'd be living in angst that you were about to leave it. If flies know what's going on, they should all be nihilists (someone who believes that nothing matters and that life is pointless). Not even evolution has been good to them. If they believe in reincarnation, their last run at life must have been a really bad one. I suppose their one place for hope is that things really can't get any worse.

One of the clear distinctions between us and the rest of created life is that while insects, reptiles, birds, fish, amphibians, and even mammals are content with surviving, humans are not content to simply survive; we are driven to thrive.

It's not enough for us to merely exist; we are compelled to achieve. This drive would not even exist without a concept of time. We understand that each day is not a reoccurring cycle of static events. The human experience is not only that time moves, but that we do too. We have been created with not only awareness, but a need for progress.

There may be no greater proof that we are not the random results of an evolutionary process but, in fact, the unique creations of a personal God.

We cannot function effectively without a belief in that which does not exist. And I'm not talking about God. You believe in tomorrow; you believe in progress. You live your life with an unconscious awareness of time. The reality of past, present, and future is an unexamined given, which you simply accept as reality.

There is empirical evidence that the past exists, although we could make an argument that it is nothing more than social hysteria and cultural memory created in our own minds to give us the context from which we can exist. There are some who would advocate that history is nothing more than propaganda. Most of us would accept that archaeology gives us proof of a past.

Most of us would agree that the present exists, although there are those who would challenge even that assumption. They would say that there is nothing that can be known for certain, that everything is an illusion.

I remember once sitting in a meeting of young leaders when the speaker began asking if there was really a red chair in front of him. He claimed that we really couldn't know for certain. His contention was that everything was subjective. The other day I was playing basketball and got hit in the face with an elbow. Maybe I have abandoned my philosophical roots, but that was proof enough for me that the external world actually exists.

Besides, when I drive by the McDonald's and I see a sign that says, "Over one billion served," I have to ask myself how one billion people could step into the same ill-conceived illusion if it were all just in our heads. And right behind that I have to ask myself a more profound question: If this is all make-believe, why would we make up McDonald's? Oh, and could you supersize that thought?

ENTRY #11 Running Out of Time

No, whether we like it or not, I think there is way too much evidence that the past and the present exist, even in their present and unhealthy condition. What's startling, though, is that even the most skeptical empiricist would accept and even assume the existence of the future. The future doesn't exist. It's not there yet. It's being created at this very moment.

Without any proof, we believe in the future. Yes, we have precedent. We certainly have anecdotal evidence. In the end we step into the future as an act of faith and hope it's still there when we arrive. But it's more than that. We not only assume the future and believe in the future, but we're all searching for a future. And while you may not believe in anything overtly religious, it takes faith to believe in the future.

Why are we most alive when we are pursuing a great dream?

Why is it that we need a reason to live?

Why do we need to feel that we are in some way unique?

Why is it that when we conclude our lives don't matter, we lose the will to live?

The maddening reality is that each and every one of us has been created with a soul craving to become—to become something—something better, something different, something special, something unique, something admired, something valued, something more than we are.

At the same time, we are faced with the reality of our own mortality. We are pulled by both eternity and brevity. We act as if we will live forever and are constantly facing the painful truth that life can end at any moment.

For my son, Aaron's, seventeenth birthday, I bought him that poster of his favorite icon, James Dean. I'm pretty sure it's because James Dean reminds him so much of me. Underneath a black-and-white photograph of what my daughter, Mariah, has determined is a picture of human perfection, these words are written: "Dream as if you'll live forever. Live as if you'll die today." Dean's words are even more poignant when we remember that he didn't live to see his twenty-fifth birthday.

We are all chasing daylight. Our lives are but a brief moment in time. Blink and it's gone. As soon as we are fully aware of life, we become fully aware of death. The more moments we live, the faster they speed past us. And if this life is all there is, the more we make of this life, the more we have to lose when we leave it. The fact that we're all time-dated should lead us nowhere but to desperation. We are all running out of time. If that isn't bleak, I don't know what is. Yet in some strange way even our awareness of death can powerfully work in our favor.

A friend of mine introduced me to a classic foreign film a few years ago. It has become one of my favorites. It's called *Chungking Express*. In one of the subplots, a man scorned by love concludes that everything has an expiration date. Tomatoes, milk, eggs, film, pills, passports, faith, hope, love—everything has an expiration date, or at least so it seems.

You don't have to search far for people who thought love would last forever and watched it fall apart right before their eyes. I have also seen in life that many who are most antagonistic against the idea of faith had at one time been the most sincere of the faithful. When milk hits its expiration date, it turns sour, but when we come to the end of hope, it's our souls that turn bad. There are some things that are not supposed to expire before we do. At the same time, the expiration date that we fear the most and that looms over us all is that of life itself.

Earlier I mentioned one of my favorite people and speakers Chip Anderson. Chip had a Ph.D. in education and for years taught at

UCLA. Through his work in educational psychology, he had become the father of strengths-based education. Over three thousand people at Mosaic in Los Angeles have discovered their strengths as a result of Chip's investment in our lives. One of his extraordinary talents was seeing the best in people. He spent his whole life calling out greatness in others and applauding it, even when he saw it expressed in the smallest of ways. The last time he spoke to our community here in Los Angeles, the title of his talk was simply "It's All About the Dash."

Take a few minutes sometime and find your nearest cemetery. Walk through the memorials there representing the lives of a countless number of people who lived before you. You will see different dates of birth and times of death, but they all will have one thing in common—the dash in between the two. To everyone who is a stranger, our dash will be just that, a space holder in between the pertinent information. But for those who know us, the dash represents the totality of our lives.

Chip reminded us that we are all born with a terminal condition.

It's called being human. He knew that all too well. Raging within his body was a violent and aggressive cancer. He hoped he would have a few more years to spend with his wife, Irma, and to pursue his passion of helping others discover what they're best at, but in the end he had only weeks. If it was about desire to live, he would still be with us. He was full of life until his last breath, and we all have a last breath. We're all born with an expiration date.

ENTRY #12 Despair's Only Hope

WHAT IS FASCINATING ABOUT THE HUMAN SPIRIT IS THAT we can live with a conscious awareness of death and not be paralyzed. In fact, it can actually inspire us to live a life of passionate urgency. It is only when we lose all hope that we find ourselves incapable of moving forward. Whether we believe in God or not, whether we accept that we are created by God or not, it is undeniable that we are incapable of functioning effectively without dreams. Again, it hardly seems to matter about what.

Even the smallest of dreams will keep us moving forward. It doesn't even need to be rooted in reality; just our belief that we can get there keeps us inspired. But when we give up hope, when we allow ourselves to internalize despair, we shut down. We simply give up trying. Despair not only takes us to the wrong place, but it keeps us from going forward.

You were not created to run from challenges, to live in angst, or to drown in despair.

This is not a good place for your soul.

You also can't move forward into your future when you are paralyzed by fear.

Over the years I've heard many people condescendingly describe faith as the activity of the weak. Is it possible that the reason we find God in our deepest despair is that this is when we are most earnestly listening? The word *despair* means "to live apart from hope." It can then also be translated "to live without a future." No one knows better than God that we cannot live like this. Despair is to the soul what toxic waste is to the body. Overexposure is lethal. When we find ourselves hiding in a cave, we should not be surprised that our souls begin to long for God. What should cause us to question what's going on is that this happens even when we don't believe in God.

Why should despair make a person open to God?

It's a troubling thing when your soul demands what your brain rejects. I guess if you think about it, if it wasn't for God, we might find ourselves capable of drowning in despair and thinking it was our natural habitat. Instead, we will always be haunted by this soul craving, this seemingly irrational need for hope. We should be able to live perfectly well without God and without hope. But neither proves to be the case. Ironically, when we should least believe in even the existence of hope, when we are most consumed with a sense of our insignificance, it is here we will crave it the most. You can't give up on hope and go on with life. Without hope your life may not come to an end, but it does come to a stop.

It is when we are hiding in a cave that we desperately want someone to call us out and cause us to believe there is still a life to be lived.

ENTRY #13 Imagine

YEARS AGO I WAS INTRODUCED TO THE WRITINGS OF Viktor Frankl. Frankl, who lived during World War II, was one of the many Jews who endured the horrors of the Nazi concentration camps and one of the few who survived. I have been deeply affected on both personal and professional levels by the insights he gained through his struggle. His most famous book was originally titled *From Death-Camp to Existentialism*. It was first published in Austria in 1946. I am indebted to him for the lessons he learned through the brutality of Nazi oppression. While his writings are rich with insight, one observation stands as paramount:

Hope is essential for life.

Frankl makes a powerful observation that those who still believed they had something yet to accomplish, something that required them to exist in the future, found the strength to endure what those who had lost all hope could not:

> "Whenever there was an opportunity for it, one had to give them a why—an aim—for their lives in order to strengthen them to bear the terrible *how* of their existence. Woe to him who saw no more sense in his life, no aim, no purpose, and therefore no point in carrying on. He was soon lost."

Frankl goes on to explain in addressing the issue of despair, "What was really needed was a fundamental change in our attitude toward life. We had to learn ourselves and, furthermore, we had to teach the

SOUL CRAVINGS

despairing men, *that it did not really matter what we expected from life, but rather what life expected from us.*"

Ironically Frankl's most powerful insight was most likely inspired, or at least informed, by Nietzsche's observation, "He who has a *why* to live can bear with almost any *how.*"

Frankl's writings became an introduction to his development of logotherapy, and from that his book was retitled *Man's Search for Meaning.* But I think rather than moving his fellow prisoners toward meaning, he instead took them past meaning to purpose.

Their despair was overcome not by making sense of life, but by believing in the future. After all, how could you have made sense of their lives? How do you make sense of the fact that on a beautiful Monday afternoon you and your family are ripped out of your home, stripped of all that you've worked for, thrown into a train, and placed within a concentration camp where you would be starved, tortured, dehumanized, and perhaps even incinerated? How exactly do you make sense of that? How do you keep from losing hope—from giving up on hope altogether?

Their resolve and resilience to endure the unimaginable came out of souls that believed that their destiny could not be thwarted by their present tragedy.

This is true for all of us, and it affects us on both ends of the life spectrum. A sense of destiny gives us the strength to face overwhelming obstacles and hardships. At the same time living a life with a powerful sense of purpose gives us the energy and enthusiasm to get up in the morning and face the day. It is in the worst of situations that we are able to discover the best in us. It is also in these moments that we are able to see most clearly what is true and what is real and what it means most fully to be human.

ENTRY #14 On Becoming Human

I'VE COME TO LOVE THAT WORD—*HUMAN.* I MEAN, HUMANity can be a pretty bleak place to live, but when you begin to see what we're really capable of, our potential for good, it can be breathtaking. For the past two thousand years, Christianity, along with pretty much every other world religion, has made the primary focus the sinful nature of us all. In some ways I think this has led to a not-so-subtle self-hatred.

Several years ago a young filmmaker came by my office eagerly wanting to show me a private screening of his film. The story was about a couple of angels struggling with right and wrong. One chose the path of good and remained an angel; the other chose a dark path, and as his punishment, he became a human. It was beautifully shot; it was visually stunning; even the story was captivating.

But his view of what it means to be human was tragic. Being human was a punishment. Being human is what happens to fallen angels. I think more of us see humanity like this than we think. In fact, it is a gift to be human.

The Hebrew imagery is that we were created out of the breath of God. We are the products of a divine kiss. When Ezekiel the Hebrew prophet spoke of the change that was needed in the human heart, he simply said that God would take our hearts of stone and give us hearts of flesh. In other words, all God is going to do is to make us once again truly human or maybe fully human. When we live beneath our humanity, we become inhumane. When we live genuinely human lives, we become translucent reflections of divinity.

entry 14

I think a lot of us turn to reincarnation in hopes that one day we might escape the curse of being human. Some of us even hope that one day humans might actually become gods. The Church of Jesus Christ of Latter-day Saints, otherwise known as the Mormons, holds this as humanity's best hope. If you are a Mormon and a man, you will become a deity like Jesus, and in some future world you will reign as a divine being. Talk about visions of grandeur! We're back with Leonardo on the bow of the Titanic. It seems pretty clear to me that we will never become gods, and I think somewhere deep down inside we all suspect this.

The good news is that we don't have to become gods to become something worth loving, worth respecting, worth valuing. Don't let your shortcomings and flaws convince you that you need to become something other than human. Our brokenness is not proof that God could not or would not love us, but proof that what we need is the God who both created us and loves us. What our souls long to become is not something other than human, but to become beautifully human.

ENTRY #15 A Reason to Live

VIKTOR FRANKL DISCOVERED THAT STRENGTH IS unleashed within us when we are convinced our lives have a purpose yet to be fulfilled. This reality is magnified when we choose a purpose beyond ourselves. When we begin to give ourselves to a cause or a purpose greater than us, it changes us; it makes us better. When we dream of a better world, we become better people. When we give ourselves for the good of the world, we find that doing so brings to us a world of good. We are not disconnected by the destiny we pursue.

Even if we never achieve our dreams, we are always shaped by those dreams, and the higher the purpose, the stronger the person.

Just a few months ago my family and I were having dinner at PF Chang's in Pasadena with one of the guys from our community named Peter and his family. It would only take you a few minutes to realize he was different from most twenty-two-year-olds. Both his parents were humanitarians who had chosen to live in underdeveloped countries. He had traveled just a year before to Indonesia with my wife, Kim, and an educational team that worked with Muslim educators, even though the U.S. team did not adhere to Islam. It might seem unorthodox that a group of devout Christians were working with a group of devout Muslims for the purpose of helping the children in Indonesia to receive a better education and, in turn, have a better life. The focus of the trip was helping the teachers move from a process that focuses on standardization and repetition to a learning model that emphasizes creativity and uniqueness.

This trip seemed to confirm to Peter that for him, coming back to

Los Angeles and enjoying the sweet life of the West Coast could be only a short-term luxury. Just a few months ago he packed his bags and prepared to move to Aceh. His intent was to work with an NGO (non-governmental organization) for the purpose of rebuilding the community of Keduh.

Within days after his arrival he was bitten by a mosquito, which, by the way, happens a lot in Indonesia. The mosquito clearly had a philosophy of take a little, give a little. It took a little blood and gave Peter dengue fever. Before he knew it, he was in a hospital bed fighting for his life. Along with a brutal attack on the respiratory system, medical articles say that two months of discouragement and depression can linger after having dengue fever.

About here a lot of us would stop and ask ourselves some serious questions. What am I doing in Jakarta instead of Laguna? Imagine if you add to your confusion that you felt you had a divine appointment to serve the people in Aceh. Who could blame Peter if the moment he found the strength to pull himself out of his hospital bed, he decided to take the first plane home? There are a lot of mosquitoes in Indonesia and a lot of bikinis in Laguna. It would not only make sense, but would be much easier just to turn back and rethink the whole thing—but not for Peter. He had never been raised to think like that. His life wasn't all about himself.

He had a contribution to make, and until he breathed his last breath, he was going to make it.

This week I learned that Peter saved two girls from drowning in the waters off Bali, which was not all that surprising when you consider that just the week before, he had rescued a man from drowning in the waters off Aceh. Maybe it is possible to save the world one person at a time. At the very least, you will save yourself. It would have been easy and reasonable for Peter to give up on the future he had envisioned for himself when he was lying in a hospital fighting for his life.

But if Peter had given up on the future that had gripped his soul, would he have had the strength to overcome the poison that had gripped his body?

Peter had something yet to do, something still to accomplish.

He had a reason to live.

The amazing thing is that his death would have resulted in the deaths of others, but his life and his refusal to retreat meant that others would live. Because Peter did not give up on his future, there are at least three people who now have one.

ENTRY #16 A Crisis of Success

THE LIFE THAT IS MOST POWERFULLY LIVED IS THE ONE that finds passionate urgency fueled by a sense of destiny. We must become. This is both something we need and something we long for.

One of the most quoted proverbs of Solomon is that without vision the people will perish. He also said that hope deferred makes a heart sick. He seems to be telling us that we need to have a dream we are pursuing and at the same time experience enough of that dream to keep us inspired.

We need both to aspire and accomplish. Without a vision for your life, without a sense of purpose, you will begin to die a slow death.

At the same time, if hope seems only an illusion, if you give up on hope, your heart, your soul, will become sick. It is not only essential to keep hope alive; it is hope that keeps us alive.

Hope is the fuel through which we create the future.

When you give up on hope, you become paralyzed in the present and begin to live in the past.

If you are not looking toward the future, you do not have one.

The baby boomer generation seems to have perfected the cultural phenomenon described as midlife crisis. The classic scenario is, you turn forty, and all of a sudden you start reconsidering everything. You begin having this haunting sense that you've wasted your life and will never fulfill your full potential.

Really there are only two scenarios that lead to midlife crisis.

First, you've given all your life to pursue certain goals and dreams. You've sacrificed everything to get there, maybe even your marriage and children. You've placed everything on the altar of success. Now you're nearing forty, and you realize that you have given everything you have and are still going to fall short of your dreams, goals, and ambitions. So you panic. You find yourself in the middle of a life crisis.

The second scenario is exactly like the first, except for one difference. As you turn forty, you realize that you got there; you accomplished everything you set out to do. You were so sure that it would be worth the sacrifice. Even when you left people behind, you told yourself it was necessary for the mission at hand. Stay focused. Don't get distracted. Win at all costs. And there you were a success.

You have become the perfect picture of accomplishment without fulfillment. You have everything, and you are empty. It all came to nothing.

So you find yourself in the midst of crisis wondering if this is all there is, asking yourself, maybe for the first time, *Is there anything worth living for?*

Sometimes this crisis is solved by moving from success to significance. We've outgrown success. Now we know it's not about that. We've grown up. We just want to be significant. We want to make a difference, to make our lives count. We hope it's not too late. Every day we move just a bit closer to death and a lot farther from birth.

So we redefine our values, reorganize our priorities, and once again begin our search for a future.

Though we have a new compass, we are still essentially on the same journey, trying to become something worth remembering, trying to be someone worth admiring, trying, oh, so desperately trying, to become someone. We are strange creatures, we humans. We strive for success, search for significance, look for purpose, and dream of our destiny.

Why do we need it? Shouldn't we be able to live without it?

ENTRY #17 A Search for Significance

OVER THE YEARS, I HAVE BEEN ASKED TO SPEAK AT conferences on this very subject. Each time in the middle of my lecture I would ask one of the more well-known speakers to come up and help me for a minute. I would try to choose someone the people saw as a symbol of success. Someone who, in a transparent moment, the audience would confess they wanted to be like. I would begin an interview and explain that the only rules were that the person had to be honest. The dialogue would go something like this:

"Elvis, it's good to have you here today. I want to ask you a couple of personal questions. Is that all right?"

"Sure, that's fine."

"What I need from you is for you just to be perfectly honest. Okay?"

"Of course. Yes."

"You're a pretty successful guy, and everyone here admires you. A lot of people would rather spend their lives imitating you than actually finding their own unique voice."

"That's true. Viva Las Vegas."

"Elvis, has there ever been a time when you have felt insignificant?"

(*Long pause.*) "Yeah."

"So there's been a moment in your life when even with all of your success, you've wondered if your life had any value, any real significance? In spite of all of your success, these insecurities have haunted you? In other words, you're nothing but a hound dog?"

"That's right."

"How did you get through those moments?"

Not mentioning alcohol or prescription drugs, he responds, "Love. People around me, Priscilla, you know, the people who care about me helped me through those moments."

"And they told you what?"

"You know, that I'm the King."

"In other words, that you're significant, that you have value, that you're important?"

"Exactly."

"Well, Elvis, I do some counseling sometimes—not often, but occasionally—and I'd like to help you through this. You know that moment when you felt insignificant, that moment when you wondered if you had any value at all, if your life really meant anything? That was the most honest moment you ever had, because you are insignificant. You're just a speck of dust against the backdrop of the cosmos. You are an evolutionary tragedy, a gnat with self-awareness heading straight toward the windshield of inevitability. All your future holds for you is splat and then it's over.

"I know what you're thinking, but look at all that you've done. You're the king of Graceland, the king of rock and roll, the king of rhinestones. And what about all the people who tell you that you're so important? That's because we all live in this illusion together. If you're not significant, then what are we? We affirm you're important in hopes that we are too. But we're all deluded by the same drug. If we all came to our senses, if we could all sober up, we would see the truth—we're born, we rock, then we die. Welcome to my own version of reality therapy. So, Elvis, how are you feeling?"

"Not good."

"Oh, by the way, everything I just said is absolutely true if there is no God."

Maybe you can't prove God in a tube, but you can find him in your soul. When he's missing, you can feel it in your gut.

ENTRY #18 Driven, Destined, and Determined to Change

IF THERE WERE NO GOD, IT WOULD BE INANE FOR US TO search for significance or to be ambitious for success. Our need to become points us to where we've come from. The reason we struggle with insignificance, the reason we fight to accomplish something, the reason we aspire and dream and risk is that God created us with an intrinsic need to become.

This thing that haunts you, that never seems satisfied, the cravings in your soul that you are unable to satiate through all the success that the world can bring—this is your soul screaming for God.

Only God can take you where you were born to go. There are a lot of roads you can choose, but one path chooses you.

One universal phenomenon I've discovered each time I've had this conversation is the reaction of those listening in. The moment I tell a person that he is insignificant, you can feel it in the room. The crowd feels I have done something unthinkable, something even immoral. Maybe you felt it just a minute ago: something in your gut went tight and a voice inside you said, *Wait a minute; this is wrong.* Most likely you had already picked up on the fact that I've never actually had a conversation with Elvis, but even that didn't matter.

Something inside tells you it's wrong to say to another human being that he or she is nothing.

But again, the question begs to be asked, If there is no God, if we're just drifting through time and space, if we're actually not going any-where, if there is no progress, why should it matter and why should we care? If it's the truth, isn't it best for all of us to come to grips with it, to come face-to-face with this harsh reality? Even if we are at the far end of the continuum with God on the other side, it doesn't change it at all.

Atheist, agnostic, existentialist, humanist, Buddhist, Muslim, Hindu, Christian—we all need to believe that somehow our lives matter.

There is a reason for our existence, a reason to live, and if we can't find it, we'll just make it up. And if we lack imagination, then we'll just medicate ourselves, sedate ourselves, intoxicate ourselves, indulge ourselves, deceive ourselves, or just simply come to the end of ourselves. Without a reason to live, we don't even have a reason to get out of bed.

One of my friends was telling me that koalas sleep twenty-two hours a day and are awake just long enough to eat and poop. By the way, they pretty much live in a state of intoxication, living on nothing but eucalyptus. I've had friends like that. Wouldn't this just be easier? No, we have to be driven to accomplish something, which is the amazing thing about success and significance. Put a hundred of us in the room, and we'll come up with a hundred different definitions of what success is and what makes a person significant.

The only unifying theme will be that all of us long for it and live for it. Some of us have become frustrated by our inability to achieve the dreams that haunt us. Some of us are disgusted by our willingness to throw away everything that is important to us and settle for something of far less value. In either case, we find ourselves giving up on our dreams.

But sometimes we go further than that. We stop believing in progress. We then become the enemy of hope. We move toward becoming cynics, pessimists, and nihilists. And once you're on this list, you not only believe in nothing, but you quickly begin to have nothing to look forward to.

I was watching HBO's weekly *Inside the NFL* wrap-up to get my weekly adrenaline shot, and they had the rookie quarterback for the Chicago Bears, Kyle Orton, miked for sound. He was on an incredible streak of wins, yet there were still a lot of questions about whether his play was strong enough to keep his starting job once the play-offs began. The Bears were once again about to win another close game where the defense pulled them through. Orton runs to the sideline filled with enthusiasm, begins to talk to what appears to be an offensive lineman, and says without explanation, "I'm a nihilist. I don't believe in anything." This evidently was good news.

Even then it's not that we don't have a goal, a dream, or a sense of destiny. We've just inverted it. Our mission is now to stop progress—to bring an end to empty optimism and foolish idealism. The danger, of course, is that whatever you choose to become is what you begin to call others to. Remember, Thoreau didn't just go to Walden; he called us all to go there with him.

Our need to become is intimately connected with our need to create. You cannot engage the future without activating your creative nature. The more proactive you become in pursuing your destiny, the more responsibility you will take for your life. When you choose to become, you become an enemy of the status quo. To become is to change and to bring change.

ENTRY #19 Becoming the Change

We take the characteristic of becoming for granted, but actually it is something quite unique to being human. What is natural to us is not natural to everything else that breathes. Gazelles are not driven to pursue a better life; lions are not lying around contemplating their personal destiny; and while even mother hens have an instinct to protect their chicks, they do not feel compelled to create a better world. This is something that is uniquely human. Granted, there are some individuals who have allowed their souls to be consumed by the part of us that is most corrupt and destructive.

Most of us, no matter how badly we've messed up our lives, want to create a better life for ourselves and for those we love. If we have the privilege to live our lives free of the struggle for survival, this instinct within us begins to take our focus to the broader world. We somehow know we're supposed to be conduits of good. We're supposed to make the world a better place. Yes, when we connect to God, we begin to care more deeply about the world around us. But I'm convinced it's more than this.

Even when we do not believe in God, something within us calls us to be humane. Isn't that really the core of humanism, trying to find a justification for our need to live differently than the rest of the animal kingdom? Somehow we know it's not supposed to be a dog-eat-dog world. If it's all evolutionary, then we should be motivated only by survival of the fittest. While some decide this is the way of the world as it should be, most of us know instinctively there's something very wrong about this. We don't know why, and without God we certainly don't have a justification for it, but we feel compelled to care about others. When we see or experience the suffering of others, it compels us to do something. If we ignore it, if we just walk away and decide the problem isn't ours, it sears our consciences, and we know deep inside us that something has gone horribly wrong.

When Katrina hit the Gulf Coast, swallowing up the shores of Louisiana, Mississippi, and Alabama, those of us here in Los Angeles felt compelled to help those devastated. A large number of evacuees were sent to Houston, so we decided to make the Astrodome the focus of our effort. Throughout our weekend gatherings, I simply made people aware that we wanted to do something as a community. I encouraged them to continue giving to the Red Cross and other trustworthy organizations, but we also asked them to consider going and supporting a team that would take time off from work and serve on location. I told them that it was absolutely essential that those who identify themselves as Christians show up at a time like this. I knew that our community cared; we just needed to make it practical. Over forty people volunteered, and we quickly pulled together about $25,000. We ended up sending a team of twenty-one.

Later we had the team over to our house and simply listened as they shared their stories. All of them had been profoundly affected by their experience. All were deeply moved by the opportunity to connect their lives with those who had lost so much. Our team was like an international coalition: Americans whose backgrounds were of African, Asian, Latin, and European descent. They were a small microcosm of the world coming together. In spite of all their different backgrounds, they had one common ambition—to give their lives to help total strangers and do whatever they could to help them find a better life. Of course, the whole point of this is: Why should they care? What is it about us that compulsively needs to make the world a better place? That's just not very Darwinian of us.

One of the team members, Charity Marquis, sent her reflections in an e-mail. Here are some of her thoughts:

> I'm back from Houston and it was an incredibly difficult trip. The people I had the privilege of serving have been through an experience that is unimaginable. Their grief is only beginning. As they find new places to live, families are further being torn apart.
>
> When the water spilled onto the streets of New Orleans . . . hell literally broke loose in that city. Prisoners were let out of jail, gangs went on a rampage and the spirit of death was everywhere. The violence and atrocities that took place in the Superdome are unfathomable. This all happened in the United States of America while we watched it unfold on TV. New Orleans became a war zone.
>
> After this experience I can't NOT think about it. I can no longer pretend that everything is okay because it is NOT. My eyes were opened to this reality and now I have to figure out what to do about it.

While Charity's e-mail is filled with important issues that need to be dealt with, there's only one part I want to bring to the forefront here: *"My eyes were opened to this reality and now I have to figure out what to do about it."*

Why? What is it inside the human spirit that tells us something must be done?

Why can't we just leave things well enough alone? Why should we care about someone when there's no benefit to us? Why should suffering or tragedy or poverty or injustice move us in any way? It's simple really—because we're human, and humans are created in the image of God. Because within all of us there's an intrinsic need for progress.

There is within all of us the need to believe that things will get better. We will get better. Our lives will get better. Even the world will get better. Doesn't every beauty queen hope for world peace?

Unless you have been severely jaded, there is something inside you that either drives you to make the world a better place or makes you feel guilty that you aren't doing anything about it. You are designed to accomplish. Your soul cannot live without progress. We are jaded because we have lost hope. If this is you, remember a time when you believed in your future. There was a time when you longed to make a difference.

What holds us back is that we can't make the world a better place if we ourselves are not moving toward a better place. It was Gandhi who implored us to become the change we seek. I totally agree. I guess the question is: How?

ENTRY #20 The Secret Longing of the Soul

MAYBE NO ONE HAS EVER PUT WORDS TO OUR LONGING to make a difference more aptly than J. D. Salinger in his classic *The Catcher in the Rye.*

In the words of Holden Caulfield, who is a study in cynicism and aimlessness:

> Anyway, I keep picturing all these little kids playing some game in this big field of rye and all. Thousands of little kids, and nobody's around—nobody big, I mean—except me. And I'm standing on the edge of some crazy cliff. What I have to do, I have to catch everybody if they start to go over the cliff—I mean if they're running and they don't look where they're going I have to come out from somewhere and *catch* them. That's all I do all day. I'd just be the catcher in the rye and all. I know it's crazy, but that's the only thing I'd really like to be.

All of us have a deeply rooted longing not only for our lives to be different but to make a difference in the lives of others. We are created with a need to have hope and to give it. When we become jaded, we ignore the voice to catch those who are falling over the edge, but it is still there within us and it haunts us. And even when we know something should be done, we just hope someone will do it.

Yes, it is possible to deaden your soul, but not to silence it. The farther we move from God, the more likely we are to actually give up on progress. A superficial assessment would lead you to conclude the exact opposite, given religion is often the enemy of progress, but God never is. When we stop believing the world can become a better place, when we stop caring about the lives and conditions of others, we lose a part of ourselves.

God created us for progress. His intention for us was always that we would be conduits of good. We can insulate ourselves from the problems of the world, but in doing so, we become less than human. When we give ourselves to create a better future, when we choose to become instruments of change, when we refuse to accept the status quo and commit to make the world a better place, something resonates within us. It is beyond reason. It is something far deeper than that. Somehow we know that this is right. It satisfies something deep within you. It's as if your soul has been craving and you didn't know for what. And there it was. Your soul was starving for hope—not just to have it, but to give it.

This is the mystery of the human spirit, that God never intended for us to live hopeless lives. When we treat the future as something that happens to us, we become passive, apathetic, and even paralyzed. When we embrace our unique place in creation, when we believe that God has created us to create, it begins to change everything for us. It not only empowers us to live, but it holds us responsible for life. Not only our lives, but the lives of everyone we could affect for good.

To live an aimless life is to live an unfulfilling life. You're just not wired that give up on life. The best evidence that your soul craves a destiny is that when you no longer believe you were created with a purpose and for a purpose, your soul is never satisfied with the life you have. You can't get enough, make enough, or buy enough to pay it off. Your misery owns you.

By the way, Charity's name is the Middle English version of the word *love*, which is a great reminder that when a person gives her heart to God, she is given a heart for the world. To go beyond feeling, to go beyond compassion, you have to believe that it is right to act, that you were created to bring change. If Jesus was nothing else, he was an activist for change. To be a follower of Christ is to believe that everyone's life can be different. No one is defined by the status of birth. Our destiny is not limited to our pedigree. Every human being is of equal value to God. No one must remain a prisoner of fate.

ENTRY #21 A Fresh Start to a Dead End

I WAS INTRODUCED TO REINCARNATION AT A YOUNG age, but the Western version. You know, the one where you were someone famous in a past life and it only gets better from there. Reincarnation was the spiritual version of a roller coaster—it was one wild and fun ride. Most Westerners who believe in reincarnation see it as a gift rather than a curse. I can no longer see it like that. I began to see things differently long before I walked the streets of Delhi, but certainly my time in India, Thailand, and Cambodia has helped me see why the way of Jesus is so much more powerful and empowering.

A person who genuinely honors the teachings of Buddha or the beliefs held by devout Hindus understands that reincarnation is a cycle that must be broken or at least completed. To be reincarnated is not a gift, but a declaration that you have not yet lived your life well enough. The ultimate gift in Buddhism is to complete the cycle and move to nothingness, the end of you. A part of this process is the end of all desire. This is one reason why reincarnation is no longer acceptable to me.

For me, the teachings of Jesus are far more compelling and resonate more deeply. In the Eastern view of humanity we are no different than a rat or a dog or a roach. We are all souls in transit, longing for release of self-awareness to become a part of a cosmic nothingness. A cow would be considered more sacred than any human. If you were born an untouchable, that is what you are for all of this life. There is no hope for progress; there is no chance for change. It is wrong for you to war against the status to which you were born. It is all about karma and dharma.

While many of us in the Western world have placed a great deal of focus on the apartheid of South Africa, the caste system of India, which keeps people trapped in poverty, has been virtually overlooked and ignored. I've found at times we are tempted to try to glamorize poverty by claiming that poverty-stricken people are more fulfilled than all of us trapped in materialism, but the truth is, they are ignored and without hope and we are allowing a human tragedy. In this system, a person's only hope is to live out this life so that things might change in the next. In other words, if a person is born wrong, his or her only hope is in the next cycle.

Jesus offers something quite different. If you know in your gut there's something broken, something missing, something needing to be changed, you don't have to wait for this to begin taking place in your life. In a phrase that has often been misused and misunderstood, Jesus promises that you can be "born again"—be given a fresh start in this life. What an amazing possibility to be able to start over in this life.

At the same time, reincarnation makes no distinction between a human and an insect. It's funny how oftentimes Christianity is seen as more judgmental and less forgiving than either Buddhism or Hinduism, yet we overlook the fact that this belief system accepts without blinking an eye that billions of souls at this moment live in the state of being roaches. If this is true, there are more of us who are sewer rats in Manhattan than there are brokers.

Don't be so quick to agree.

The teachings of Jesus are dramatically different in this area too. There is a clear distinction between the uniqueness of one human being and the rest of all created things. You are not the same as a dog. I know this isn't a particularly popular view. Popular culture has moved quickly to seeing animals as not only equal to humans, but even of greater value. We are no longer dog owners but pet parents. Whatever your views on choice may be, you should stop and ask yourself, *Why have we come to value a sea turtle's egg more than a human fetus?*

The Hebrew view of the human spirit is one of uniqueness. From the very beginning the Scriptures define the creation of man and woman as a distinct act of God. Only you were created in the image and likeness of God. While all creation is to be valued, while everything that breathes is to be treated with respect, while the earth itself is a sacred stewardship, everything is not equal. You are not equal. You are human. You are given one life, and it translates into eternity.

ENTRY #22 Standardized Testing

IRONICALLY, ONE OF THE VERY THINGS THAT SHOULD DRAW people to God has actually repelled them from Christianity. Over the last two thousand years, the Christian religion has abdicated its unique view of the individual and has fallen in line with every other world religion. It's easier to run a religion if you can standardize everything, including the people. Religion, after all, has become one of history's most powerful tools for controlling people. If you were thinking of a strategy to keep people in line, religion would have to be at the top of the list. In this, Christianity has become no different.

If you were to interview people who have come out of churches and have no intention to return, you'd find some common themes. One of them is the controlling nature of the churches they came from. Somehow we've equated conformity with holiness. Spirituality is more identified with tradition and ritual than it is with a future and a hope. Too often discipleship equals standardization. It's almost as if God's solution to the human problem is cloning, making us all the same, extracting from us all that is unique, destroying that which makes us different.

The tragedy, of course, is that this has nothing to do with Jesus. It would be an understatement to say that Jesus was unique. Even if he were not God, he would have been history's most extraordinary human being. He was a nonconformist; He was anti-institutional; He surrounded himself with outcasts; He was everything except what they expected. Jesus' life was a model of uniqueness, and his movement was nothing less than that. The people he chose to entrust his message to had to have been the unlikeliest of candidates. They were nothing if not unique. The son of a carpenter gave the responsibility that would typically be entrusted to priests and theologians to an unqualified group consisting of fishermen and even a tax collector. Furthermore, his inner circle also consisted of a woman who was once a prostitute. From background to temperament there was nothing about Jesuus' disciples that reflected conformity—neither did his message.

When Jesus spoke to the crowds in what has become known as the Sermon on the Mount, he described the masses in a way that no one else saw them. The thousands who pressed against each other to listen to the teachings of Jesus were the social outcasts of their time. They were the unwanted, the poor, the criminal, and the sick. Yet when Jesus described them, his words were filled with both affection and admiration. "You are the light of the world," He told them. Their lives should not be hidden, but open for the world to see.

These masses were the invisible.

They were part of the countless number of people who are lost in the shadows of great civilizations. They were the throwaways. They were seen as liabilities, burdens to society, but not to Jesus. He saw them as lights hidden under a bushel. He knew that there was something deep inside them waiting to come out, something beautiful, something breathtaking.

They were created by God to be luminous if only Jesus could make them see it.

"You are the salt of the earth," he also told them. But here there is a different danger. When salt loses its flavor, it has no value. It's thrown out and trampled upon. I think a lot of the people listening understood that. In fact, they had probably experienced it. In the sight of those who were powerful, they were considered worthless. It was easier to walk on them than to waste a good bag of salt. But they themselves may have been their worst enemies. If they did not recognize their own worth, if they relinquished the uniqueness of being human, if they denied their own value, they were like salt that had lost its savor.

In both these images, Jesus appeals to the intrinsic value of every human being.

You may not agree with this, but you should take time to consider it. While religions have historically tried to make us the same, Jesus calls us to be different. If you have ever experienced this, you know your soul bristled at the demand to quietly get in line and conform. But something in your gut told you this was wrong. If there was a God, his value would not be uniformity, but uniqueness. And you were right. Imprinted on your soul is the fingerprint of God. There is something inside you that resists surrendering your soul to legalism. The good news is that all that time it wasn't you fighting against God; you were fighting for what God has created you to become.

To come to God is to discover the uniqueness of your being.

When you come to God, you begin a process that re-creates you from the inside out. You begin a journey that is nothing less than life transforming. While there are some things we will share in common, the journey God has prepared for you is uniquely yours with him. Don't be confused about this—everything around us pushes us toward conformity. Whether it's communism or Islam, Calvin Klein or McDonald's, we are all pushed toward standardization and quickly find ourselves as assembly-line humanity.

We have to choose.

Liberal or conservative? Democrat or Republican? Evolution or creation? Pro-choice or pro-life? The environment or development? Coke or Pepsi? Coke Zero or Pepsi One?

Choose your box and stay there.

ENTRY #23 Creatives

IT'S SO MUCH EASIER TO ORGANIZE US, TO CONTROL US, when we allow others to standardize us. It shouldn't surprise you that your brain eventually revolts from being pressed and shaped like processed food (or you go brain-dead). Imagine how your soul is reacting to a processed life. Now we have 100 percent pure beef and natural spring water. I don't even want to think about what we were eating before. Or maybe more important, what kind of religion have we been swallowing? Your soul will end up vomiting everything you shove down its throat that violates who you are created to become.

You can choose to believe that your spirit has lived a thousand times before and that in a previous life you were a bug—or even worse than that, it's the life to come. Or you can choose to believe that you are the result of some kind of genetic mutation that arbitrarily happened through the evolutionary process. But remember this, what can settle your mind will not settle your soul. It will stir it up. You are a unique creation made by God to live and not simply exist. Your soul longs to find its ultimate purpose. It will not rest until you do. Your soul craves its destiny. Your soul desires. It always will. You were created as a creative being. You were made to grow, to dream, to achieve. Your soul is letting you know you come from God and your life is intended to be God-sized and God-inspired.

If this weren't enough to change my mind, all it would really take is the contrasting views on desire. To be truly holy in Buddhism or Hinduism is to be free from all desire. Personally this has never worked for me, and thank God, not even God expects that, nor does he desire it. In glaring contrast, Jesus was a man of amazing passion. Love, compassion, mercy, anger, disgust, and even hate found expression in the person of Jesus. Just in case you're wondering, it was people he loved and evil he hated. He wasn't all that happy about hypocrisy either. Then there was a time he made a whip and chased out all the money changers from the Temple, but that's another story.

If Jesus is God, then God is a God of passion. He is not a force or energy—indifferent to the human condition. He has created us like him—with passion and desire and emotion. God is like a fire that burns within your soul.

It isn't an accident that we are filled with desire. It's one part of being made like God. The problem, of course, is that we have raging passions and desires without the character and inherent good of God to channel them properly. Nevertheless, the solution for God has never been to neuter us or move us toward living apathetic lives. The goal of spirituality is not to extract from you all desire and passion. The call of Jesus is the exact opposite—delight in him and he will give you the desires of your heart. The destination of your spiritual journey was never intended to be nothingness.

Jesus kept inviting those who seemed to think it was too good to be true to follow him and experience nothing less than life, and life beyond measure.

ENTRY #24 Pathos

FOR BETTER OR WORSE, FOR RICHER OR POORER—THAT'S the commitment I made back in 1977 when I first saw *Star Wars*. I've been there through them all. If *Star Wars* was the honeymoon, then *Attack of the Clones* nearly caused our divorce. I was with a group of my friends in line at midnight just to be a part of the opening. But it hit me most fully at the *Revenge of the Sith*. We had flown all night from Los Angeles to Sydney, Australia. We were exhausted, jet-lagged, and committed to finding our lifelong colleague Obi-Wan Kenobi and bringing our journey with him to completion.

I have always been very much aware that Star Wars carries at its core George Lucas's Hindu view of the world. Certainly over the last thirty years while God has been going down in the polls, the Force has been steadily climbing. It's not hard to understand what's so attractive about the Force, an untapped source of power that enables us to become more than we ever could alone. Our attraction to the Force is just further proof that our souls long for God. At our core, we know that something is missing, that there's more to us than just flesh and bone.

The challenge is, Which side of the Force will you choose—the good or the dark side? So far so good, right? Of course, you're going to choose the Jedi way. Which one of us would even want to be a Sith? Well, in a world of metrosexuals, the Siths do have better costumes. I mean, Darth Maul had by far the best mask. But as the story unwraps, it all starts to become so clear. I found myself torn by Anakin's dilemma. Anakin, we discover, becomes the infamous Darth Vader. He is being trained to be a Jedi knight. The way of the Jedi is a life of honor but also a life of detachment. You must give up your right to love, to feel, and even to be loved. You must learn to live a life absent of desire. This is the way of the Jedi. This is what it means to choose the good.

The way of the Sith is the only other option. There is darkness there, and this is where your passions will lead you if you do not relinquish them. Anakin, of course, had a dilemma. He was in love with the young Queen Amidala. This presented a problem. Given, he had a lot of other problems too. But really this was the choice before him— live a life of detachment or live a life of passion. How can you disagree with this? Our passions have left an endless trail of devastation. Left to ourselves, it seems, desire leads us only to the dark side. I understand how this view can be compelling, but Jesus gives us another way.

Let him change you at your core, then let your passions fuel your life.

Spirituality and desire are not in conflict from the perspective of Jesus. In fact, he teaches that a genuine spirituality results in the passionate pursuit of life. I'm convinced one of the reasons so many have given up on pursuing genuine spirituality is that they didn't know what to do with their desires and passions. No one ever told them that they were placed there by God, that they were intended to be the fuel that would drive them to pursue their dreams and visions. At the same time we must heed the warning of the Sith, that unrestrained passions, passions lacking a moral compass, will lead us to a life that is self-destructive and will hurt anyone who chooses to come near to us.

Our greatest danger is living for whatever we can take and devour now and destroying our future in the process. Sometimes we find ourselves seething in anger because our desires cannot be satiated. When our dreams seem out of our reach, it is easy to simply choose apathy. Our worst-case scenario is that we become enemies of hope. We have to come to grips with the longing of our souls to become something that requires a metamorphosis, which is why no matter what we become, it is never enough. Our souls always crave more. It's not because they're insatiable, but because we know there's more to be had.

ENTRY #25 A Place of Hope

PROBABLY THE MOST FAMOUS METAPHOR TO EVER COME from the early followers of Christ is the butterfly. The imagery is that if people entrust their lives to Jesus, God will make them new creations. When you come to God and allow him to re-create you, from that moment the old is past, and all things are made new. The word describing this is *metamorphosis,* the image of a caterpillar becoming a butterfly—same species, completely different. This describes a change that literally moves us from crawling to flying. It is a necessary change if we are going to journey to the future we were created to live, to experience, to enjoy.

Sometimes, we choose just to be a worm; at other times, our preference is to hide in the cocoon, but every now and again we choose to engage the difficult struggle of breaking out. It's painful; it's frustrating; it's hard work. We might even wonder why God would make the cocoon so hard to escape from, never realizing it is the process itself that strengthens our wings and prepares us for flight.

Once you have lift, once you have takeoff, it just might hit you—on its worst day, a butterfly flies better than a caterpillar on its best day.

Wilbur and Orville Wright's history-making first flight lasted the whole of twelve seconds. Twelve seconds that forever changed their lives and changed the course of human history. Who could have guessed that twelve seconds could change your life? The key here is to get liftoff. You might not be Charles Lindbergh or Amelia Earhart right away, but your dreams will eventually take flight. Remember it was way back in 1485 when Leonardo da Vinci was dreaming and drawing over one hundred illustrations based on his theories of flight. It took us awhile, but his dreams were the basis for the modern helicopter. And never forget the bumblebee. All God wants to do is to take you where you cannot go alone and make you what you cannot be alone. You were not created to live your life absent of God. There is a dream for your life you can't even begin to imagine without God. Without him you are settling for less.

If you were meant to fly, not even running really fast is that impressive.

You can spend your whole life trying to become what your soul longs for without God. You might resent him that he's made it so hard for you to live out your dreams or fulfill your destiny. It's never quite hit you that it's in the struggle, in the process, even in the search for God, that e is making you strong enough to take flight. What in the world enters the mind of a cocooned caterpillar that would make it want to break out?

Maybe there's an instinct somewhere deep within it that lets it know something's happening, a change is taking place. It is no longer the same; it is somehow different.

Somewhere in the walls of a prison known as Shawshank, Red warns Andy Dufresne that hope can be a dangerous thing, which we soon discover is the whole point of *Shawshank Redemption*—that fear can hold you prisoner and hope can set you free. There's a power in hope that goes beyond explanation. It lifts us out of the rubble of our failures, our pain, and our fear to rise above what at one point seemed insurmountable.

Our ability to endure, to persevere, to overcome is fueled by this one seemingly innocuous ingredient called hope.

Everything that drives us,
   every effort to succeed,
      every attempt to be significant,
every moment we pursue a dream,
   advance a cause,
      or work to make the world better in any way
is an act of hope.

Every week when I drive from my house to the gatherings across Los Angeles, I pass a billboard advertising City of Hope, one of the premier centers for cancer research and care.

It simply says, "Where There Is Hope, There Is Life." I agree.

MEANING

Meaning

Curiosity

Imagination

Questions

Believing

Reason

Truth

Trust

Mystery

Faith

ENTRY #1   Is It All Just Dumb Luck?

THE GUN WAS IN MY HAND AND SHE WAS DEAD. A POLICE report would leave no doubt that her death was premeditated. I loaded the gun. I aimed. I pulled the trigger. One bullet was all it took. Only I knew it was an accident. I never thought I would actually hit my mark. It was my first time to ever hold a weapon. All I could think to do was to dig a grave in my backyard and bury her. Bury the evidence, bury the memory, and bury my regret. I wasn't even out of sixth grade, and I was face-to-face with the hard reality of life and death. In this case I was the grim reaper.

There's an old spiritual that says of God that "His eye is on the sparrow." Well, it didn't seem to help this one all that much. I think it goes on to say, "And he watches over me." Somehow that thought is not particularly comforting if this sparrow is any indication. I don't want to know if God is watching. I want to know if he's actually involved in how all of this plays out. If he's just watching, then we're all unwilling participants in the universe's biggest reality show—the original *Survivor*. Humanity here for your viewing pleasure! Hope we're not already into reruns. What a horrible thought that we are here for nothing more than God's entertainment. And you thought you were addicted to reality television.

There it was—helpless little bird, doing nothing more than flying around, enjoying a beautiful Miami day. So much sky to choose from, and it picked the space that aligned with my scope.

Talk about dumb luck.

You have to wonder, *Is this really how it is?* Can life and death be this arbitrary? Flying high one minute, then lying upside down with your legs pointing straight to heaven the next? And the question isn't so much about death as it is about making sense of life.

Remember how thirteen coal miners in West Virginia were trapped in a mine? It was reported widely that twelve survived the blast and one died. While this, of course, was great news, I found myself wondering, *Why those twelve? Why not thirteen?*

Seems so random. Why one? Why that one?

The papers were rightfully filled with celebration. "Alive! Miners Beat the Odds," "Miracle in the Mine," "Miracle at Sago Mine: 12 Miners Found Alive" were the headlines spreading across the country. And so it seemed for everyone but that one . . . Three hours later the families learned what officials already knew—it wasn't that only one died; only one survived.

Randal McCloy, who at twenty-seven years old was one of the youngest of the group, was carried out in critical condition. The others were killed either by the blast or by carbon monoxide poisoning. I woke up to this news and felt sick to my stomach. It seemed wrong to have even thought the question. It was as if my heart was breaking from sorrow.

Still, I had the same question, but now for a very different, more painful reason:

Why one? Why that one?Is it all just dumb luck?

Is life really this arbitrary? Are pain and joy, love and hate, and life and death just random? Is there method behind the madness? Does life have meaning, or is it all just meaningless?

entry 1

ENTRY #2 Making Sense of This Mess

TRYING TO MAKE SENSE OF LIFE CAN DRIVE YOU CRAZY. There was a time when I was doing just that—trying to make sense of my life and going crazy.

So there I was sitting on that proverbial couch while a complete stranger tried to help me make sense of my life. From IQ tests to determine if I could think well enough to identifying ink blots to figure out what was locked in my subconscious, I endured a battery of tests whose end goal was essentially self-discovery. It was like having someone excavate my brain. Sometimes it felt like walking out of the shower with the door open and having someone see me completely naked, except it was my soul that was exposed.

Funny thing about it is that I wasn't the one confused about what was wrong with me. It was clear to me that the world as it was being presented just didn't make sense. It was as if the universe was out of whack, but everyone else was oblivious to it—which I know makes me sound crazy. I wasn't sure which scenario was actually real. Either everyone was part of a grand conspiracy, or everyone had all memories erased. I didn't know what happened, but I knew that everything was not as it seemed.

All I wanted to know was the truth. I didn't even care what it was or what the implications might be; I just wanted to make sense of life—or more specifically, my life.

When I finally understood, it was such a relief. Some of it is too personal to share on the pages of a book. But it came down to the kind of pain and confusion that often comes through marriage and divorce. The missing piece for me was the memory of a father I had never heard mentioned. Like the sparrow, he had been buried and forgotten. Well, the problem was that somewhere deep inside me, he wasn't forgotten.

Without going into painful detail, I spent my first years with my grandparents in El Salvador. Years after a divorce, my mom remarried, and my stepdad stepped right in and became a father to us. As the years passed, memories of a life before Bill McManus disappeared. It just became easier for my family to act as if there had never been a "before," but my soul told me there was one. I had grown so close to my stepfather that they were afraid to tell me what had happened.

I knew something wasn't right. The pieces didn't quite fit. I kept asking questions, but no one was talking. The military has a phrase, "It's on a need-to-know basis." The implication, of course, is that you don't need to know. I had a memory of something lost that I could not understand. I used to love *The X-Files* with Scully and Mulder. Like them, I knew the truth was out there. I just didn't know what the truth was. But I would not rest until I found it . . . What we don't seem to get is that when it comes to truth, our souls always need to know.

I didn't need everything fixed. I certainly didn't need all the answers. I just needed to know the truth. We underestimate the healing power of truth. We also underestimate how desperately our souls long for truth. Our souls crave truth. We want to know the truth. We need to know the truth. The human spirit isn't designed to live a lie. Ironically, the only reason we are capable of lying is that we are able to know truth. Even without any external guidelines or boundaries, we know a lie when we tell one.

We have a filter within us that separates truth from falsehood.

We assume this is simply a part of being human, but we shouldn't underestimate what this says about us as a species. We are creatures of truth. We can form thoughts and create language, we can imagine possibilities and create technology, we can explore the created world and create medicine, but we also can distinguish between that which is real and that which is false. Not only can we know the difference, but it is critical to do so. Whether it's from an economic or a sociological perspective, the ability to discern between a lie and the truth is essential for survival. We cannot live in healthy, functioning relationships when we choose to lie to each other.

The more that deceit, deception, and dishonesty pervades a culture, the more unhealthy and destructive it is.

Not only is it unhealthy to be lied to, but it is corrosive to our souls to lie and deceive others. We weren't designed to live a lie or even to tell one. Even if you don't believe in God, don't believe in objective truth, and don't believe in any moral absolutes, you still have to grapple with the unusual human phenomenon that we become psychologically and relationally sick when we live a lie and we find health in an environment of truthfulness, even when the truth is more painful than the lie.

Probably one of the most memorable lines in any film occurred in the moment that Jack Nicholson looked at Tom Cruise in *A Few Good Men* and pushed back against Cruise's attempt to find the truth: "You can't handle the truth." A lot of us believe that. We tell white lies, distort the truth, hide the truth, or just create our own truth. The thinking, of course, is that the truth is just too painful. Sometimes we avoid the truth at all costs, yet to run from the truth costs us more than we can imagine.

Our souls crave to know the truth, and we need to pursue it at all cost. Whatever the implication, wherever it takes us, we must search for meaning, strive for understanding, struggle to make sense of life, never give up on the belief that the truth is out there.

ENTRY #3   What's the Meaning of This?

THERE WAS A TIME WHEN I WONDERED IF MY LIFE WAS A waste. No matter what I did I couldn't shake the irrelevance of my existence. Too many things were just so arbitrary. No matter how I tried, I just couldn't make sense of it.

I've learned something about us humans: we just don't do well when we feel our lives are meaningless. Something inside us drives us to meaning. Why is it that when we have no meaning for our lives, something inside of us gets really sick? Conclude that life is meaningless, and you'll find yourself struggling with fear, angst, and doubt.

While mystery is a wonderful thing that makes us more alive, meaninglessness has a paralyzing effect. We demean ourselves when we give up on finding meaning for our lives.

Our souls resonate with meaning. Our souls search for meaning.

Meaning has a healing effect.

Without meaning we find ourselves consumed by phobias and controlled by superstitions. We all need to make sense of life. Whether we satisfy our craving for meaning through faith or reason, the one place we do not live well is in a life that seems arbitrary, random, or senseless.

Don't get me wrong. We are more than capable of living with uncertainty, mystery, and the unknown. In fact, much of life requires that we do. And if you're anything like me, you love adventure, surprise, and even risk.

What's perplexing is that we'll believe in something that is false just so that we don't have to experience the destabilizing effect of not knowing. We want something to be certain, something to be sure. All

entry 3

of us organize our lives around what we believe is true, and it makes our lives manageable and gives us some sense of control. It helps us deal with everything that is out of our control.

We try to compensate for our lack of control either by increasing our sense of power or by creating greater predictability in our lives. We often flesh out our need for certainty through our need to control.

Thirty-eight times the word *meaningless* is used in the Scriptures:

meaningless meaningless

Of those thirty-eight, thirty-five are in the book of Ecclesiastes. It's a strange thing that the man the Hebrews knew as the wisest person who ever lived is the one who struggled the most with doubt. Solomon should have been the master of meaning, but he became history's first nihilist.

His opening words in the book of Ecclesiastes are—"Meaningless! Meaningless! Utterly meaningless! Everything is meaningless." He writes, "What a heavy burden God has laid on men! I have seen all the things that are done under the sun; all of them are meaningless, a chasing after the wind."

Eleven chapters later, as he moves toward his conclusion after having explored all the possibilities for the meaning of life, he comes back once again to "Meaningless! Meaningless! Everything is meaningless!" In between he gives us eleven chapters of endless dead ends.

He pursued pleasure and in the end found it leaving him empty.

His conclusion—meaningless! He pursued ambition and worked himself into the ground accomplishing great things, and it left him empty. His conclusion—meaningless! Solomon pursued wealth, power, and fame, and he found that it was all meaningless, meaningless, and yes, you guessed it, meaningless.

The peculiar thing about Solomon's journey is that it began undeniably with God. It was God who gave him the gift of wisdom, but wisdom didn't remove the doubts and questions that haunt us all.

Instead of running *to* God, he chose to run *from* God.

He searched for meaning everywhere except in God, and it nearly drove him out of his mind. Ecclesiastes is filled with cynicism, bitterness, and hedonism. It is also strangely empty of God, except to question God.

Solomon traveled far from where he began, only to return there in the end.

Having searched the world
for meaning,
he concludes that life
is meaningless
without
God
and that only in God
will we ever find
the meaning
our souls long for.

ENTRY #4 Open Our Coffins and We're All Just Well-Meaning Vampires

As he walks through the decayed house, his eyes are expressionless.

"And my story ends there. But in fact it ended a long time ago, with Claudia's ashes in that theater. My love died with her. I never really changed after that. What became of Lestat I have no idea. I go on, night after night. I feed on those who cross my path. But all my passion went with her yellow hair. I am a spirit with preternatural flesh. Detached. Unchangeable. Empty."

THESE ARE THE WORDS OF THE INFAMOUS VAMPIRE LOUIS (Brad Pitt) as scripted by Anne Rice, author of the bestselling novel *Interview with the Vampire.* What in the world can a vampire teach us about being human? Can anyone relate with a person whose life ended long before he stopped breathing?

Have you ever known someone who went through so much pain that all life and love and meaning were lost? Is it possible that more of us are vampires than we know? When we give up on life, we become the undead. Life can be like a stake through the heart.

To the surprise of many, Anne Rice was being interviewed in regard to her rediscovery of faith. It may appear to the casual observer that her new focus on Jesus Christ would stand in direct opposition to her more controversial works in the *Vampire Chronicles.* For Anne there is nothing irreligious about them.

She explains, "I think they are very Christian books by somebody outside the church, lost in darkness, striving to find meaning and sometimes being rebellious."

We are all on a journey to make sense of life, and when it doesn't make sense, it is maddening to our souls.

If you conclude life is meaningless, your story ends before you do. You may never make the connection, but the cynicism, bitterness, despair, and emptiness eating away at you have everything to do with your need to believe in something or someone. As antiquated as it may sound, it's not that some people choose to live by faith, but that all human beings must live by faith, even if it's faith in reason.

We all live by faith.

If we were all just a little more honest or maybe a little humbler about this, it would be easier on all of us. Certainly it would be better for all of us. It's not that we're copping out; it's that we don't have any other option. Anyone who is not all-knowing has faith in their future.

Some people take leaps of faith; others go there kicking and screaming.

In either case, we all find ourselves in the same place.
We have to make choices,

      draw conclusions,

          embrace beliefs,

              that in the end are

                    acts of faith.

Even if you choose not to believe, that in itself is a HUGE leap of faith.

If you step back and extract the emotion and look at it objectively, you begin to realize that faith and reason have a lot in common. Oh, they come to different conclusions, but they're both trying to do the same thing. They're trying to make sense of life. They're trying to establish what is true, what is real. Again, I think this is far more important than even looking at the outcome.

Drowning in the end of the conversation, we might miss the beauty of the middle.

    Both the person who trusts in reason and intellect
    and the person who trusts in faith and intuition,
    while coming to very different conclusions,
    are asking the same question:
    What is true?

Reason and faith look very different but are more alike than we would care to admit.

ENTRY #5 I've Got a Frog in My Throat

FIGURING OUT WHAT IS REAL, WHAT IS AUTHENTIC, WHAT IS trustworthy in everyday life is hard enough; it gets a lot tougher when we bring faith into it. We have an endless number of world religions, and they all claim to have the truth.

Somebody's wrong.

Maybe everyone's wrong, right?

At least it would seem so when it comes to the answers. Somebody way back there decided to try to make sense of life, you know, to help people. He didn't have all the pieces, so he filled in the blanks wherever needed. After a while what was true and what was filler became indistinguishable, and both took on equal value. Over time it all became sacred because it helped people cope with life.

Life is difficult enough. It's almost impossible when it doesn't make sense.

We create our own version of truth. Maybe we do it by accident. We wake up one morning convinced there is a rain god, and he won't let it rain unless we dance the night away.

Or somehow some guy figures out that the volcano god is boiling mad over the fact that no one offered him a virgin. Or maybe some guy is mad because he couldn't get the virgin and, out of spite, decides to throw her into the volcano.

Call me jaded, but someone early in the process had to know he made things up. I really do believe that religions are filled with sincere people. In each religion there had to be a first genuine convert.

But the guy right before him, he knew.

He knew it wasn't all real.

 entry 5

He knew at best it was a hopeful guess.

It's not that I'm a cynic. It's just that I question everything.

My Snapple bottle cap (my postgraduate educational system) just informed me that frogs can't swallow with their eyes open. There is a lot of stuff out there you'd have to have your eyes closed to swallow. Me—I would rather swallow with my eyes wide open.

So maybe this guy was sincere and delusional.

Now that's so much more comforting.

To his credit, though, he also somehow knew that everyone was on a search for meaning. Maybe he was completely sinister and created a belief system to control people. Or maybe in some dysfunctional way he was genuinely caring and was just trying to make life easier on the people he cared about. Or it may be that he was reacting against a greater falsehood, a greater deception. Maybe that's what motivated the likes of Buddha, Confucius, Gandhi, and even Nietzsche.

They were just sick and tired of watching people be manipulated by the prevailing false view of reality. In reaction to it, they created a new way of thinking, a new way of believing, a new way of living. The truth of the matter is that Colonel Nathan R. Jessup was exactly wrong. It's not that we can't handle the truth; it's that we can't live without it. We can't function effectively without making sense of our experience. You're searching for meaning, but maybe you haven't recognized it as a part of a spiritual quest.

We live in a time when philosophers question even the existence of reality.

It has us all wondering . . .

if anything is true.

if anything is real.

if anyone is right.

if anyone can be trusted.

ENTRY #6   Junk Food and the Search for Truth

THE QUESTION THAT DRIVES SO MUCH OF OUR PRESENT-DAY thinking is, *What can we know?* On one end of the spectrum are those who say nothing can be known. We can't be certain of anything. The natural conclusion is that there is no truth—at least any objective truth. All we are left with is what we perceive. Everything becomes subjective. You can't really know anything; you can only think or feel or believe something is true. It's your personal truth. It's true to you, and that's as far as it goes.

On the other end of the spectrum are those who are entirely committed to objective truth—and nothing else. All that exists is what can be tested. For example, "I'll believe in God when they prove his existence in the laboratory." It's all about empirical evidence.

Ironically, both of these views—*nothing is real* and *only the physical world is real*—even though they're diametrically opposed, tend to be the two acceptable positions among the intellectual elite.

This just reminds me that our search for meaning is more complicated than we think.

It's not just religion that is floundering in the end. Philosophy and science aren't doing any better. We can argue all day about who has the best view on meaning, whether it's science or philosophy or religion. Put a hundred people in a room, and we might find ourselves with a hundred different philosophies, religions, and scientific perspectives.

There are a lot of answers out there. It's like an endless smorgasbord, one of those all-you-can-eat deals, and boy, have we learned to overeat.

Eventually we get sick of gorging ourselves (some of us not as quickly

entry 6

as others). It's amazing how much we can put down. We'll just stuff our-selves and shove it down our throats way past when we're full. And I'm not talking about food. We are all standing in the line of an endless buf-fet. It's technically called pluralism, but it's basically an all-you-can-eat salad bar of beliefs. An endless number of belief systems surround us. The issue is not so much that we have to choose between them, but that we can pick and choose the parts we like the best from each one.

This phenomenon known as pluralism has created more than an end-less number of options; it has also led to the customizing of faith (which, by the way, is very different from having a personal faith).

There once was a time when everyone who lived in the same com-munity shared the same beliefs. We were all part of a tribe and had a tribal shaman who would pass on to us the beliefs, values, and culture that held us together. We didn't really have a lot of options. It might not even occur to us that there were other ways to think, other ways to see reality, other ways to believe. Today we have more than an endless number of options; we have opportunities. You can have it your way.

I remember when it all began. Burger King freed us from standard-ization. Imagine the possibility of ordering a burger specifically made to order. Most of you have no memory of a world without options.

When I was a kid, if you wanted to buy someone a stuffed bear, you just went to the toy store and bought a stuffed bear—pretty simple and straightforward. Now we have "Build a Bear." It's a toy store where you get endless options of the bear you want to create. After you've picked up all of your accessories, a store employee stuffs it and sews it up, and you're off. It's pretty much the same with religion. You don't need to find one; you can just make one.

Once only the cultural elite would engage in philosophy; now everyone is a philosopher. What's strange, though, is that we seem more motivated to create our own truth rather than search for it.

This is where it's important to remember that more is not always better.

AND WHEN YOU ADD THE COUNTLESS VOICES WHO have become our cultural experts in pop psychology, even the most compulsive of us are beginning to conclude that less is more. At the same time, this moment gives us a great opportunity for self-discovery. If there ever was a moment when we could see that proof of God is not in the answers, it is now. If anything, the endless number of opinions only moves us toward disbelief.

We can't put a finger on it,
      but what is happening is that
          our souls are being spammed.

ENTRY #7   The Answer Is the Question
(or the Other Way Around)

THERE IS PROOF OF GOD IN ALL THIS, BUT WE'VE BEEN looking in the wrong place. Before you can find God in the answers, you have to find him in the questions.

Maybe the answers come from us, so we come up with a million of them. But the questions . . . there's something mysterious about the questions.

We all ask them;

we all have them;

and no matter where we come from

or what time in history we have lived,

the questions are always the same.

As important as the answers might be,

what's even more revealing is that we even have

questions: ??

Why do we need to know?

What drives us to search for answers?

Where does the "ask" come from?

Every one of us is on a search for meaning.

We are all on a quest (ion).

The arrow that points the way looks not like this: $\rightarrow$ but like this: ?

All of us, no matter what conclusions we've come to, are driven by the same thing—**we have to find the answers!**

Everything we experience, everything we learn, every bit of information we process, is being integrated by our brains, and we will not have peace of mind until we create some kind of cohesion.

Whatever your view of the Bible may be, whether you believe it is divinely inspired or the product of human effort, you would have to at least acknowledge that it, like all other religious texts, is a part of the grand story of humanity searching for meaning.

Every world religion, every philosophy, every belief system—from anthropology to astrology to sociology to psychology to mythology to science itself—is trying to propose a cohesive view of reality. They're all trying to make sense of life. We're all trying to figure out who we are, why we're here, what this whole thing is about.

If you're sophisticated, you can see the flaws and fallacies of so many different belief systems. You might even look down with condescension at those who believe what you would consider simplistic answers to the complex problems in the world. We once were convinced that the world was flat; that if we danced, the rain would come; that the stars determined our fate in life.

We have outgrown so many fairy tales that we once believed were reality. Maybe it's an inherent flaw in the human species, but we are all predisposed to believe. We'll believe in just about anything.

If they catch us young enough, we'll believe without consideration—

Santa Claus	crystals
tooth fairy	spirits
Easter bunny	demons
ghosts	angels
vampires	Buddha
bogeymen	Allah
karma	Krishna
reincarnation	Jehovah
feng shui	Jesus

entry 7

The list is endless.

While we may be able to systematically eliminate everything we believe that later we discover isn't real, we can't escape the very thing that's right in front of us. Every one of us, regardless of race or language or education or generation, regardless of all the variables possible to make us different, is still inclined to believe in something.

While we may disagree on what we believe in and we may argue violently about what is true, what we can't escape is that we are all on the same quest and our soul craving is to find something we can believe in.

ENTRY #8 I Don't Understand Why I Must Understand

It's significant that Jesus said the kind of person God is looking for is one who worships in spirit and truth. God does not see these in conflict with each other. Both guide us on our search for meaning. And this is not something we even do consciously.

Searching for meaning is like breathing.

It is something intrinsic to the human spirit. It's inside all of us, and it is there from the very beginning. Or is it only my children who are so inquisitive? Barely able to walk, they were already asking the most profound philosophical question known to humankind:

Why?

It's the question that drives every parent insane.

Everything is *why?* It isn't even the most important question at that stage in life. How about asking *where?* "Where do I put all the poop in my diapers?" I've never had a child ask that one. Or how about asking *how?* "How are you able to get to the potty on time?" Or you expect them at the very least to ask *what?* "What in the world is that smell?"

If you think about it, all the other big questions—*who, what, when, where, how*—can be explained by our struggle to survive as a species. Evolution easily addresses the development of these questions. Who got eaten? What ate them? Where did it go? When did it come? And most important, how did you get away?

Why, on the other hand, just doesn't fit. It is not really necessary for survival. I just can't see early humans needing to ask, Why did the raptor eat Krug? Why did it have to happen to him? Why do they have to be carnivores? Why did we have to be made out of meat? It would have been so much easier if we had been made out of a polyester blend or synthetic.

Yet the more we seem to advance as a species, the more we're able to eliminate our need to ask all the other questions. Calculators do our math; computers do our research; restaurants do our hunting; malls do our gathering; movies do our living.

Still, no matter how much is done for us, no matter how much is provided for us, we can't escape the nagging question of *why*. Even when life comes easy, it doesn't seem to make this part any easier. Eventually something's going to happen that makes you pop the question: Something's going to disrupt your personal utopia.

Even when you're just trying to have a good time and enjoy your life, something will come and disrupt your conscious slumber and put you face-to-face with the question that haunts us all—*why*? Why did this have to happen? This doesn't make any sense. What is the meaning of this? And ultimately how can God exist and allow things like this to happen? Whatever answers we come to, they all expose that we really need to ask the questions.

Asking *why* isn't about the survival of the fittest; it is about the soul's craving for meaning.

Ironically, since the Enlightenment we seem to increasingly find ourselves groping in the dark. Our desperate search for truth has become increasingly more elusive. The more we know, the more we're unsure. Our philosophers went searching for truth, and when they returned, they told us that there is no truth to be known, that nothing is true, and that all we can do is create our own truth and hope for the best. *Is this really true?*

The modern world built laboratories and told us that we could trust science with truth—that scientists would search for it vigorously: In this it has returned a failed experiment.

Our leading minds kept insisting that if you can't prove it, you can't believe it, but then they kept stepping way past their own criteria. From anthropology's infamous Leakey family, who kept claiming they found the missing link—only to have another sibling discredit them—to Stephen Hawking, who made science the new philosophy, science keeps trying to answer more than it can prove.

Science can't even begin to touch the most important question to us, which, of course, is *why*.

Is there a bigger question than *why*? It overshadows all the rest. Knowing *how* it happened is fascinating, but knowing *why* it happened is essential. You can live without knowing how it happened, but when you can't figure out why, it's absolutely maddening.

Why are we here?

Why is there evil in the world?

Why is there so much suffering?

Why would God allow this to happen?

Why would we allow it to happen?

Why don't we change?

Why don't we do something about it?

Why does it matter?

Why is the question that haunts us.

ENTRY #9 I Don't Know How I Know What I Know

WHEN LIFE DOESN'T MAKE SENSE OR WHEN WE GIVE UP trying to make sense of life, we find places to run and hide.

Usually religion is accused of being the place where people go to escape reality. I'm not going to argue with this. Overall I agree with it. I would suggest, though, that it's not the most popular place to go anymore.

There are two places where I find people retreating. While a healthy faith openly embraces mystery, allowing room for the unknown, our new places to escape attempt to eliminate everything that is uncertain.

Option number one is the path where you have to prove something or it doesn't exist. We try to make sense of life by concluding that this is all there is. We become what we might call materialists (only the physical world is real). All that exists is what can be proven.

If you can't see it, touch it, taste it, smell it, or hear it, it doesn't exist.

What is real is what can be empirically proven—the proof has to be scientific. While I fully understand how a reasonable person would come to this conclusion, it makes me wonder about other deeply meaningful dimensions of knowing.

If we were honest with ourselves, we would admit that love is far more real to us than, let's say, Venus. I don't mean the Greek goddess, but the planet. Most likely you've never actually seen Venus; you just know it's there. Maybe you've seen pictures, but how do you know that they're not doctored? There are people even still who don't believe Elvis is dead (haven't seen it) and people who don't believe we've ever landed on the moon (they might actually be the same people). And even if the pictures are not doctored, how do you know it's really Venus?

But you know when you have loved.

You know when you've hated.

You know when you've been jealous, bitter, and angry.

You know when your heart has been broken,

when your spirit has been crushed,

when your gut is telling you something your brain can't make sense of.

You know deep things within your soul with more certainty

than you know that Venus, Jupiter, and Mars exist.

If we conclude that all we can know is what can be tested and proven in a laboratory, how can we explain all that our hearts know? Intellect is a wonderful thing, but there is more to us than what our heads can hold.

You can't escape the reality that you know things deeply that have nothing to do with rational thought. And if that were not enough, you can't escape the dilemma of life itself. You can't function without putting your faith in something or someone.

You get on a plane; you put your life in the pilot's hands. It's kind of silly to strap that seat belt if the pilot just had a fight with his wife, decided he couldn't take it anymore, got drunk, and then somehow slipped into the "driver" seat. Even knowing this is a real possibility, you take your seat and calmly put on your headphones.

Every moment of your life you breathe. You've said a thousand times, you can't trust in something you can't see. Of course, you're talking about God, not about oxygen.

Oxygen doesn't count.

You clearly need oxygen. You can't live without it. So you breathe, you inhale and exhale, never even contemplating if your next breath will be your last. What about if it just runs out? What if the breath you just took right this minute was the last one you're ever going to get? You wouldn't exhale it so callously, would you? You wouldn't be so casual about breathing if you knew we were down to the last 1 or 2 percent.

Take a deep breath. Enjoy it. It's an act of faith, you know.

Could be toxic.

Probably is.

Killing you slowly.

But you're okay with that, or at least you seem to be. You just keep right on breathing. You have to. You don't have a choice.

The only real option is to stop breathing and die or to live by faith and just keep right on breathing what you cannot see and really do not know.

The word for "spirit" in both the Hebrew culture and the Greek is also the word for "wind" and "breath." Is it possible that our souls are suffocating, desperately trying to inhale, to breathe in God, but we're afraid to trust in something we can't see, something we can't prove?

While there are some who decide that the best way to search for meaning is to depend entirely on objective proof, there are others who are looking to a very different filter to determine what's real. Instead of depending on objective evidence, some of us, instead, turn to our own personal experience. This could be defined as subjective validation.

Instead of depending on our senses, we depend on our sensations.

What is real is now determined not by what we can prove, but by what we experience. And it could be argued that the only real proof we have is experience. The difficulty is that we become our own source and validation for what is real—for what is true. Let me say emphatically that emotions are as real as thoughts, ideas, or even knowledge. They're just real in a different way.

The problem occurs when truth becomes a slave to our emotions.

When you feel something deeply, it's a true feeling, but it doesn't mean that it should become the basis of all reality. Our emotions can be a turbulent ocean constantly changing in response to our circumstances.

We reject objective truth because we are uncertain of what can be known, unsure of what we can trust. At the same time, we find it's no different inside us. If you think it's hard to know what's real in the world outside you, stop and take an honest look at your inner self.

There's more mystery inside you than there is in the entire universe outside. We are a mystery even to ourselves. And it is this mystery that our souls long most to understand. Much of our search for meaning is shrouded in the secondary questions of life—*how, what, when,* and *where.*

The more perplexing questions, the ones our souls long to find answers to, are *who* and *why.*

The scientific method depends on objectivity and detachment. While these are essential for good science, the shortcoming is that science, no matter how advanced it may become, cannot even begin to engage the most profound questions of *who* and *why.* At the same time, science can't seem to help itself. Science seems to continually stumble awkwardly into philosophy and religion.

Science is obviously ill-equipped to deal with the subject of God.

But that's not where its inadequacy comes to an end. Science is incapable of addressing the deepest issues of the human spirit. Everything that is human is not material. If you don't believe in the human spirit, you would have to concede that there is the complexity of human emotions, that there is the uniqueness of human intuition, and that there is more going on here than meets the eye.

Science can explain the human brain
      flounders in attempts to explain the human mind
           and fails completely when it comes to the human spirit.

ENTRY #10 If It's Pitch Black, Does It Matter If You're Blind?

IRONICALLY IT'S ACTUALLY SCIENCE THAT HAS DRIVEN US to becoming increasingly subjective. The rationalists (all head-proof) and the romantics (all heart-passion) are antagonistic stepsisters. I'm just not sure which one is Cinderella. When you believe only what you can see, and you can't trust what you see, where does that leave you?

Blind.

In a very dark room.

It isn't that hard for us to see that science is inadequate to explain the whole of human experience. At the same time, we're not ready to make what seems like an irrational leap of faith. We're stuck between the proverbial rock and a hard place. The bottom line is, we don't know who or what to trust. Either way it's a huge risk that we're not all that eager to take. So instead of expanding our level of trust, we constrict it and contract it.

We move from having once trusted in the eternal, the invisible, the spiritual, the unseen, to trusting only that which is visible and tangible.

Now

    take

        one

           step

back.

We no longer trust science. We no longer believe in objective truth. History is just propaganda or mythology. The only thing we have confidence in is what we experience. While these two approaches to finding truth might seem to have nothing in common, at the core they are very similar.

In the end it is about limiting who we trust.

Whether we are trusting in our research or our experience, we are still trying to get to the same place. We are trying to work our way through the other questions to get to the ones that are burning within our souls:

Why am I here? Is there meaning to my existence? Am I here by accident? If not, who put me here?

And by the way, God, if you're out there, would you mind speaking up!

If there is a *why* to our lives, then there is also a *who*. If there is a *who* behind our existence, then there is meaning to our lives. But life doesn't always make sense. So you begin to wonder, If there is a God, can he be trusted? Here, I think, is where we begin to address the challenge of faith.

Faith is simply the word for trust when used in relation to God.

In a brief conversation one evening with a guest, this became even clearer to me. I knew he was uncomfortable, and I wanted to respect his space, but I wanted to give him a chance to share his story. After politely letting me know that church and God just weren't his things, I asked him what was. He went on to describe himself as a secular humanist. He added that he was very much an existentialist and saw no need for God.

The conversation could have gone a lot of places, but I saw something in his eyes that I had seen many times before.

I'm sure my next question must have seemed to him to come from nowhere. But if my question was a surprise to him, his answer was even more surprising to me.

I asked him, "You must have really been hurt at some time in your life?"

Over the years, I found that cynicism is a way of escape. You've believed, you've trusted, you've put yourself out there, and you've gotten hurt. Someone lied to you, or betrayed you, or maybe it was even God. He just didn't show up when you needed him. So you retreat to the only place you know to go. You go hide inside your own soul and decide that you can trust no one but yourself. In the end, this is at the heart of the path that leads us to trust only in ourselves.

So instead of asking him a philosophical question, I just asked him about his own pain, his own past, his own story. His response has never left me. After a long pause, I could almost hear his brain working overtime.

He simply answered, "Maybe."

"Maybe": what a strange answer.

If I asked him, "Do you know that God created you in his image and likeness?" I could see him answering, "Maybe."

Or if I proposed that God had stepped into human history in the person of Jesus Christ, lived a perfect life, was crucified, buried, and raised from the dead, I could hear him saying, "Maybe."

The only knowledge this question required was to know his heart.

But he was lost in the land of "maybe."

It was Friedrich Nietzsche who concluded, "There are no facts, only interpretations."

The real struggle is not with knowing the world beyond us,
but with knowing the world within us.

ENTRY #11 We Are All Decoding

IF DESCARTES GOT US STARTED WITH, "I THINK, THEREFORE I am," then we have moved far past that to "I feel, therefore it's true." You hear this in our everyday language. We talk about our own personal truth, or we deflect another person's opinion by saying, "Well, that's just your truth." Truth is now a personal possession. Where at one time we searched for truth, we now just create our own.

The problem is that our souls are more difficult to deceive than our minds.

We can talk ourselves into believing almost anything, but it's the spiritual equivalent of living on Prozac. Everything seems fine until twenty years later when you wake up and realize you don't feel anything. Don't confuse your soul's need for truth with your being the source of truth. Your soul craves to believe. The danger is not to take this seriously enough and to settle for believing in just anything.

We live in a time of endless information and unparalleled knowledge, and we have become increasingly incapable of knowing ourselves. We don't just doubt the existence of God; we are drowning in self-doubt. The search for truth is more than an intellectual pursuit; it's the longing of the human spirit. If we find ourselves frustrated in this pursuit, we become vulnerable to surrendering our quest and choosing to circumvent our search by either giving up on truth or, even more dangerous, convincing ourselves that we are the source of truth.

We are even compulsively connected to meaning. We give meaning to everything. Grab your pencil or pen and start tapping it against your desk. Just start listening to that arbitrary, meaningless clicking sound you're making. Back in the 1800s, Samuel Morse and Alfred Vail developed a code sequence that began to connect dots and dashes into letters. This system of communication through what would seem to be meaningless sounds became a primary way of communicating through the telegraph. What were once just long and short marks, tones, or pulses soon became a foundation for language.

Speaking of language, here's another place where humans are able to create meaning. Really, if you break it down, language is nothing more than a specific number of sounds used to construct and communicate meaning.

Or just turn on Korean television or Telemundo or submerge yourself in any language that you don't know at all. It's nothing but meaningless noise to you—unintelligible, indistinguishable sounds. But as you learn a language, all that noise moves to sound, and that sound soon begins to communicate meaning.

Oh! And when you open that dictionary or as you're reading these pages, what are you really looking at? Nothing but symbols.

It was a fifteen-year-old boy, blinded by a tragic accident, who found sixty-three ways to use a six-dot cell to communicate meaning. By the age of twelve, Louis Braille had begun a journey that would lead to the development of a system of reading and writing for the blind. Imagine finding a way to make six dots tell any story, communicate any theory, bring meaning into a world gone dark.

Here, read this: Fjislghiel. Mean anything to you? I didn't think so; doesn't mean much to me either. How about this: /SKWROEU? Mean anything to you? Now to Holly, that's different. What we're looking at is the stenographic version of the word *joy*. So when Holly hears me say the word *joy*, her court reporting equipment translates that into /SKWROEU, which means nothing to us until

SOUL CRAVINGS

it's retranslated into these three symbols, J-O-Y. And we know exactly what that means.

While I am sitting here at the computer, my wife, Kim, hands me a glossary of terms. It takes me a few minutes to recognize the language. Check out your language skills:

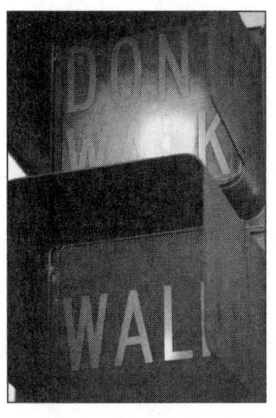

GMTA

FYE

WDSLM

LOL

TMI

YOYO

In case you need help: "Great minds think alike;" "for your entertainment;" "Why doesn't she love me?;" "laugh out loud;" "too much information;" "You're on your own."

All of these characters are no different than the unintelligible symbols. They are lines and curves and angles organized together in a pattern that somehow communicates a specific meaning to every person who understands that specific language. This, by the way, is all the English language is—individual characters brought together to create meaning. Open your dictionary, and instead of reading the actual words, just go down the page reading nothing but the phonetic spelling. It gives you a clear picture of what's going on. The Chinese Kanji, on the other hand, is an art-form language with a seemingly endless number of symbols, each of which contains a story.

We give meaning to taps; we give meaning to sounds; we give meaning to symbols; we even give meaning to smells, colors, facial expressions, hand movements, and touch. We are meaning machines. We even sometimes read meaning that isn't there or try to read between the lines. We are so nuanced we will even ask ourselves, *I heard what he said, but is that what he really means?*

Recently I saw a report on how Disney has opened up Disney Tokyo. It's a lot like Disneyland in California or Disney World in Florida, except that they had to bring in a feng shui expert because design has spiritual implications for their Asian clientele. We give meaning to space and place. From binary codes to dress codes, everything means something to us. Truth be told, our need to define and describe, to understand and explain, to prove and refute, is out of control. We are designed for meaning and desperate for it.

We even give meaning to meaningless things. That, of course, is called superstition.

Superstition is, at the very least, an improper relationship between cause and effect. You know, step on the crack, break your mother's back; seven years of bad luck for breaking a mirror; wearing a cross but living like hell; 777 is good, but 666 is bad, unless you're Asian, and then fours are bad and eights are very good. By the way, I was born on 8/28/58. I'm feeling very good about that. Superstitions are endless and everywhere, which is where our need for meaning can become tragic.

ENTRY #12 It's All in How You Look at It

THE NICE THING ABOUT A SEARCH FOR TRUTH IS THAT WE can keep it impersonal. Our language can make it look like our interest in what is real is just a matter of inquiry. It's all just an objective pursuit. But there is a subtle difference between truth and honesty. We can be on a search for truth but never be honest with ourselves. There is no such thing as a purely objective process, at least as long as a human being is involved.

Whether we like to admit it or not, observation is always affected by not only the objective, but also the subjective. We bring our own perceptions to the research. If somehow our observations could be purely objective, our opinions and predispositions would inevitably affect the conclusions drawn. Data are not information until data are interpreted. In other words, for something to make sense to us, it cannot remain outside us. We do not simply study information and then come to a conclusion; we absorb it and come to a personal interpretation of what is real.

I was listening to a lecture in which the speaker referred to studies in neuroscience that describe the process from which the human brain gathers and holds information. He explained that when the human brain absorbs information, that information is one part data and six parts emotion. Now that's a fascinating thought—that everything we remember is wrapped around everything we experience. When you reflect on this, it makes perfect sense.

You spend hours and hours studying books, reviewing lectures, and listening to tapes in hopes that you can ace a chemistry test. But even though you didn't take any time at all trying to memorize your childhood, the memories are vivid. I can tell you exactly what my wife, Kim, was wearing the first time I met her. It was a black dress with purple flowers on it, black shoes. By the way, I had no idea she was going to become my wife.

The more emotions attached to an experience, the easier it is for us to retain the data.

If neuroscience is right, there isn't one iota of objective information in your brain; it's all wrapped around by experience and emotion. Maybe it's not just that we like math when we're good at it; maybe it's also that we're good at it when we like it. The very fact that we have a positive experience makes it easier for us to retain large amounts of information.

So how does this affect our search for meaning? What are the implications when it comes to our quest for truth? Truth is never simply objective. It is never purely impersonal. Whatever we conclude is true comes to us through a process that is informed both by our experiences and by our perceptions.

Our search for truth is deeply personal.

No matter how much we like to think of ourselves as entirely objective, everyone's search for meaning begins in the subjective and ends in the subjective. However you decide on the best process for evaluating what is true, it began with your asking the question, *What's really going on here?* And whether you are comfortable with openly acknowledging it, it always ends with *This is what I believe to be true.* The journey for everyone is subjective-objective-subjective, which makes me wonder if our search for truth is nothing less than an S.O.S.

When I was around eight or nine, I loved reading science fiction. Robert Heinlein, Andre Norton, and Ray Bradbury join the list of the more well-known authors, J. R. R. Tolkien and C. S. Lewis. Somewhere along the way I read about a man who was driven insane not by his ability to count every raindrop that fell, but by his maddening ability to count the spaces in between them. Since then I have always been fascinated with how we process information—not just how we come to know things, but what things we choose to know.

Clearly we can't know everything. Even the attempt at it results in insanity. Genius might be less how much you know and more the ability to know the right things.

Does anyone really need to know how many raindrops fell on Seattle last year? If you think about it, it's as important not to know certain things as it is to know anything. My understanding is that Attention Deficit Disorder is the result of an overload of information. To function effectively, we have to be able to filter information out.

Donald E. Broadbent did some studies in the late 1950s on human perception. Basically he proposed that our perceptual system processes only that which it believes to be most relevant. Every one of us has selective sensory perception (SSP). It keeps us from counting the raindrops and remaining entirely unaware of the spaces between them. When it works well, we don't even notice it. But sometimes our SSP betrays us.

You're driving through an intersection. Next thing you know, you hear a loud crash. You never saw it coming. In fact, in the police report you describe the driver as "coming out of nowhere." What really happened was that your SSP filtered out critical information by treating it as irrelevant.

Thomas Kuhn, whose theories developed around the same time as Broadbent's, introduced the concept of paradigms. In his landmark work, *The Structure of Scientific Revolutions,* he proposes that all scientific work requires an established framework from which reality is perceived—in other words, a paradigm. A paradigm is essential in that it allows us to engage the outside world with the constancy necessary to observe it and make predictions.

At the same time, it defines reality and discredits or reorganizes any information that contradicts our present view of reality. While our paradigm helps us deal with reality, it also blinds us to new realities.

Our paradigms can make us incapable of seeing what is real. Both Broadbent and Kuhn raise important cautions in our search for meaning. Like when our SSP doesn't see the car coming right at us or when our paradigm blinds us to an ever-present reality, our present beliefs and experiences may actually make us unaware of the overwhelming proof of God all around us.

It was Rene Magritte who observed, "Each thing we see hides something else we want to see."

Yet in a slip of the tongue, psychologist Thane Pittman inadvertently declared, "I'll see it when I believe it."

We might find that this is truer than the reverse.

ENTRY #13 Home Alone

PROBABLY THE REOCCURING QUESTION I GET FROM people who are struggling with the existence of God concerns the issue of evil and human suffering. It's kind of hard to believe in God when he lets us screw up the world so badly. It's like kids wreaking havoc because they're home alone. Yeah, the kids should have been more responsible, but the parents should have known better. Or were they absolutely oblivious to what their kids were capable of?

The short version of the argument sort of goes like this: *If there is a God, why does he allow such horrible things to happen?*

So let's say there is no God.

If we agree that there is no God, is there still evil in the world? Are we still living on a planet filled with violence? Is our history still marred by murder, oppression, and corruption? Are there still hundreds of millions of people starving while we callously throw away our leftovers?

If there is no God, is there still evil?

The answer, of course, is yes.

Well, if there is no God and we still have a problem of evil, who should we hold responsible?

> **The good thing about God
> is that we can blame him
> for everything.**

But the question remains: Who's to blame?

Who's to blame that millions of people are going to die of AIDS in Africa? That millions of children are left orphaned and starving without any help or hope? That women are set on fire in India so that their husbands can be free to marry someone else and pick up another dowry? That millions of people are buried in the killing fields of Cambodia? That millions of children are living in urban garbage dumps throughout Latin America, homeless and alone?

There's no God, so we can't blame him.

Now that we've eliminated God, who's left?

All we have left is us.

Part of our problem in making sense of life is that we can't even make sense of ourselves. We want to blame God because we don't want to take responsibility for our mess. We stop believing in God because he won't change it. Is it possible that God does, in fact, exist, and we are still fully responsible for the human condition?

Is it possible that God created us with the power to create the world of our choosing?

In truth it is not we who have a right to be mad at God, but it is God who has a right to be mad at us. Usually what follows is our God-is-still-to-blame catch-22. Even if it's our fault, why doesn't God fix it? Exactly how would he do that? Let's consider the options.

For God to create a perfect world, there seems to be a limited number of scenarios possible. The first scenario is, he could just get rid of all of us. That would pretty much fix the problem right away. I'm personally not for that one, so let's move on to the next option. He could control our every thought, our every emotion, our every motive, our every action. Because he's God, he could do it in such a way that we would feel as if we have free will.

We would be the products of a divinely created illusion, a utopia. This version would be a planet-wide version of the *Stepford Wives*, you

entry 13

know, the place where everything is perfect because you really can't choose for yourself. I'm not for a world where we do not have free will, where choosing is an illusion. I am personally grateful that God has created us as thinking creatures with the capacity to choose.

For God to create us in such a way that we can choose that which is good, true, and beautiful, he must also allow us the freedom to choose that which is corrupt, false, and destructive.

Most of us want God to fix every wrong choice we make without taking from us our right to choose wrongly. We want to make God into our own personal pooper-scooper following right behind us, cleaning up our mess. God lets us make our bed and makes us lie in it.

There is another option, however. Given that there is a God, he cares about humanity, and he is deeply troubled by the human condition, how could God proceed to actively engage the human dilemma? If God refuses to take from us our free will and he refuses to leave the world in its present condition, what can he do?

Here's an interesting possibility: He could change our hearts. He could take us through a process that would move us from greed to altruism, that would move us from indifference to compassion, that would move us from hate to love, that would move us from apathy to activism. If he could change us, he could change the world (other version: By changing us, he can change the world).

There was once a Roman citizen named Saul of Tarsus who was a religious fanatic and murderer, and he eventually had an encounter with Jesus Christ. He is best known as Paul. He turned from a life of condemnation and violence to becoming a champion of love, hope, and faith.

It may seem way too simple, but the world will change when we change.

ENTRY #14 The Truth Is, It's About Trust

THE WORLD WILL GET BETTER WHEN WE GET BETTER. WITH all the progress that we've made since the Enlightenment, we've got to be honest with ourselves and admit that we're not getting better, which is one reason we're quickly losing our confidence in science. There was a time when science was our promise of a better world. We would outgrow our worst primal instincts. This, in part, was the hope of the Enlightenment, that we would educate and elevate ourselves out of violence.

We were the masters of progress, and one day we would no longer hate each other, abuse the powerless, instigate wars, or in any way be inhumane. Science was a promise of progress. We had outgrown God. We no longer needed him to make us good. We could not only be good without God, but through our achievements, we could actually make ourselves better.

Then there were Hiroshima and Nagasaki. Even if we found ourselves standing on the winning side, something in our gut told us that we were all losers in this. Science wasn't creating a better world for us, but a more dangerous one. It seems as if we can improve on everything except ourselves.

If science and God are enemies, how come we tend to blame God even for what science corrupts?

Even Einstein acknowledged the problem was within us: "The release of atom power has changed everything except our way of thinking. The solution to this problem lies in the heart of mankind. If only I had known, I should have become a watchmaker."

 entry 14

In other words, it is better to keep us stupid if we can't become good. The less technology we have, the less damage we can do.

It was in the middle of the last century when we knew that all the technology in the world would not create for us the paradise that had been lost. Maybe it was right to conclude that we can't trust religion or philosophy or history or government or institutions, but what we know for certain is that we can't trust science, and all for the same reason. They're all connected to people, which brings us to the inseparable relationship between truth and trust.

When I was a philosophy student in college, I was struck by how every writer and each belief system had something within it that was compelling. Yet it eventually became clear that every system of thought had gaping holes and shortcomings. Even before I became a follower of Jesus Christ, even when I considered myself a Socratic, I could see that in the end it all comes down to faith. I found myself moving from one view to another and then to another. And I had all the passion of youth to back it up. After a while I began to see beliefs as fluid, interchangeable, and disposable. I couldn't help wondering if Locke or Hume or Rousseau really knew any better than I did. They were clearly smarter than I am, but I felt certain that behind closed doors, they were just as uncertain.

We were all wanderers in the same forest trying to find a fresh trail to truth.

Some believed God was down the road ahead. Others were convinced it was all a dead end. Maybe we had nothing in common except that we were all lost and trying to find our way. It's hard to be the guide when you don't know where you're going.

In the midst of all this uncertainty, we made a shift from looking for the answers to looking at the questions—which is why I liked Socrates so much (not to mention that he was willing to die for his convictions).

Even when we don't know what is ultimately true, most of us would follow someone whom we absolutely trust. There's an inseparable relationship between truth and trust, and God, it seems, is lost in between the two.

Accuracy is less important to us than authenticity.

If no one knows the answer, does anyone know the way?

I began looking for truth in an entirely new way. I was no longer looking for the best idea but the best life. Whatever I would come to believe in, it could not simply change my mind; it had to change my life. Was any truth out there not simply worth believing in but becoming it? What does an idea look like when it is fleshed out? That's where Jesus came into the picture. His words were straight to the point. His was more than a claim to know the truth; He claimed that he *was* the truth. The implication of this claim is huge. Is it possible that truth is more than an idea and that it is found in God? What Jesus is telling us is that truth exists in God and comes from God.

When we search for truth, we search for God. Our souls crave the One who is true.

Truth does not exist in a vacuum. Truth exists because God can be trusted. When our souls drive us to search for truth, we are actually longing for God. It's easier just to trust in myself. If you think it's easy to believe in God, you can't even begin to imagine how hard it is to put your trust in him. I had moved from searching for a system of beliefs to searching for someone I could believe in. Somehow I had moved from truth to trust.

This is at the core of our search for meaning.

ENTRY #15 Bloody Sunday Leads
to Cheap Monday

SEVERAL YEARS AGO, I WAS INVITED TO A DIALOGUE WITH Dallas Willard, professor of philosophy at the University of Southern California, where he proposed a thought that was both refreshing and breathtaking. He looked at a group of philosophers, academics, and spiritual leaders and proposed that followers of Jesus Christ were required to pursue truth wherever it leads them.

Jesus pursued truth regardless of where that quest took him. Truth defined his journey regardless of the implications or the consequences. He calls us to nothing less. He would have it no other way. I was profoundly affected by that thought. The implications, of course, are astonishing . . . To be true to the way of Jesus, you cannot follow with blind allegiance.

You can never justify any belief or action where you consciously deny what is true, even if called to do so in the name of God.

The name and reputation of Jesus have absolutely been dragged through the gutter by the actions of those who have hijacked the Christian faith. Earlier today I was reading about a new jean company in Sweden whose owner is an activist against Christianity.

Cheap Monday is a punk-rock, trendy, tight-fit jean that is both popular and controversial. Its logo is a skull with an upside down cross on its forehead. The jeans maker calls it more of a joke, but its designer says there's a deeper message.

"It is an active statement against Christianity. . . . Atldax insists he has a purpose beyond selling denim: to make people question Christianity, which he calls a 'force of evil' that he blames for sparking wars through-out history."

Get ready. They're already in Norway, Denmark, Britain, the Netherlands, France, Australia, and are on their way to the United States It would be a tragedy to have people missing out on Jesus because of unthinkable things done in his name. And while being a follower of Christ requires a life of faith, it also requires a love for truth. To represent Jesus well, we cannot live thoughtless lives.

Jesus never called us to follow him without thought or reflection. This is important because so many things have been done in Jesus' name that history has proven were not only ill-advised but even inhumane. You can't just write it off as, "Well, the church told me to do that." History would have been a much better place without the Inquisitions and the Crusades, not to mention the KKK, but all of them have used a cross to lead the way. It's a fascinating thought that Jesus would rather have us do what is right than what is "Christian."

Earlier I mentioned I killed a bird. It might have been a mock-ingbird. I hope not, because it's the Florida state bird and I think that makes it illegal. I'm reminded by Harper Lee's classic novel that it's a sin *to kill a mockingbird* because they don't do one thing but sing their hearts out for us. Great, it just keeps getting worse. With all the violence ever done in the name of God, you need to know Jesus clearly taught us another way. We are not supposed to be like the condemning and murderous citizens of Maycomb, but rather like Atticus Finch's movement, defending the innocent and fighting for justice.

Whether you like it or not, you need to believe.

entry 15

You get to choose in what and you get to choose how much you will believe or how little. You are already a universe of belief. Whether you believe in science or Buddha or Jesus or Oprah or yourself, you believe in something. While you may have thought yourself above the need to believe, you're just like the rest of us.

You get to pick what you believe in, but you have no say over your need to believe. You shouldn't really need to make sense of life to enjoy it, but there it is every day nagging at you.

Believing as an intellectual exercise is difficult enough, but our need to believe goes much deeper than that. The Enlightenment changed what it means to believe. To believe can mean nothing more than to agree with the data. When Jesus spoke of believing, he meant something very different. To believe is to wrap your soul around something. To believe in God has to do with trusting. What you believe in is what you trust in and, more important, who you trust.

The loss of truth isn't so much rational as it is relational. When you conclude you can't trust anyone, you'll find yourself quickly concluding that there is no truth. The rejection of absolutes has as much to do with our distrust for authority as with anything else. We have created a new kind of paranoia—everyone is out to deceive us. When we decide there is no one left to trust, all we have left to do is run and hide. When we declare that truth cannot be known, we're really saying that no one can be trusted.

"That's just your truth" is another way of saying, "I don't trust you." You are not a valid source of information. What you consider fact, I consider opinion. Personal truth doesn't require any outside validation—only sincerity. It is a retreat from our search for meaning. It is our attempt to escape the barrage of deception and betrayal that has led us to run and hide from the very thing our souls long for.

When all you stand on is subjective truth, you're really declaring you are the only one you can trust, which is a pretty scary place to be when you realize that all of us are filled with self-doubt and are limited in what we know.

In the end, it's all about trust. Can anyone be trusted? Is there anyone who is trustworthy? Truth is a very personal thing. Truth is not simply something we come to know, but something that becomes a part of us. Whatever we conclude is truth directly affects not only what we believe, but also who we become.

Margaret Wheatley reminds us that information both informs us and forms us. This is especially true when it comes to our search for meaning. Anything that is not true is irrelevant and unimportant; it just doesn't matter.

So if you don't believe God exists, he becomes irrelevant to your life.

If you don't believe there's actually a famine in Africa, it's irrelevant to your life.

If you don't believe there's an environmental crisis with the decay of the ozone, it's irrelevant to your life.

No famine, no need for generosity.

No ozone crisis, no need for emissions controls.

No God, no need for humanity.

**Truth isn't something you conclude;
truth is something you become.**

Who you decide you can trust
   inevitably becomes
      your source of truth.

ENTRY #16 Truth Eventually Gets Personal

OUR NEED TO TRUST GIVES US INSIGHT INTO OUR SEARCH for truth. Several years ago, I was invited to speak at a national conference for Wall Street investors in San Francisco. I remember someone mentioning the smallest fund was somewhere around $9 billion. That was about $9 billion larger than my personal investment account. One of our spiritual and business leaders had secured the opportunity for me to speak on future trends and on the need for ethics in the world of Wall Street. We were sitting at dinner the night before my presentations were to begin, and before the table was complete with all of the assigned guests to be seated, the others began talking about the one investor who had not yet come.

To summarize the description, he was brilliant, tough, successful, and a professor of economics and a graduate of Harvard. He finally joined the party, and within a few minutes he asked me who I was and what I did. Rick Yamamoto, who had brought me, explained that I was the futurist who was to speak the next day. We had met no more than three minutes earlier, and he already felt free to mock me openly.

I love how people warm up to me, feel right at home.

He taunted the concept of a futurist. He went on to elaborate that futurists had projected the American population and had been off by a hundred million. His conclusion, of course, was if futurists can't even get how many people are going to be here right now, is there anything they can get right? I went on to explain that there's a difference between a futurist and a psychic. My particular expertise was to look at human values and project where our values will take us.

I don't really think he was listening at first, just waiting for me to breathe so that he could pick up where he left off: "You want to know what makes the world go round. You want an explanation for what is happening around the world and what will determine where we're going? It's all economics. It's nothing but economics."

This was a huge surprise, coming from an economist. Even the table filled with investors began to protest, if only mildly. I think to their surprise I resisted their support and told them I totally agreed if he would concede one thing—economics is nothing more than the agreement of value. In other words, nothing has value until two or more people agree on what it's worth. It's only when that worth is determined and agreed upon that there can be any form of trade.

He immediately agreed: "That's exactly right."

So I went back to my original point: "All economics does is place a value on things. All I do is look at what people value. We could stop there, but that's only the surface.

"If I'm going to do my job well, I need to go deeper, to ask why we value these things, and to press against those values and think through their implications.

"Everything is about economics if economics is simply the external application of values.

"But if this is true, then to understand economics, you have to understand what humans value, why they value those things, and how we change our values."

This was the beginning of a great conversation. It lasted for hours, long after the dinner was over, long after the tables were folded and the chairs put away. We sat there together talking about economics—or maybe it was a conversation about human values.

Eventually I explained to him that my primary focus was the human spirit. He was fast to respond, "I don't believe in the human spirit,"

SOUL CRAVINGS

which led us to the same conversation we're having in this book, that there are intrinsic evidences of God and that God has placed within us undeniable proof that he exists. The economist was as inquisitive as he was brilliant, and he graciously invited me to continue. We finally came at this point to a conversation about truth and trust.

I suggested that an intrinsic evidence of God is that all of us are searching for truth; we're all trying to make sense of life.

We took this a little further and moved this to the need for trust. His immediate response was that trust is necessary for commerce. I had to admire him for his consistency. He believed in money, like I believe in God. He could explain away our need to trust by simply explaining that we have to trust each other for trade to happen. Whether we like it or not, we are required to trust or we'll starve.

I said, "Yes, this might explain why you have to trust someone. This might also explain why you need people to trust you. Now can you explain why you have it in your heart to want to be trustworthy?"

I admitted I was making an assumption, but I told him I believe he is no different than me in this. I do need to trust people. You can't live without trusting people. I do need people to trust me. You can't accomplish anything without gaining a level of trust. But I also knew there was something inside me that longed to be trustworthy. I asked him if he was different than that.

He had two very clear options—I have no desire to be trustworthy, or it's more than something I simply need to be. I have a longing to be trustworthy, and I have no idea where that comes from.

It's a strange thing, but unless your heart has been totally hardened and your conscience entirely seared, even when you lie, there is something inside you that knows this is beneath you.

In the worst of us there's still a desire that aspires to be the best of us.

We are designed to trust, to gain trust, and to aspire to be trustworthy.

All of this is a part of how God has created us.

Our search for truth, our need to trust, and our struggle to be trustworthy are all evidences of the human spirit.

We will never escape these because, whether we believe in God or not, we are still created in his image and likeness.

Because God is true, our souls will never find rest until we are also.

ENTRY #17 You've Gotta Know Who to Trust

We were driving home one afternoon and were bringing our nephew over to enjoy the day with us. My whole family was being entertained by this bright, inquisitive nine-year-old conversationalist. But he kept repeating a phrase over and over again. Now, in LA there are certain phrases that are beaten into the ground. Every other word is *like* or *you know what I mean*. But his was different.

He kept repeating the word *honest.*

After every sentence he kept saying *honest,* as if he felt a need to convince us.

I was struck by this pattern, so I finally asked him, "Why do you keep saying 'honest'?"

He responded without hesitation, "It's just that I really want you to believe me."

Then, without taking a breath, he added, "Or maybe it's because of all the lies I've told in my life."

Now that's an honest kid.

This was one insightful nine-year-old. The trustworthiness of any information is only as good as its source. If you discover that the source cannot be trusted, you will naturally conclude that nothing he said is true even if he told you the truth. The reason for this is simple—no matter how rational or objective you try to make a process to conclude something is true, it is always an act of faith.

**The more trustworthy you can determine the source is,
the shorter the leap of faith.**

MEANING

 entry 17

When we are searching for truth,
what we're really trying to do is figure out
who can be trusted.

When we conclude no one can be trusted, we find ourselves struggling with doubt and being afraid to commit. I've had this conversation over and over again—singles who are afraid to commit to marriage, students who are afraid to commit to a career, Christians who are afraid to commit to a church, seekers who are afraid to commit to God. This doubt is in all of us.

The less you trust in someone, the less likely you are to commit. The more you trust someone, the easier it is to commit your life to that one.

This is one reason why the approach of Jesus resonates so powerfully with my soul. Jesus didn't come advocating a better idea. While history is filled with great teachers, being the best of them was never Jesus' goal or ambition. He never said to his disciples, "This is the truth. Follow it." Instead, he said something far more compelling. Jesus' claim was nothing less than "I am the truth."

Jesus moves truth from impersonal to personal.

He moved it from rational to relational. He was telling his disciples the truth isn't an answer; it is a person. You don't come to know the truth as a result of an academic pursuit. You might discover an endless number of things that are true along the way, but this is not the truth your soul is craving. No matter how many true things you come to know, they will never leave you satisfied until you find your way to the One who is the very source of truth.

Jesus didn't come to show us a better way or point us to a better life, but instead invites us to know him as the One who is the way, the truth, and the life. If all God wanted was to make sure that we knew the truth, Jesus didn't have to come. It would have been more than enough to carve commandments from stone or to have scribes pen the pages of the Scriptures. But as sacred as I might hold the Law of Moses or the words of the prophets or the writings of the apostles, they are simply not enough. It's simply not enough to know what is true. We need far more than that.

We need to know the One who is true. Jesus walked among us not so that he could get to know us but so that we could come to know him. God himself stepped into human history so that we would know that he is not only the source of truth, but that he is utterly and completely trustworthy.

ENTRY #18 Why Crawl When You Can Jump?

AARON WAS AROUND TWO YEARS OLD, IN THAT STAGE between crawling and walking. We heard somewhere that the longer your kids crawl, the better they will be able to read, so we encouraged the scooting and let him take his time on the walking. Seems like a strange connection, doesn't it, between crawling and reading? But the longer I live, the more I've come to realize that seemingly unrelated things are far more connected than they first appear.

The only part of the crawling stage that was driving me crazy was that he kept insisting on crawling up the stairs to the second floor of our house. This was a problem because he was great at crawling up but incapable of crawling down. So day after day, sometimes hour after hour, I would hear Aaron crying from the second floor, pleading for someone to come and help him back down the stairs.

This was cute the first couple of times, but cute only goes so far.

At first I tried to calmly explain that he was not allowed to climb up the stairs. It kind of makes you wonder who's denser, the two-year-old who can't seem to understand the rules or the thirty-two-year-old who actually thinks the two-year-old will listen. So it became my daily ritual to retrieve Aaron from upstairs. Since we couldn't get him to cooperate, we decided to buy a gate that would block the staircase. Before we knew it, Aaron had pried the screws right out of the wall, removed the gate, and found his way to freedom, which, of course, left him trapped on the second floor.

Come to think of it, it's not much different from the way a lot of us live our lives. We use our freedom to get where we want to go and then find ourselves trapped and can't get out without help.

Anyway, the gate idea was an inadequate solution to a grand problem. I hate climbing up stairs—bad knees, you know. This was going to require an intervention. I was going to have to catch him in the act and take control of the situation. One afternoon I watched him scooting around behind the furniture, and I knew exactly where he was heading. When he was convinced I wasn't paying attention, he made a break for the stairs. I let him climb about halfway up, and then I sneaked around the corner.

In my best I-am-your-father voice, I stepped out and commanded him to stop and to immediately come down.

I began to think to myself, *He's only two. He probably just doesn't know any better.* But I could see it in his eyes. He knew better. He knew exactly what was going on. He was absolutely clear that he was violating the no-trespassing zone. It wasn't a lack of understanding; it was an act of defiance. That just made me even angrier.

With fire in my eyes, I said, "Aaron, you get down right now."

I could almost hear his brain working. He was considering his options. He looked up, assessing the probability of whether he could make it without being stopped. He looked down and seemed only to remember why down was never an option.

Then he did the strangest thing.

He rose to his feet and turned toward me and, with a look of desperation, simply said, "Daddy, carry me." I almost gave in, but somehow I knew this was a defining moment. This was an epic battle for who would rule. If I gave in now, he would control me forever.

So I said, "No. You got up; you get down."

He paused, seemed to reflect, and repeated, "Daddy, carry me."

I knew I needed to stand firm, so I repeated, "No. You get down."
He asked me once again, and once again I refused.

Then it happened. I never would have expected it. It took me entirely
by surprise.

He jumped.

He jumped right to me. Even when I refused to carry him, he somehow concluded that I would catch him.

Well, we couldn't have that. So as painful as it was, I just moved out
of the way and let him go crashing into the wall across the hall.

I'm just kidding.

Of course, I didn't. It never even occurred to me. All I did was act
on instinct.

When he jumped, I just reached out my arms and caught him. I
brought him close and held him tightly. It was one of the best moments
of my life. I don't know when I've ever felt so close to a my son. He was
only two. If I asked him to tell me who God was, he would have had
no idea. Imagine if I had asked him to explain how the world came into
existence. The truth is, he knew very little about the world around him.
In fact, he knew very little about me.

He didn't know my history, had never looked for a police report, had
never done a background check. As far as he knew I could have been a
mass murderer or an escaped convict or a hockey player. Clearly, though,
he knew more than I thought.

He knew if he jumped, I would catch him.

He was afraid to even attempt to climb down but was more than
confident to jump off.

He had more confidence in me than he did in himself.

Sometimes we try to make truth sound like it's all about information, but really Aaron didn't know much about me when it came to information. He didn't even really know my name. I was just Daddy. The truth is not about data. Truth is more than the gathering of information.

Truth is about trust.

If nothing can be trusted, then there is no truth. Then life really is arbitrary and meaningless. But the truth is, Aaron was right. He could trust me with his life. He knew something deeper than information.

He had come to know something far deeper than knowledge. He knew me.

Aaron knew he could trust me. There was so much he didn't know, so much that was uncertain to him. Most of the world was a mystery. You would think all that doubt would paralyze him, but he didn't really have to know everything. In the end, if the only thing you know is who you can trust, it can take you a long way. If you would come to trust God, you might find yourself jumping right into his arms.

ENTRY #19 A Healthy Faith in Doubts

YOU WERE CREATED WITH AN INSATIABLE THIRST FOR TRUTH. You will always crave it, even when you run from it. It is always God's desire to move you toward truth. He created you with a drive to pursue it.

From your first breath, you have been on a journey, and a significant part of it has been a search for meaning. Contrary to what you may have been told all your life, God is not offended by questions, even questions about his existence.

God created you to question.

He made you inquisitive and curious and has placed within you an unquenchable thirst for knowledge—not for information, but for meaning. We need to know.

As we were reminded weekly by Mulder and Scully, the truth is out there.

When Aaron was about fifteen, he and I were driving in the car to an event, and in one of the many dad-son conversations we've had, he began to open up his heart about his spiritual journey.

"Dad, I think if I hadn't been born in a Christian home, I wouldn't be a Christian."

I have to admit I wasn't really ready for that. He caught me totally off guard. You might be able to imagine, as a pastor, this wasn't the most exciting news to hear. It seemed like in that moment my heart broke in two—half dropped to the bottom of my gut, giving me a sick feeling, and the other half became a lump in my throat.

Aaron has always been able to talk to me about anything, and I didn't want that to change now, so I calmly responded, "Really, buddy, why's that?"

"I have so many doubts and questions."

I have to admit, that response was a huge relief to me. I can live with that one.

But what would have grieved me is if he had said, "I just don't see it in your life," or "I've been around this stuff for a long time and I just don't think it's real."

I'm more aware than anyone that I'm a flawed human being. It would have just broken my heart to think that Aaron might not believe in God because of inconsistency in my life. Isn't the overwhelming accusation against Christianity that the church is full of hypocrites? I have always hoped that sincerity would override imperfection.

Doubts and questions—what a relief.

I said, "Oh, doubts and questions—I have those too." He seemed to find a certain assurance in my common experience. We sat silently for a moment as we were driving down the road.

Finally, I broke the silence by asking him, "So what do you think you're going to do?"

I'll never forget his response. "Well, I've met God, so what can I do?"

I simply nodded in agreement and said, "Yeah, I know what you mean. Once you've met God, what can you do?"

It really wasn't that different from over a dozen years before when, at the age of two, Aaron decided to jump into my arms. I'm sure his little two-year-old mind was filled with doubts and questions. There was just one thing he knew—me—me in relationship to him.

But now it wasn't between me and him; it was between him and God. I'm glad I had the privilege to be the father he could trust, but far beyond that, way past how important it is to me that my son knows I'm there for him, I'm grateful to know he has come to know and trust the God who tells us to call Him Father. Maybe that's exactly why Jesus chose this particular metaphor to describe God to us.

There are a lot of words attached to God—*Lord, Master, King, Almighty, Sovereign.* This one just seems a misfit on the list—*Father.*

Is it possible that thousands of years before we found ourselves where we are today, God already knew that our search for truth would lead us back to a far more human question: *Is there anyone I can trust?*

A few months back i had the opportunity to consult with New Line Cinema about one of their upcoming films entitled *Nativity.* Among the many questions that were asked popped up this one: "Why does the Bible call God Father?" My answer was simply, "I guess it was popular back then."

entry 19

ENTRY #20 It's Not Supposed to Make You Sick

What's so frustrating is that so many things that have the name of Jesus on the label have nothing to do with Jesus in the end. This is a real problem when we are trying to make sense of life. Most people I meet, whenever they learn of Jesus, are deeply drawn to him, yet many of them keep themselves at a distance from Jesus all the same. It doesn't take long to realize that what restrains them from trusting in Jesus is not the compelling nature of Hinduism or humanism or Buddhism or even atheism. The real obstacle that most people struggle with when it comes to Jesus is this thing called Christianity. I've never been a real fan of religion anyway. Once during a series of lectures at Borders in West LA (near UCLA), a very kind and compassionate woman told me that I shouldn't be so hard on religion, that it was a great halfstep in a person's journey toward God. I told her that my experience was exactly the opposite.

Usually religion is a halfstep away from God.

Another time a self-proclaimed atheist e-mailed me the most surprising letter. He sent me a passionate argument for the value of religion. He accused me of being too hard on religions in general and advocated their value as a psychological catharsis. I e-mailed back that I found myself in a surprising place in my relationship with him. He was a religious atheist, and I was an irreligious pastor. I tried to explain to him as a follower of Jesus Christ that I felt it was important to expose and oppose corruption anywhere I found it, whether it was in Islam or in the U.S. government, whether it was in Catholicism or in evangelical Christianity.

Whenever religion is used to manipulate or control people, I consider it the enemy of humanity and the enemy of God.

I just don't have a lot of patience for people who use the name of God to try to control people through guilt and shame. If God's love isn't freely given, it's not worth receiving anyway—because then it wouldn't be real. It's a curious thing that Jesus is like a cold drink on a hot summer day, but Christianity can be like spoiled milk.

I took an international team to Damascus, Syria, in the summer of 2000. What an amazing place to travel and experience standing in the middle of one of the oldest cultures in the world, not to mention the capital for global terrorism. We were warned before we entered that choosing to go there was inherently dangerous and could even be lifethreatening. To my unfortunate surprise, they were right. The trip almost killed me. In fact, if I remember correctly, three of us were fighting for our lives.

We had been poisoned.

We traced it back to what we thought was the most innocent of things. All three of us drank Diet Coke. The can said "Diet Coke" in big, bold American-like print. It was the fine print that was far more important—"bottled in Syria." We thought we knew what we were getting, but we were tragically mistaken. Some mistakes don't cost you much; this one cost us everything we had, or at least everything we could heave. It looked like the real thing, but three of us lived as witnesses that it was a counterfeit.

There are unfortunate similarities between Syrian Diet Coke and Western Christianity. You can't let the name on the label fool you. You're not getting what you think you're getting. Just because Jesus and his logo are imprinted on the outside of the container doesn't mean that what you're drinking is the real thing. If you find yourself keeled over in agonizing pain, wondering why you're sick to your stomach, it may be that what you got was a counterfeit version of Jesus.

In the Apocalypse, Jesus speaks to a church in Laodicea, describing

entry 20

them as being neither hot nor cold, and he bluntly tells them, "Because you are lukewarm—neither hot nor cold—I am about to spit you out of my mouth." It may come as a surprise to you, but there are some expressions of Christianity that Jesus just can't stomach. It's like bad Diet Coke—either you spit it out, or it's going to make you sick.

It seems almost counterintuitive that there are people who are running hard and fast away from the church and are, at the same time, desperately and earnestly searching for God.

If you stepped into a toxic religious environment, you were right to run, even if Jesus' name was attached to it. And by the way, when you did that, you weren't running farther from Jesus, but closer to him. You just have to be careful not to come to the tragic conclusion that just because you've experienced something that was false and maybe even toxic, there is nothing that is good. Even when you find yourself frustrated, even when you feel that you've been duped or deceived, even when you think something is true and later discover it is false, you should take solace in this: something inside you knows the difference.

Something within you not only compels you to search for truth, but has a soul reaction to it.

ENTRY #21 Driving Blind Full Speed Ahead

ON MY FIRST TRIP TO INDIA WITH A GROUP OF FRIENDS, we had the opportunity to go from New Delhi to Agra. For years the road to Agra was considered the most dangerous road in the world. The whole team that was with me wanted to see the Taj Mahal, so we felt it was worth the risk

To make our journey safer and easier on us, we paid extra for a van that had air-conditioning and was guaranteed to be of the highest quality. When the van arrived, it didn't have air-conditioning, and it had only one working headlight.

It wasn't a problem on the way down to Agra; it was daytime.

Though the road was crowded with not only cars but various other modes of transportation (it seems Agra is the transportation system for not only cars and motorcycles, but for elephants and every other possible form of transportation you can imagine), it was the way back late that night that was perilous.

It was pitch black, there were no streetlights, and the width of the road was best suited to serve as a one-way but had traffic moving in both directions.

We thought we were at a deficit with only one headlight and soon discovered that we had one more than almost all the others on the road.

Tragically, when I returned to Los Angeles, I discovered that a young girl from our neighborhood in LA was killed in a car accident on that very same road during that same time.

Sometimes our search for meaning can feel a lot like being on the road to Agra—

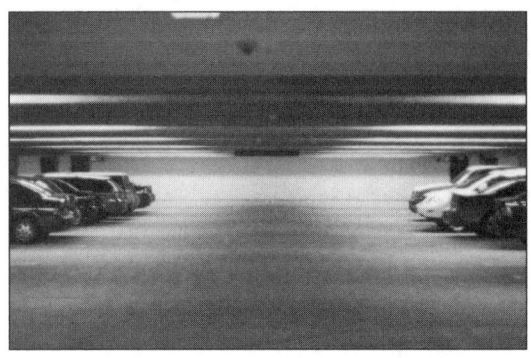

pitch black,
no headlights,
driving blind, and
desperate to find our way back.

Sometimes the only reason we keep going is that we don't want to stay where we are or go back to where we've been. But when life begins to fall apart, what do you do then? How do you make sense out of life then? Surely that would be a reasonable place to ask if God has any idea what he's doing or to demand to know what in the world is going on.

When we are drowning in the counterfeit, our souls become sick. When we are immersed in what is true, we begin to experience wholeness and health. Even when you feel like you're driving blind, full speed ahead in the middle of the night, you have to keep going; you have to continue searching for truth; you have to keep looking for meaning; you have to keep trying to make sense of life. When life doesn't make sense, it becomes all about trust. Sometimes you're driving full speed down a very dark road. All you can do is trust the driver and let him take you home.

ENTRY #22 Just Follow the Signs

IT COULDN'T HAVE BEEN MUCH DIFFERENT FOR THOSE early disciples investing everything in Jesus, trusting him with their lives, leaving everything to follow him. They believed in his message; they believed in him.

Then he was gone.

What do you do when Jesus dies right before your very eyes?

His followers evidently just went back to life as they knew it before they met him.

Well, not quite.

No, it was worse.

They went back to fishing, to surviving, but they were also hiding. They were afraid.

If this could happen to God, what in the world could happen to us? they thought.

And then it happened—Jesus appeared.

They were shocked, confused, and terrified.

They didn't know what to believe.

This didn't make any sense.

The first time Jesus showed up, Thomas was missing. Can you imagine spending the week hearing all your friends declaring adamantly that they had seen Jesus alive from the grave? I don't know if I would be convinced either.

Thomas's response was that of any thinking person. When they kept insisting, "We saw the Lord,"

Thomas drew the line in the sand: "I will not believe it until I see the nail marks in his hands and put my finger where the nails were and put my hand into his side."

A week later a handful of followers were meeting again, but this time Thomas was with them. The doors were locked, but there was Jesus. Somehow he came in and stood right in the midst of them. Once again, Jesus greeted them with calming words, "Peace be with you." It was almost as if Jesus felt for them, I know you're confused. I know nothing makes sense right now, but trust me. He then looked to Thomas and said to him, "Put your finger here, and look at my hands. Put your hand here in my side. Stop being an unbeliever and believe."

There wasn't really much left for Thomas to do. It must have been really hard to inhale right then. But somehow he managed the words that are so hard to say and yet so important to confess: "My Lord and my God!"

Never let anyone tell you that God is offended by your questions. Your questions will lead you to God. Your soul craves meaning even as it longs for God. To search for one is to find the other. Go ahead—question everything. We're all trying to make sense of this life that we've been thrown into. A lot of times the world doesn't help the process at all. We experience pain, disappointment, tragedy, betrayal. It fills us with doubt and bitterness and leaves us confused. I love that God understands that, that he knows life's a struggle.

And by the way, don't forget to listen; don't forget to look; the signs are all around you.

It was my daughter, Mariah's, fourteenth birthday weekend—February 3, 2006. She is really very talented musically, and I wanted to encourage this area of her life. The timing was perfect. I picked up her gift, then we caught a flight to Nashville where I was speaking at a conference. I told her the gift would be waiting in LA for her when she got back home.

She didn't want me to tell her what it was, but she kept asking for clues.

I gave her over a thousand signs pointing her to her gift. In fact, from the time we landed to the moment we left, she was barraged by signs but could never put the pieces together—until we were on the plane going home.

It was as if a light came on. She looked at me knowingly and said, "It's a guitar."

It wasn't just a guitar; it was a Gibson. Nashville is the home of Gibson. We stayed next to the Gibson Showcase where they make and repair their instruments. We actually visited the store, and she held the exact model she had waiting back home. Even as we walked the streets downtown, we saw Gibsons everywhere.

I think sometimes searching for God is like looking for a Gibson in Nashville.

The signs are everywhere. You just have to know what you're looking for.

We are all searching for truth.

We are all looking for God.

We crave meaning.

We long to trust.

We need to believe in something.

We need to believe in someone.

We need to believe in God.

Is it possible that God is like a father waiting for us to read the signs?

entry 22

SEEK

Sometimes I feel like my soul is nothing more than a leaky faucet. You know, the kind that drips all night long. It's not really a loud sound, but after hours and hours of *drip, drip, drip*, the sound not only echoes, it begins to intensify. The more silent the room, the louder the sound becomes. Before you know it, it consumes the whole room. You would give anything if you could just shut it off.

After a while, if the water keeps dripping long enough, it moves from deafening to silence. You just can't hear it anymore. It becomes white noise, backdrop. It's still making noise; it's still calling out, but you can't hear it anymore. It goes from thunder to silence and, then when you least expect it, back to thunder.

Soul cravings are like that. They scream in your head until your ears hurt. But after a while, it's a silent scream. You can't hear it anymore, and you could almost deny it completely except for the echo deep within the hollowness of your soul. You don't know what your soul wants. You can't find what your soul needs, so you lose your soul. You just have to ignore it and go on.

The Foo Fighters put my frustration to music.

All my life I've been searching for something
　　Something never comes
　　　Never leads to nothing
　　　　Nothing satisfies but I'm getting close
　　　　　Closer to the prize at the end of the rope.

Remember when you were a kid and all you wanted was dessert? Ever watched someone eat all the candy or ice cream he wanted until he never wanted to see another piece of candy or a cone again? That's what feeding my soul is like. It keeps confusing what it wants with what it needs. Or maybe my soul just isn't convinced until I'm sick to my stomach that the former is not the latter.

Buddha was right about desires: they really can make you sick. Sometimes the worst thing for you is to get what you want. Desires and passions can lead you down a very dark path. Buddha must have experienced the same frustration as I did and decided the only way through this was to get rid of all his desires.

Now millions of his followers pursue the elimination of all desires. I guess for him it was pretty simple: if your desires keep making your soul sick, get rid of them—all of them. Personally, I have found this impossible, but I understand the sentiment. I'm not even Buddha, and I've figured out that what my head, heart, and body desire is not necessarily what my soul needs.

We can get lost in desires and never find what our souls long for.

Instead of facing the hard reality that what we're pursuing is not what our souls crave, we just try to solve the problem by getting more—more toys, more money, more power, more prestige, more sex, more stuff. We spend our lives trying to satisfy our souls. Some things are only a facade. Some things satisfy for a moment. Some things deaden our souls.

It's kind of weird when you think about it—to gain the whole world and lose our souls.

Sometimes it feels less like we've lost our souls and more like we're lost inside them. Our souls are an endless universe but can become an abyss.

Scientists tell us that the cosmos is ever expanding, that it's an infinite amount of space waiting to be explored and discovered. I think that pretty much describes the human spirit. There's no end to how far you can travel inside yourself. With every breath you take, with every day you live, with every new experience you have, your soul expands.

You are on a journey of the human spirit.

There is as much mystery inside as there is outside—maybe more. We've spent billions of dollars in search of what's out there, and it seems that a lot of us won't even give the time of day to figure out what's going on inside us. If you look carefully inside people, you'll find both luminaries and black holes. And if you choose to walk with someone for a lifetime, you'll find that no matter how well you know him or her, there's still so much you don't know.

I've been married to Kim for over twenty-two years, and I can tell you she's an ever-expanding universe. The more I get to know her, the deeper I realize she has become. I'll never know her completely, and in fact, she'll never know herself completely because she's not a stagnant being. You can't completely know someone who is always growing, always changing, always expanding. This is what I love most about Kim. She's not the woman I married over twenty years ago. She's far more than that.

I wish I could say that's true for everyone, but I don't know that it is. Some people seem to live in a very small universe. Their world has room only for themselves. While their souls have every potential to be ever expanding, they seem instead to be the center of a collapsing universe—no room for dreams, for hope, for laughter, for love, for others—room only for themselves.

They find themselves very much alone, and they are very lonely. Strangely enough, they don't know why. Their souls crave too. And the way they have gained the whole world and lost their souls is that they have made themselves their whole world. They have sold out.

Most of us don't sell our souls to the devil; we just give them away.

You can play it safe and hide away behind indifference and choose the path of mediocrity. Remember you can swallow almost anything. The question is, can you keep it down? We live in a world filled with indifference, apathy, detachment, conformity, compliance, and acquiescing to the status quo. We swallow, but it doesn't settle well. The human spirit has no appetite for the bland, the mundane, or even the passionless. When you stop believing you are unique, something begins to die inside you.

What is it in the human spirit that insists on its uniqueness?

It is not enough for us to simply exist. That every one of us has a unique fingerprint means more to us than simply improvements in forensics. We are nothing less than driven to find our own paths, make our own way, be our own person. While we love to have things in common with others, we desperately need to believe we are in some way unique. We want to be the same as and different from those around us.

We want to have things in common, but we don't want to be common.

We are made up of nothing but ordinary material. Yet something inside us cries out that there is more to us than what meets the eye. We are like a cloth made of burlap and cashmere. We are without question on our way to becoming dust. Is this all it means to be human, or is there more?

Even as you read this, there is a voice coming not from your head but from your gut, screaming that you are more than water and disposable material. So much of your life journey can be explained by your soul cravings. Your soul knows its uniqueness. And a voice somewhere deep inside you longs to discover it. It calls you out and beckons you to pursue it.

There is something out there to be found, and our souls are restless to find it.

All of us begin our lives fueled by curiosity, yet far too many of us replace it with conformity. We are born unique but can die standardized. Henry Ford offered his Model T in any color customers wanted as long as it was black. He was the master of standardization. This wasn't even a sustainable idea for cars, much less for people. We are not supposed to look like or act like and certainly not live like we are the products of an assembly line.

It's way too easy to live our lives by default. If we are not careful, we can become the sum total of all the expectations others impose on our lives. We allow ourselves to become generic, standardized, homogenized.

We maintain the status quo. Conform to the expectations of others. Suppress our curiosity. Stop questioning. Keep from stirring things up. Line up and march in single file. We just get in line, never asking why we're even standing there at all.

My son, Aaron, and I were in London last December. One night we decided to catch a movie over in the Piccadilly Circus area. It was rainy and cold, and there was a long line of people waiting to buy tickets. I didn't want to stand in line and get wet, so I looked for an alternative route. Just to the left of the queue I noticed another window that appeared available with no one waiting in line. I asked the person manning the booth if he was open, and he said yes with a look of surprise on his face. We asked why no one was in his line, which was empty, and everyone chose instead to stand unquestioning in the rain. "I have no idea" was his response. While I was buying our tickets, Aaron felt compelled to free those trapped in the other queue. They were reluctant to believe him.

Why are we more likely to get behind someone in line rather than start our own?

Eventually we find ourselves a part of a human assembly line surrounded by standardization, routine, and predictability. We find ourselves miserable in the mundane. One day we find ourselves looking in the mirror, wondering who we are and why we are. Is life arbitrary, or is there meaning behind it? Am I unique or incidental? Screen writer and actor Zach Braff captures the struggle to find uniqueness while wallowing in the blandness of everyday existence.

Garden State follows the lives of a group of people who seem to be going nowhere, yet the death of Andrew Largeman's mother and the intervention of one person who refuses to give up on her own uniqueness awaken him out of his slumber. The story reminds us that it is easy to become an echo instead of a voice. Yet we discover even one meaningless act that stands alone as unique can give us hope that our lives can be different. Funny how we can be absolutely uncertain about what we are looking for and yet be absolutely certain we haven't found it. We know we are searching for something; we just don't know for what or even why.

What we are searching for is rooted in where we come from and in who we are.

From your first breath you have been on a journey. There are things your soul longs for, and whether you have yet recognized it or not, your life is shaped by your search for them.

You are on a quest to discover your own uniqueness—who you are, why you are here, and where you are going.

Eric Bryant and I were on our way to Adeleide from Sydney when we finally saw the writing on the wall:

> not expected, not replaceable, not bland, not usual, not common, not typical, not standard, not humdrum, not parity, not obvious, not predictable, not similar, not comparable. What makes you special?

Thank you IBM.com/au/innovation for reminding us what we are not, which reminds us of who we long to be.

Unique.

If we find ourselves endlessly thwarted in the search for our uniqueness, we may choose to end our quest and settle for a sterile life of empty existence. We must be careful not to mistake surrender for rest.

We seem destined to be tormented by cravings we cannot satisfy or to live dissatisfied lives dead to our deepest longings.

We tend to think of childhood as the period of time when we're preparing for life. It seems to me life pretty much comes at us from the very beginning. No warm-up; no pregame. It's the real thing from the first breath.

I don't really remember when I was born, so I have to pick up a few years afterward. It's humbling to realize my earliest memories are not independent thoughts. All of us are shaped by people and events that we may not even remember. I don't remember my biological father, but whether I like to admit it or not, he still affects me decades later. So I know my earliest thoughts were not shaped in a vacuum, but I also know they didn't simply come from the outside.

My earliest memories were longings coming from somewhere deep within me. I didn't have a language for them then, but that doesn't mean they didn't speak to me as forcefully at the age of eight as they have at the ages of twenty-eight and forty-eight.

When I was only a small child, I believed in God, in love, and in laughter. To believe in these things is natural to the human spirit. For a child, more is unknown than known. To believe in God, in mystery, in the unseen, is not difficult for a child. Children are born to believe. They are the perfect candidates for myths and fables and fairy tales. As adults, we see this as a weakness, proof of the naïveté of childhood.

As we grow older, we know better. It's funny how as adults, we struggle with faith. We need evidence to justify our belief in the invisible. We attempt to build faith systems constructed with our logic and reason. As children, we just believed. Faith was so natural. Yes, our innocence left us vulnerable to believing things that are not true, but is it possible that this same innocence exists so that we may find that which is most true? We are created with a natural inclination to believe.

We don't grow *into* faith; we grow *out of* it.

We have within us both the ability and the disposition to look beyond the material and search for the eternal. If God exists and we were created to know him and faith is the means by which that happens, wouldn't it make sense that we would be born with this inclination? For some, to believe in God is way too much of a stretch. They consider it an insult to their intelligence. For them believing in something they cannot see is absurd. And if you talk about the effect of God on people's lives, they will insist that secondary evidence is not enough. It has to be primary, or it's not real.

So then there is love.

Some people who do not believe in God are consistent and don't believe in love either. No primary evidence. In fact, my nonscientific research has found a direct correlation between losing faith in love and losing faith in God. But for many people it is at this point where they simply live with the inconsistency. You can't see God; you can't prove God in the laboratory. Believing in God is a stretch, but they believe in love. But you can't see love. You can't prove love. The only evidence available is secondary. No primary evidence. Yet when you love someone, you are more certain of that than of almost anything else.

Love reminds us that there is a knowing beyond reason.

We are born to love. Children love unconditionally. You can beat the love out of a person, but it's impossible, of course, to beat it into someone. Just like faith, love is intrinsic. It's not taught or transferred—it just is. You can't make a person love you. Heaven knows, a lot of us have tried. There might be nothing more painful than loving someone who doesn't love you in return.

For love to exist it doesn't even require reciprocation.

You can, in fact, be in a loveless environment and still love. Children love their parents when tragically their parents don't love them. If love is something developed over time, it wouldn't be like this. It's not the result of becoming a mature adult. Sometimes it seems adulthood becomes the enemy of love. I'm not saying that love doesn't deepen with maturity. What I am saying is that the impetus for love is in us from the start; we're all born with both faith and love—not to mention hope.

Have you ever experienced an entirely blissful moment? A moment when everything was right in the world? Can you remember how you didn't have a care in the world? Or at least so it seemed. I've had many times like this. And ironically it wasn't because everything in life was exactly as I wanted. I have never had that moment—maybe because my expectations are too high. But what I did have was a wonderful sense of optimism. When you lack hope, you feel powerless to change anything and certain that nothing will change. When you have hope, you are able to see the beauty and potential of every circumstance. Life is filled with wonder. Hope empowers us to pursue our dreams.

Dreams are the art form of hope. They paint a picture of the life we desire.

It's impossible to enjoy life fully without dreams. And we were created to enjoy life. You don't have to teach a child to laugh. Joy, celebration, and even happiness are the natural environments for the human spirit. Have you ever noticed it's pretty much impossible to fake a real laugh? You might have faith in the wrong thing and you might later discover it was just puppy love, but you never are confused about whether something is really funny to you. If you think about that long enough, that can be a very depressing thought. I mean, I'd rather be right about what I believe or who I love than have a keen sense of comedy. What really is the evolutionary value of laughter? Yet somehow it's strangely true that laughter is often the best medicine.

When you study any life form, you can determine its proper environment by what brings it health.

Some trees require shade; others direct sunlight. Some species are designed to thrive in deserts, and others can exist only in tropical rain forests. Move them out of their natural habitat, and you find that they quickly deteriorate in both health and vitality.

Human beings are no different. Place them in an environment filled with despair or bitterness or detachment, and it doesn't take long to see the negative effect. It may seem superficial, but the human spirit thrives where there is laughter. We really do need to take happiness more seriously. We live in a world where those who have the highest percentage of human wealth have the highest concentration of people medicated for depression. It just goes to show that you can't buy happiness. That doesn't stop us from trying, though.

I remember laughing when I was young. I remember when I stopped laughing even better.

Nothing seemed funny. I was in pretty sad shape. Trapped in a universe I couldn't get out of, I was quickly losing hope. I didn't realize how essential hope was to getting up in the morning. You're in trouble when you stop believing in hope. No matter how hard your life is, if you can imagine a different one, it somehow seems to pull you through. You can stomach who you are, no matter how much you hate yourself, if you can somehow believe that one day you'll become someone different.

Your soul craves truth, beauty, wonder, love. Your soul craves to dream, to imagine, and even simply to understand. Your soul craves to connect, to commune, to create. And once you are fully convinced all these things are illusions to be dispensed of, your soul becomes sick. When you cannot see the possibility of these things, when you give up on them, when you are no longer changed by the pursuit of what seem to be ideals outside your reach, you starve your soul and you lose yourself.

One ink blot in particular clearly gave me a choice between a bat and a butterfly. I saw them both, and I fully understood the implications. Which would I choose? But frankly what do you do when your soul wants butterflies and the world keeps sending you bats? Maybe you become Batman. You take your worst fear and make it your strength. Ironically, those half dozen sessions excavating my soul actually made a difference.

I didn't get any answers, but I left convinced that asking the questions was a good thing.

I began to realize that all of us have a common struggle. While there may be an endless number of philosophies and religions in the world and while we may all disagree on the answers, all of us have the same questions, the same longings, the same cravings.

When I was just a small child, I believed in God, in love, and in laughter—and then I didn't. I think love went first, then laughter. Then since God couldn't help me with the first two, I went ahead and threw him out with everything else you need to get rid of when you are no longer a child. But before you think too badly of me, you might want to know I wanted them all back. I just didn't realize how they were all connected together. Imagine my surprise when I began to discover that the things that came so naturally as a child were the very things my soul was craving.

I gave my soul away at a very young age. By this I mean I gave up on myself. When you give up on yourself, you start throwing out things like dreams, optimism, hope, intimacy, love, trust, truth, meaning, and faith. Looking back, I realize I was paralyzed by fear. I now know I was afraid of nothing. I was terrified that I was nothing and that I would never amount to anything. Deep inside this ever-expanding universe known as my soul, I was drowning in a quickly rising ocean of self-doubt and despair.

I know from experience that it isn't enough just to survive.

Solomon once wrote that God has set eternity in the hearts of men, but that in the end we can't seem to make any sense of it. He somehow knew deep within us is our greatest evidence for God and our greatest connection to God. Jesus said the kingdom of God is within, yet for two thousand years after him, we have kept looking outward for this kingdom rather than inside us. I am absolutely convinced of this one thing: God has placed cravings within your soul that will drive you insane or drive you to him. Your soul longs for God; you just may not know it yet.

I lose things all the time. I've spent hours looking for whatever I lost. When I was a kid, I used to think God was punishing me by hiding the missing object. I was sure I committed some heinous crime against God and humanity, and now God was punishing me by hiding my shoes. My mom would be furious. It must have been frustrating to have a son who lost everything.

Losing things drove me to prayer. I would spend every minute of my search begging God to help me find whatever I had lost. I would think of everything I did wrong and try to make it right—make my bed, clean the closet, take all the stuff I'd hidden under the bed, pull it out and put it in the right place. I would scour my mind for anything I possibly could have done wrong and do whatever I could to make it right. I was frantically trying to find the one thing God was holding against me so I could get him to give back what was missing.

You might think this was a ridiculous thought process, but frankly it worked a lot. Most of the time I was able to get God off my back, repair whatever breach in the cosmos I had created, and find the missing pair of shoes or watch or wallet or whatever happened to be lost at the time. Looking back, I realize that the one thing that seemed to be lost all the time was me. I kept looking for me. Or really for who I was.

Somewhere along the way I became lost.

We try to fill ourselves with everything we can grab, and yet there remains an inescapable emptiness within. Even when we've looked everywhere else, even when there's nowhere else to look, we still somehow neglect to consider the possibility that what our souls long for is God. We can't take enough or make enough to fill the hollowness within us. No matter what we try or do we can't avoid the void.

Maybe that's what Jesus meant when he said, "What is it worth to gain the whole world, but to lose your soul?" Was he describing someone like you or me? We spend our whole lives as slaves to our desires, determined to somehow satisfy the deepest longings of our souls. We take everything we can get; we keep everything we can grab; we become human versions of a black hole.

There's something inside us that pulls us toward God, something our souls long for that we cannot fully understand.

Doesn't it make sense that if we were created for relationship with the Creator of the universe, he would leverage everything within us so we would search for him, reach out for him, and perhaps even find him?

So we're back to hide-and-seek. You might be asking yourself, *If God wants me to find him and my soul craves to do so, why doesn't he make it easier than this?* Have you ever gone searching for God? I have. Frankly I didn't feel like he was cooperating at all. And when you add my propensity toward losing things, how in the world was I supposed to find God?

When you lose something, you have to backtrack.

Don't you just hate the question, "Where did you have it last?" If you knew that, it wouldn't be lost, would it? But like an investigator from Scotland Yard, you start retracing your every step. When that doesn't work, you go to Plan B—blaming others. "Who moved my —— [you

 SOUL CRAVINGS

fill in the blank]?" Oh, that's right, we're talking about God. "Who moved my God?" Or, "My God, where did God go?"

It's a very bad thing to misplace the Creator of the universe. He could be just about anywhere. Or maybe in this case everywhere. Sometimes hide-and-seek isn't a game.

Imogen Heap has a song called "Hide and Seek." It captures the frustration of a game gone bad:

Where are we?
What the hell is going on?
The dust has only just begun to fall,
Crop circles in the carpet
Sinking, feeling
Spin me around again
And rub my eyes
This can't be happening . . .
Hide and seek
Ransom notes keep falling out of your mouth
Mid-sweet talk, newspaper word cut-outs
Speak no feeling, I don't believe you
Hide and seek
You don't care a bit, you don't care a, you don't care a bit
Oh no, you don't care a bit
Oh no, you don't care a bit
Oh no, you don't care a bit
You don't care a bit
You don't care a bit

So I asked around and I looked for God the last place someone saw him—in religion. After all, millions of people around the world go to see

God every week unless, of course, you interview them and you realize they didn't see him either. They were just there looking for him, hoping they could find him. There may be nothing more confusing or frustrating than having tried God and walking away with nothing but the bad taste of religion in your mouth.

My grandmother was Roman Catholic, and so I began my journey in a Latin Mass. I remember seeing that crucifix and feeling very badly for God. It's hard to be mad at God when He's in worse shape than you. I felt great empathy for him. I also felt a huge sense of gratitude to hear that Jesus died for the sins of the world. I knew very little about sin at the time, but from what I heard, it was a real problem. I, on the other hand, had other issues I was trying to resolve. I know it sounds selfish, but I really needed someone who could help me, and God seemed to have his own problems.

I remember once when I was ten, trying to run away from home, getting caught, getting in trouble, getting grounded, sitting in my room, and yelling at God from the top of my lungs. I remember telling God off and then pausing to see what would happen. Nothing happened, and that seemed to be the worst thing that could happen.

So many of us spend our lives worrying that God is going to punish us or hoping that God is going to help us, but neither one of those things ever seems to happen. For all the activity that there is in the world trying to get God's attention, it can leave you wondering whether it's all just a horrible waste of time. You couldn't really blame God, though. I never really got mad at him or anything like that. I figured he was just way too busy with more important stuff or maybe more important people. So much of my life I felt invisible. It seemed pretty arrogant and presumptuous of me to think God would actually see me. Probably God is only a big picture kind of guy. Maybe he's just not that into details. Or maybe, just maybe, there's more going on than we know.

Over and over again Jesus taught the value of the one to God. He described God as the shepherd who leaves the ninety-nine sheep to find the one that is lost; the woman who searches for the one coin that is missing until she finds it; the father who waits for his wayward son to return home to him.

The one matters to God.

Steven Spielberg explores the theme of the one in several of his films. From *E.T.* to *A.I.* to *Schindler's List* to *Saving Private Ryan,* Spielberg seems almost consumed with the journey of the solitary individual. In *Saving Private Ryan* we find a true story of how a troop of men marched through a world war to find and secure the safe return of one soldier. The movie raises important questions: What is the value of one human being? To what extreme should we go to save one person?

I used to think that I was desperately searching for God. I've changed my mind about that. Looking back, I realize that God was desperately searching for me. I used to wonder why my soul ached and God wouldn't do anything about it. Now I know that it was that very pain that drove me to God. Life without God is starvation of the soul. I thought for a while that God could meet my needs and stop my soul cravings. Now I know that isn't the case.

My soul doesn't crave something from God; my soul craves God. And by the way, so does yours.

That's why everything else will leave you unsatisfied in the end. But don't let this frustrate you; just let it fuel you. All the evidence you need to prove God is waiting within you to be discovered. We have traveled together through these pages, but the journey does not end here. We are not at our destination but at a crossroad. There are decisions to be considered, choices to be made, steps to be taken. You might want to take a moment to turn your head and look back. You have journeyed farther than you know.

If you are still with me, you are very much the kind of person Jesus spoke of in the highest terms. He calls you a seeker and assures you that if you seek, you will find.

He also promises that if you knock, the door will be opened, and if you ask, it will be given to you. He isn't talking about material possessions here as much as meeting the deepest longings of your soul. So continue to seek, knock, ask, and don't stop until you find, enter in, and come to know the answer your soul has been asking all along.

Your soul craves, and it's God you are longing for. So listen carefully to the conversation going on inside your head. Don't worry. You're probably not going crazy. I do know in this case you're not talking to yourself. God is trying to get your attention and bring you into relationship with him. If you will pay attention to your soul, it will guide you to God.

Cheng Yi said, "To exert thought is like digging a well. At first there is only muddy water. Later on, after one has done some drawing, clear water will come out. One's thoughts are always muddy at first. After a long while they will naturally be nicely clear."

This past August we were traveling through Australia, and I had the privilege of meeting a Greek Aussie named Yanni. He was not a follower of Christ, but he was a very honest and sincere seeker. I was speaking at a leadership conference that was spiritually focused, and I was pleasantly surprised to see Yanni there at every session. He shared with me later that he had called his brother with whom he had not spoken for a long time to tell him about the conference.

His brother's immediate response was one of concern.

He first asked him if he was getting involved in a cult. In a country with about 5 percent of the population openly believing in God, anything spiritual seems like a cult. His brother then warned him about being brainwashed, which seemed to offend Yanni since he was very much a free and independent thinker. I asked him how he responded, and with all the confidence you would expect from a Greek Aussie, he said, "I told him, 'What does brainwashing have to do with this? All he's doing is reaching inside of me and pulling out what's already there.'"

What an incredible insight.

If God is real and you are created by him, your soul already knows it.

You may be in denial or even genuinely unaware of it, but if you take the time to explore nowhere else except deep within yourself, I have no doubt that you will come face-to-face with God.

In the movie *Contact*, Jodie Foster asks the question, "Do you think there's life out there?" The theme of the movie, of course, was that if there's not, it would be a terrible waste of space.

There is more unexplored space within you than there is in this ever-expanding universe.

I am certain that if you will take the time to journey to the depths of your soul, you will not leave there disappointed, and perhaps to your surprise and astonishment you will find God there. I hope *Soul Cravings* has at least helped you start your journey.

Then what will you do?

Have you found yourself face-to-face with God and felt his presence touch your soul like a gentle breeze against your face? How will you respond to him?

To trust in God, you have to know that he loves you without condition. This is the beauty of Jesus' death on the cross. It is God's declaration of love for you. His love embraces you wherever you are on your journey, and he does not leave you there.

He launches you on a quest to pursue the life you were created to live. Your soul knows there is a greater purpose for your life, a God-sized dream waiting to unfold and become your future.

We're all on a quest for intimacy, for meaning, for our destiny. Our souls crave love and faith and hope. We are all searching for what our souls long for, and we will be satisfied only in God.

I guess it will never be easy, but Jesus has made it possible. You don't have to be afraid to commit your life to someone who gives his life for you.

Maybe you're different than I am, but I think that we're probably a lot alike in this.

Your soul craves to believe.

You've been burned, maybe you've even been deceived, but deep in your gut, somewhere deep inside, there's a voice telling you that God can be trusted with your life, that you can trust. Someone like Jesus.

That his love is pure and your soul thirsts for him like water is needed by a crusted desert.

That there is more to life than you can know without God.

Jesus walked among us so that we could get close enough to hear him, to see him, to touch him, to smell him, to know him. To know him, this is what your soul craves.

Your journey matters to me, to our community here in Los Angeles, and to friends we have around the world. If you want to continue this conversation, we would love to make that possible.

We would also love to hear the stories of your journey of faith. We're all in this together, and I am personally grateful for that. We need each other, and besides, without fellow travelers, who will you laugh with?

Join us on the quest by coming to www.awakenhumanity.org.

— erwin

OTHER TITLES BY ERWIN RAPHAEL MCMANUS

Uprising

Stand Against the Wind

Chasing Daylight

An Unstoppable Force

ABOUT THE AUTHOR

Erwin Raphael McManus serves as lead pastor and cultural architect of Mosaic in Los Angeles, California. From the global center of change, Mosaic emerges as a reference point for the future church. As founder of Awaken, Erwin collaborates with a team of dreamers and innovators who specialize in the field of developing and unleashing personal and organizational creativity. As a national and international consultant, his expertise focuses on culture, change, leadership, and creativity. He partners with Bethel Theological Seminary as distinguished professor and futurist and is also a contributing editor for the *Leadership Journal*. Erwin's first book, *An Unstoppable Force*, was a 2002 ECPA Gold Medallion Award finalist. He is also author of *Chasing Daylight* and *Uprising: A Revolution of the Soul*, which was the featured book and theme for the 2004 Promise Keepers conferences. He and his wife, Kim, have two children, Aaron and Mariah, and a daughter in the Lord, Paty.